99¢
SOLUTIONS

99¢
SOLUTIONS

1,465 Smart and Frugal Uses for Everyday Items

Reader's
Digest

New York | Montreal

LIBRARY of CONGRESS CATALOGING IN PUBLICATION DATA

    ISBN 978-1-62145-556-1 (ppb)

    ISBN 978-1-62145-544-8 (hc)

    ISBN 978-1-62145-557-8 (e-pub)

We are committed to both the quality of our products and the service we provide to our customers. We value your comments, so please feel free to contact us.

Trusted Media Brands, Inc.

Adult Trade Publishing

44 South Broadway

White Plains, NY 10601

For more Reader's Digest products and information, visit our website:

www.rd.com

Printed in China

1 3 5 7 9 10 8 6 4 2

NOTE TO OUR READERS

The information in this book should not be substituted for, or used to alter, medical therapy without your doctor's advice. For a specific health problem, consult your physician for guidance.

Mention of specific companies, organizations, or authorities in the book does not imply endorsement by the author or publisher, nor does mention of specific companies, organizations, or authorities imply that they endorse this book, its author, or the publisher. The brand-name products mentioned in this book are trademarks or registered trademarks of their respective companies. Internet addresses and telephone numbers given in this book were accurate at the time it went to press.

WHAT'S IN THE AISLES?
of your favorite dollar store

A cozy notion that can **STUFF A PILLOW**
and also **LOWER YOUR HEATING BILLS!**

•

A terrifically **TASTY TREAT FOR BREAKFAST**
that will also **POLISH YOUR FURNITURE!**

•

A fabulously frugal tool for **REMOVING
A STAPLE** and **SCRATCHING YOUR BACK!**

•

A tried-and-true **PASTRY SCHOOL
SUPPLY** that also **REMOVES SPLINTERS!**

•

A brilliantly inexpensive item that **FLAVORS
YOUR TEA** and **SHINES YOUR JEWELRY!**

...and so much more!

SAVE TIME...
SAVE MONEY!

SAVE A
BUNDLE!

INSTANT
SAVINGS!

SAVE
BIG!

Contents

INTRODUCTION
Saving Money, the Dollar Store Way!

AISLE 1

Groceries 12

Replace the oil in baked goods with applesauce, make your copper glow and banish chlorine green hair with ketchup! Here's how to stretch that dollar and make it go much further than your refrigerator and pantry.

AISLE 2

Health and Beauty 46

Think that what's for sale in the health aisle is only good for what ails you? Guess again! Bandages are for more than cuts and bruises! Use them in your sewing room to replace that missing thimble. Quiet your squeaky floor with baby powder. Thwart thieves with a plastic pocket comb.

AISLE 3

Gardening and Outdoors 76

From flowerpots to charcoal briquettes, ice scrapers, and camping matches, there's not one thing in this aisle that can't do triple (and often quadruple) duty. Got a headache? Tie on a bandanna. Need to move something heavy? Grab some gardening burlap. Scratches in your countertop? Reach for the car wax!

AISLE 4

Cleaning and Home Supplies 102

Window cleaner for windows, and ammonia for the bathroom, right? Wrong! Why buy bug lotion if you can stop the itch with bathroom cleaner? Never mind going to the garden store to kill that moss on your walkway—use bleach instead! Ants in your kitchen? They hate dishwashing liquid!

Housewares 128

Ice cube trays? Bottle openers? Cheesecloth? You'd be amazed at the multipurpose uses these everyday items have, that will save you a bundle! Unclog a stubborn drain with a wire hanger. Detail a car with a coffee filter. Separate eggs with a funnel...and much more!

Notions 158

Baubles and beading bore you to tears? They shouldn't! Notions can do double duty almost anywhere in the house. Fix curling wallpaper with adhesive fabric spray. Quilt your windows with batting to save on heating bills. Keep a pot from boiling over with a handful of buttons.

School and Party Supplies 184

That common adhesive tape? It's not just for wrapping presents anymore! Use a piece to remove a splinter. Protect your small trees from the lawn mower with bubble wrap. Remove scuff marks with an eraser. You'll never spend unnecessarily again!

Tools 214

Tools can be used for a lot more than what they're meant for. Use a bungee cord as a yoga strap! Remove white furniture rings with car wax! Seal waterproof boots with duct tape! Wear a painting mask when you cut onions. Why buy something you don't need to?

Index 242

We've all had this experience, from as far back as we can remember, regardless of where we lived, or what the store was called.

We walk into our local dollar store (or 99 cent store, five-and-dime, Woolworth's, or McCrory's or even our neighborhood general store that seems to sell far more than just nuts and bolts), and we begin to wander the aisles. We mosey up the notions aisle, transfixed by bolts of colorful fabric and buttons, and down the health and beauty aisle, with its jars of cold cream and boxes of analgesics. We stroll through the tool section and maybe visit the school supply or toy aisle, and uncover everything from glue to marbles to pencils.

In my own family, my grandmother would pick me up at the school bus and together—rain or shine, sleet or snow or hail—we would walk down a long boulevard until we arrived on a cross street that had not one, but *two* dime stores on it: McCrory's on the western side of the street, and Woolworth's on the eastern. On some days, we'd visit McCrory's for a sandwich or a slice of cherry pie, and we'd stroll the aisles, looking at odd nicknacks that ran the gamut from the sublime to the positively silly. On other days, we'd pop into Woolworth's, which was decidedly more *serious*; you could buy bicycle tires, little red wagons, thread, Play-Doh, skeins of yarn, tooth powder, buttonhole-makers, yo-yos, jacks, cans of (white) tennis balls, knee socks,

tube socks, anklet socks, support hose, peds, nail files, chewing gum in every flavor, plastic guitars, strings for plastic guitars, Flutophones, glassware, Pyrex dishes, Christmas ornaments, holiday greeting cards, baby lotion, Corelle ware, rain boots, Keds, potato chips, baked goods, tools, bicycles, and everything in between. What we didn't know (or took for granted, anyway) was that Woolworth's was, at one time, also the largest seller of restaurant food in the world.

Other dime store operators included Samuel Kress, whose Memphis store first opened in 1896, and who eventually built his chain up to 262 branches nationwide, with $168 million in sales. Sebastian Kresge, another mogul, had over 150 stores to his name by the middle of the First World War, and then branched out into self-service discount stores called (you'll never guess!) K-Mart! Even Sam Walton launched his first retail business with a Ben Franklin store in Newport, Arkansas, and when he was unable to convince management to open discount stores, he launched...Walmart!

Today, many of these famous stores are gone... but not one of the things that continues to

Famous DIME AND DISCOUNT STORES in History

- W.T. Grant
- H.L. Green
- McLellan Stores
- G.C. Murphy
- Neisner's
- J.J. Newberry
- Ben Franklin Stores
- Kresge's
- Kress
- Woolworth's
- McCrory's
- The Dollar Store
- Dollar Tree
- S.H. Knox & Co.
- Dayton's
- Woolco

make the survivors famous: That almost everything you can find in a 99 cent store can save you money—*gobs* of money.

Think about it: Say you need a new screwdriver to replace that old rusted one sitting in your toolbox, so you pick one up at the five-and-dime. Maybe you paid a dollar for it, or maybe you paid a little bit more. Guess what? You have just bought yourself a tool that will help you accomplish *dozens* of other jobs—everything from opening a can of paint to planting seeds in packed soil to chipping ice for your annual barbecue. Why buy purpose-specific items when one simple tool can accomplish so much?

The possibilities are endless:

A simple cleaning bucket can be used to store your extension cords, create a mini-garden, and provide a convenient shower when you're camping.

A tub of car wax can make your wheels gleam, but also can fight bathroom mildew, keep fingerprints off appliances, and wax your snow shovel.

A roll of adhesive tape can help remove a splinter, emboss your library card, find the beginning of plastic wrap, and protect your wood floor.

Party balloons can help keep a bandage or cast dry when you shower, keep cats off the couch, and function as an instant icepack.

Aspirin can stop your grandson's acne, get rid of your athlete's foot, and give you a spa facial at home.

Baby powder can clean your carpet overnight, squash the squeak in your wooden floor, and help you undo a knot.

That's dozens and dozens of dollars saved, right there. And right here, in the pages of *99 Cent Solutions*, we provide you with over a thousand ways to save big, just by scouring the aisles of that old-fashioned store you've come to know and love. Read on, and watch your dollars grow!

Elissa Altman, *Executive Editor*

GROCERIES

MOST DOLLAR STORES CARRY AN EXTENSIVE selection of nonperishable foods, but do pay attention to make sure you're not buying something for a dollar that would cost less than that in the grocery store—canned beans, for example. With that warning aside, dollar store food aisles can be a terrific place to trawl for bargains. The selections can change frequently, depending on what the wholesaler has on offer, so you may find imported chocolates and jams or your favorite brand of breakfast cereal for low, low prices. Once your pantry is fully stocked with all these goodies, their uses don't stop at the kitchen door. There's a whole lot more you can do with them, both on and off the kitchen table and all around the house and garden.

applesauce

Whether sold in handy individual serving packs or in a big glass jar, applesauce in the pantry opens a host of uses besides snacks. Go for the unsweetened varieties for better taste.

Replace the oil in baking

Fat makes baked goods moist and tender. It's also incredibly calorie-dense, and if you're cutting calories, it's an easy place to start. But say you don't like your cakes and muffins dry and tough? Then applesauce is the answer. Replace up to 2/3 of the oil called for in a cake or muffin recipe with applesauce, and you'll add moisture and flavor while ditching the fat.

Make holiday ornaments

Mix equal amounts cinnamon and applesauce to make fragrant ornaments. Start with 1 cup of each and mix, adding more cinnamon if needed to form a stiff dough. Mold holiday ornaments such as wreaths or hearts or roll it out 1/2-inch thick and cut shapes with cookie cutters. Be sure to make a hole with a chopstick or pencil for a loop of ribbon. Let dry completely for several days on a baking sheet or wire rack.

Add sweetness and fiber to oatmeal

You've gone to all that trouble to make a healthy breakfast of oatmeal so don't ruin it by slathering on butter, sugar and cream. Instead, stir in a few tablespoons of applesauce and a sprinkle of cinnamon. You'll add sweetness and flavor and even more fiber, making your breakfast both healthy and delicious.

baking soda

One of the most useful items in the pantry, baking soda is a super-item. It's inexpensive and incredibly potent, both inside and outside the kitchen.

Soften beans

Afraid those dry beans have been on the shelf too long? Help soften them by adding a pinch of baking soda to the soaking water. Add a fresh pinch to the cooking water, too, and you can significantly reduce the aftereffects of bean consumption.

Get rid of fishy odors

Been chopping something pungent? The smell of garlic or fish can linger on your fingers long after the food is gone. Avoid that by scrubbing your wet hands with baking soda, just as if it were soap, then rinse in warm water. Your hands will smell sweet—and feel softer, too.

Make a rainy day toy for kids

Kids stuck inside with nothing to do? Boil 2 cups baking soda with 1 cup cornstarch and 1 1/4 cups water until thickened. Remove from the heat and cool. It makes a fun, pliable modeling clay that's good for a day.

Deep-clean a dishwasher

Faintly funky smell in your dishwasher? You can sort that out fast with a baking soda wash. Put 1 cup of baking soda in the bottom of the dishwasher and run it on a rinse cycle. If the smell persists, sprinkle a few tablespoons on the bottom of the washer to sit there between loads. There's no need to rinse it out before running the next load.

Repel rain from a windshield

You know you need new wiper blades, but now there's rain in the forecast and you haven't replaced them yet. Dissolve a couple tablespoons baking soda in 2 cups of water, dip in a clean cloth, and rub it over the windshield. Rain will slip off more easily until you buy those new blades.

De-skunk a bottle or thermos

Can't get that smell out of a bottle or flask that has been stored with the lid on? Fill it with warm water and a few teaspoons of baking soda and soak it overnight. Rinse well and the smell will have evaporated.

Make a stove top sparkle

Cooked-on food stains are difficult to remove. But you don't need a commercial spray. Far faster, more effective, and more environmentally friendly is a sprinkle of baking soda. Wipe the stains with a wet sponge to dampen them, then sprinkle on baking soda. Scrub with the sponge, and the stains will lift right off. This is also perfect for the greasy black dirt that can build up around the edges of other kitchen appliances.

Salvage a burned pot

By the time you've thought, "What's that smell?" and then remembered you left the stove on, it's often too late. The bottom of the pot is a blackened mess. You can save it, though. Scrape out as much food as you can and then fill the pan a quarter full with water. Pour in 1/2 cup of baking soda and bring the pot to a boil. Turn it off and let it sit overnight. In the morning, you can clean off the black stuff with ease.

Keep garbage cans fresh

Before you put a new liner in the garbage can, sprinkle a dollop of baking soda. When you take out the full bag, turn the can upside down to dump any dry soda still left in there, and then add more before the new bag. You've got a natural deodorizer right where you need it most.

Use it this way!

Make tomatoes taste sweeter

If last year's garden tomatoes tasted dull, take action this year to ensure your garden harvest is as good as it can be. Sprinkle baking soda lightly on the soil around the base of your tomato plants. The resulting tomatoes will taste sweeter.

Save a mildewed book

Found mildew around the edge of a childhood classic you adored? If it's a mild case, you can arrest the growth and save the book with baking soda. Sprinkle it lightly between the pages, then put the book in a paper bag and dust the outside with more baking soda. Let it sit for several days, then remove, shake out and dust off the baking soda, and let the book get a shot of bright sunlight. It doesn't remove mildew marks, but if you store it in a dry place, no more mildew will grow.

Take the sting out of sunburn

You just want the itchy pain from a sunburn to stop. Soaking in a lukewarm bath helps, but help it a bit more with a cup of baking soda poured into the water. It will take the sting out and lessen the pain quickly.

Clean a glass-front fireplace

If the glass in front of your fireplace or woodstove is blackened with soot and smoke, it's time for baking soda. Crumple a sheet of newspaper, wet it in water, and dip it in baking soda. Scrub the glass—the black stuff will come right off. Wipe with a damp cloth. You can use the same technique to get soot off the glazed bricks lining the fireplace.

Stop a mosquito bite in its tracks

Slap! You killed the mosquito, but not before it got a good bite. Rush inside and pour a tablespoon of baking soda in your palm. Wet it with a few drops of water to make a paste, then smear it on the bite area. Let it dry and flake off. If you treat the mark this way as soon as you can, there will be no red welt from the bite, and the itching will subside almost instantly. The same treatment works for bee stings, assuming you have carefully removed any sign of the stinger.

Soothe a canker sore

It's hard to believe how much pain a tiny sore on the inside of your mouth can cause. Soothe the pain away and help heal the sore faster by swishing every couple of hours with a solution of 1 teaspoon baking soda stirred until it dissolves into 1 cup warm water.

Soak your way to comfort

Hot, sweaty feet? Tired and achy toes? In the evening, plop your tootsies in a basin of cool water with baking soda stirred in. Soak for 15 to 20 minutes, then rinse and dry. Not only will this soothe your feet and help cut down on odor during the day, but it will also help dry up athlete's foot.

Soften hard-water washes

Add 1/4 cup baking soda to a hot white wash to boost the strength of your usual detergent and get your whites bright.

Ready your AC for the season

Before your window units go in, the filters should be washed. Brush off obvious dirt and dust, then lay the filters in a basin of water with several tablespoons baking soda mixed in. Swish them in the water to clean, then rinse and dry in hot sun before replacing in the unit.

Clean your brushes

Hairbrushes and combs should be washed periodically to remove the hair oils that build up. Remove any hair, then fill the sink with warm water and stir in a couple of spoonfuls of baking soda. Let the brushes and combs soak several hours, then rinse and air dry. You can also clean toothbrushes by letting them soak in a cup filled with warm water and a tablespoon of baking soda. Rinse well and air dry.

Discourage weeds in cracks

Hoping to keep grass and weeds out of the cracks between your paving stones? Sprinkle on baking soda and sweep it into the cracks. Grass will stick to the lawn instead.

Keep your garbage can fresh. Before you put a new liner in the garbage can, sprinkle a dollop of baking soda.

9 More Nontraditional Ways to Use BAKING SODA

A DIFFERENT *Solution*!

1 Revitalize Wallpaper

Did someone trail greasy little fingers down the wallpaper in the hallway? Rub the stain gently with a damp sponge sprinkled with baking soda, then rinse and pat dry. Your wallpaper will be good as new.

2 Miracle for the Microwave

Got a lot of gunk "baked" onto the walls of your microwave? Put 1 cup water and a few tablespoons of baking soda into a glass container. Microwave on high for 3 minutes. Use a sponge to wipe off all the lossened grime—it's that easy!

3 Down the Drain

Commercial drain cleaners can be hard on your pipes. For a minor blockage, pour 1 cup baking soda down the drain, followed by 1 cup white vinegar. Let it sit for 10 minutes, then pour a kettle of boiling water down the drain. Repeat as needed.

4 Be Tender to Tummies

If someone has a delicate stomach, careful use of baking soda can help you make food more palatable for them. A very tiny pinch in coffee, orange juice, or tomato soup, for example, can prevent an acidic stomach after eating. Do not overdo it or food will taste bland.

5 Don't Lose Your Marble

If your marble countertop has lost its sparkle, there's no need to fear! Brighten it with a cloth dipped in water and lightly sprinkled with baking soda. Rub gently with a circular motion and rinse with cool water. Then buff it dry. The marble will gleam again.

6 No Stick, No Rust, No Kidding!

They call it nonstick but stuff stuck. And your beloved cast-iron skillet has rust stains. Scrub the spots with a damp sponge sprinkled with baking soda. Make sure to wet the sponge well to dissolve the baking soda and avoid scratching your nonstick.

7 Eat Naked Fruit!

Give your produce a baking soda bath. Dampen fruits (or vegetables) with water, sprinkle a vegetable brush with baking soda, and then scrub before you eat them. Rinse well and dry. A baking soda wash removes wax from fruits like apples and reduces pesticides on fruits and veggies that a simple water rinse may not.

8 Green Your Baby Clothes

Do the clothes bought for your newborn feel stiff from starch and smell like chemicals? This is common in new fabric. To get rid of unwanted additives use a scent-free baby detergent and 1/2 cup baking soda to wash the garments. Nothing but soft, clean fabrics will touch your baby's skin.

9 Detergent Expander

Have only one squeeze of dishwashing liquid left? Add it to a dishpan partially filled with hot water, and then stir in a tablespoon or two of baking soda while allowing more hot water to run. The water won't look as bubbly but it will feel soapy. As you wash, you'll notice grease disappears and baked-on food comes off easily.

beans (dried)

Dried beans cost about the same at the dollar store as they do at the supermarket, but that doesn't mean you shouldn't stock up. In addition to being a delicious and cheap source of protein, they're great for a lot of other stuff, too.

Train a dog

Most dogs hate the sound of dried beans rattling in a can. Use that to your advantage when training a dog by putting a handful of beans in the bottom of an empty aluminum soda can. Seal the top with a strip of tape. When your dog misbehaves, shake the can a couple of times.

Make a close-fitting hot pad

Soothe aching muscles with a custom-made hot pad. Fill a long sock, such as a tube or athletic sock, with dried beans, and tie the top tightly closed with ribbon or string. Heat in a microwave on high for 30 seconds. Place it right on your painful spot. You can drape it around a stiff neck or wrap it around a sore wrist, and it will mold to you, providing faster relief.

Prevent a scorched pan

Got a lot of pans on the stove? Toss a small handful of beans in the bottom of a double boiler or a steamer, and as the water boils down, the beans will rattle. (This handy trick only works when you're boiling water for less than half an hour. Any longer and the beans will soften and cook!)

Make a beanbag

Put 1 cup of beans in the toe of a cotton sock, and tie a knot in the remaining material, pushing it down till the knot is closed up against the beans. Make two more and you've got a terrific juggling set or the start of a bean toss for kids. Set up your youngsters with a few beanbags and a clean, empty wastebasket, and they're ready for hours of fun.

bread

Bread was long unavailable at the dollar store, but many chains have begun to expand their grocery sections to include a small selection of fresh foods. When you're looking for uses beyond a sandwich, packaged bread is often *more* useful than a crisp bakery loaf!

Sweeten the scent of cabbage

They're good for you and they taste good, but when they're cooking, cabbage and cauliflower and other cruciferous vegetables can release an odor that does not beckon people into the kitchen. Lay a slice or two of white bread on top of the cooking veggies and put on the lid—the scent will stay in the bread, not in the air.

Train your dog by putting a handful of beans in the bottom of an empty soda can. **When your dog misbehaves, shake the can a couple of times.**

Keep cookies fresh

Homemade chocolate chip cookies can go from tasting deliciously soft and cakey to feeling hard and crunchy in a matter of days. To keep your freshly baked cookies tasting…freshly baked, put a couple slices of bread into the tin or jar where you store the cookies, laying the bread right on top of the cookies. The bread will keep that just-out-of-the-oven flavor and texture intact for up to a week.

Prevent broiler flare-ups

Put a slice or two of stale bread in the bottom of the broiler pan, and it will absorb the grease as it runs off, stopping flare-ups and easing cleanup by preventing pan juices from getting stuck to the pan.

Butter corn on the cob

Corn on the cob, that summertime treat, wouldn't taste the same without a slather of butter on top, but it's hard to spread it evenly over the nubby cob, especially for kids. Instead, spread a slice of bread thickly with softened butter and cup the bread in your palm—butter side up! Turn the corn in the buttery slice for perfect coverage.

Clean smudges off suede

Suede jackets, shoes and handbags look great but they're prone to picking up dirty marks. Clean fresh smudges off quickly and easily before they set into stains by rubbing the suede gently with a piece of fresh white bread. Use a small, circular motion. You may need a second piece of bread to get the spot clean.

Take scuffs off wallpaper and flat paint

Scuffs, fingerprints, and other marks on painted wallpapers and non-glossy paint surfaces can be hard to clean: Water can leave marks if you scrub with a sponge. Try a fresh slice of plain white bread instead, with the crusts cut off so no color can transfer. Rub gently over the mark, using a fresh slice of bread if needed, until it gently rubs off, leaving the surface intact, unharmed—and clean.

WAY BACK WHEN...

It's a Wonder

The next time you use the expression, "It's the best thing since sliced bread," think of everyone's favorite white bread in the polka-dot package. The year was 1921 and the Taggart Baking Company of Indianapolis was planning to introduce its pound-and-a-half loaf of white bread to the public. Elmer Cline, the vice president of the company, looked low and high for a marketing hook—and the latter is where he found one! While attending the International Balloon Race at the Indianapolis Speedway, Cline was dumbstruck by a sky packed with colorful balloons. "It's wonderful," he thought….and then the lightbulb went off: Ever since that time, the red, blue, and yellow balloons are instantly recognizable as Wonder Bread's package.

butter

Like bread, butter is another fresh item that's only recently available in dollar stores. Once you're done slathering some on your toast, you'll be glad to have an inexpensive source of butter—both salted and sweet—for a lot of other uses.

Keep onions and cheese fresh

They're a world apart in flavor and texture, but both onions and cheese benefit from butter when it comes to storage. Rub the cut side of an onion with butter and wrap in plastic wrap—it will stay fresh for days longer, and you can dice the buttery parts right into your skillet. Hard and semisoft

Rub the cut side of an onion with butter and wrap in plastic wrap—it will stay fresh for days longer.

cheeses will stay mold-free for weeks if you rub the cut sides with softened butter, sealing them to keep the air out before rewrapping in plastic and storing in the fridge.

Get that medicine down

Doctor says you need to take that pill—but you're wondering if it's meant for you or a horse. Whether the pill is large or you just don't love swallowing pills, try a dab of butter to ease the job. Lightly rub butter all over the outside of the pill, and it will slip gently down with a sip of water, no sticking awkwardly in your throat. To your health!

Give dry hair a real salon treatment

Return your hair to the glossy tresses it had before all that blow-drying. Smooth and soften the cuticles of your hair with a super-rich butter treatment. Rub a handful of soft butter into dry hair, working it gently down to the ends. Wrap your hair in a towel or put on a shower cap and leave in for half an hour. Wash and rinse thoroughly, and run your fingers through your luxurious tresses.

Strip off sticky sap

Whether you've been stacking firewood or collecting pinecones, the tree sap on your hands is nearly impossible to get off. Unless you rub it well

with butter. Use a generous amount and slather it on your hands like you're rubbing in lotion. Wipe it off with paper towel and wash with soap and water. All clear!

chamomile tea

Among the wealth of herbal teas on the shelf, chamomile is particularly useful. In addition to its mild and pleasant apple-like flavor and the calming effect it is said to have, there are a lot of useful things you can do with it besides drink a cup.

Repel mosquitoes

You may love the mild apple-like flavor of chamomile tea but mosquitoes absolutely hate it. Brew a very strong batch of chamomile tea and keep it in a spray bottle in the fridge. Before you relax in the back yard or run through the tall grass, spray exposed skin liberally. It's fragrant, potent, and totally safe for children.

Lighten your hair

Play up your blond highlights by using a weak solution of chamomile tea as the final rinse when you wash your hair. Combine a brewed cup of tea with two cups of cool water and pour this over your hair after rinsing out the shampoo and conditioner. Your golden highlights will gleam!

Tone your skin

If you have sensitive skin that feels dry and uncomfortable after washing with soap, try a facial toner with chamomile. It's far more soothing and effective than many expensive skin products. Boil 4 cups of water and soak 2 chamomile tea bags in it for 15 minutes. Discard the tea bags and cool the tea. Store in a glass jar in the fridge. To use, remove makeup with a soap-free remover, then soak several cotton balls in the cool tea and rub all over your face.

chewing gum

If your mother was always telling you to spit out that gum, that's probably because she didn't know how many other uses there are for gum—in addition to popping big bubbles!

Make a temporary repair

A piece of gum is more than a bubble waiting to happen. It's also the ideal material for a quick and temporary repair until you have the time and the tools to do it right. You can fill a crack in a dog's water bowl (on the outside, so the pooch doesn't accidentally suck it down!) or use a couple of wads as window putty if a pane of glass is loose. Ever have the lens pop out of your eyeglasses while you were out and about? Use a bit of chewed gum to hold them in place until you can get a proper repair.

Settle a sour stomach

Fresh out of antacids, and heartburn is making you miserable? Pop in a stick of minty gum and chew. Spearmint is ideal for settling stomach rumbles and burbles, and the increased flow of saliva from gum chewing can help neutralize stomach acids.

THE Story Behind...

Chewing Gum

In 1869, Thomas Adams, a photographer from Staten Island, New York, invented modern chewing gum. His houseguest, General Antonio de Santa of Mexico, believed chicle, a natural gum from the sapodilla tree, could make rubber less expensive. Adams bounced this idea around, but when he noticed the general chewed the stuff, he was truly inspired. He created a chewing gum that wasn't paraffin-based, like all other gums on the market. A druggist agreed to carry it, the public responded well, and by February 1871 Adams New York Gum could be purchased in drugstores for a penny per piece. Today, Americans spend more than $2 billion per year on chewing gum.

Capture a crab

Crabbing is a favorite activity of kids who summer near docks and piers because all it takes is string, a net, and a lure. Crabs are notorious scavengers who tend to be keen to grab at a bit of raw bacon, but you'll catch aplenty with gum. The scent of a bit of freshly chewed and soft gum will call all the crabs in the area. Start that pot of water boiling; it's dinnertime soon!

club soda

Soda, seltzer, fizzy water...whatever you call it, it's cool and refreshing and immensely useful for many things besides drinking. Too bad the days are gone when you could get regular seltzer deliveries right to your doorstep.

Preserve a precious newspaper clipping

Newspapers aren't made to stay intact forever, but nobody wants a wedding or birth announcement to go brown and crumbly in just a few years. Make a preservative solution by mixing one tablespoon milk of magnesia with 2 cups club soda in a wide, flat dish. Soak the clipping for one hour, then pat dry with a paper towel and dry flat.

Make your diamond sparkle

Club soda gently and safely cleans precious jewels, whether it's your wedding diamond or your Great Aunt Ruby's emerald. Put the jewels in a glass and top with club soda. Let them soak overnight. The fizzing bubbles will lift away dirt and grime that dull the gleam. Dry and polish gently with a soft cloth.

Clean dentures overnight

Gone on a visit and forgotten your denture cleaner? Don't panic or go looking for a spare toothbrush. Instead, soak them overnight in a coffee mug topped up with club soda. The fizzy bubbles will lift away food particles and leave your teeth feeling clean in the morning.

Make a "submarine tank" for kids

Are the little ones bored at the restaurant table while the grownups chat? Kids need something to do! Make them a quick and easy game with a glass of club soda and a couple of raisins. Drop two or three raisin "submarines" in the water and let the kids watch the raisins go up and down. See if they can figure out that the bubbles in the club soda are lifting the raisins.

Fight tough stains on clothes and carpets

Just got a splash of red wine or a dribble of coffee on your cream-colored cashmere? Quick, splash it again, but this time with a dousing of club soda. There's no better way to stop the stain and prevent it from setting. You can do the same with spots on rugs and carpets—pour on the club soda and scrub gently with a towel or lint-free cloth.

Pancake and waffle batter, and especially matzo balls, are much lighter when you use club soda.

coffee

You can't do without a cup of coffee to start your morning or as a pick-me-up in the afternoon. But fresh coffee grounds provide more than caffeine, as you'll see in these fun tips.

Freshen a fridge

If something soured in your fridge or the freezer failed, clean it out, then fill a wide, shallow bowl with fresh coffee grounds and leave it in the fridge or freezer overnight. The strong scent of coffee will permeate the space, eradicating any hint of what went wrong.

Feed your plants

Used coffee grounds are full of nitrogen, so it's a shame to throw them away each day. Coffee is especially good for acid-loving plants, like camellias, evergreens, rhododendrons, azaleas, and rosebushes, so be sure they don't miss out on the occasional cup of coffee—grounds, that is.

Grow longer, stronger carrots

Carrot seeds are tiny to sow, and the beds require a great deal of cultivation so the soil is loose enough for the carrots to shoot downward as they grow. Increase the odds in your favor by working leftover coffee grounds into the soil as you prepare the plot, and then mix the seeds with damp grounds just before sowing them. The scent helps repel pests, and the added bulk of the grounds helps space out the tiny plants. What's more, that extra hit of nitrogen as the seeds sprout will give you a bumper crop.

Tamp down the ashes

A fireplace is a delight—until it's time to sweep out the ashes the next day, kicking up a cloud of dust and making you cough. Sprinkle the dead ashes liberally with moist coffee grounds and then sweep away. The dampness and weight of the grounds prevents clouds of dust dancing around your living room as you clean.

That takes the bait

Up bright and early for your fishing trip? Don't forget to bring the coffee. The grounds, that is. Stir the coffee grounds from your morning joe into the soil in your bait container. Whether it's the caffeine or the scent or perhaps the texture, worms love coffee grounds and they'll stay alive and lively all day.

cornstarch

Sure, you knew cornstarch was good for thickening sauces and puddings and also as a cooling, soothing alternative to talcum powder. But did you know it's good for all these other uses as well?

Untangle a shoelace

Junior got a knot in his sneaker and pulled and pulled until it became an impenetrable mass. Sprinkle the knot generously with cornstarch, and then work the knot again. The laces will start to slip and slide, and you'll be able to get the kinks out.

Clean up oily furniture

Got a little too enthusiastic when spritzing the side tables with lemon oil? Don't live with that sticky feeling. Sprinkle cornstarch over the surface and leave it for a few minutes to absorb the excess. Wipe up the cornstarch, then buff to a shine with a soft, lint-free cloth.

Remove a scorch mark

Left a brown scorch on a dress shirt with the iron? It can happen in the blink of an eye. The cleanup won't be quite that fast but it will be effective. Douse the scorch with water (presumably not on your ironing board!) then rub a generous amount of cornstarch into the stain. When the cornstarch dries, the stain will rinse out with the powder. This same technique works on bloodstains, though a second treatment may be needed before washing.

Make a gentle silver cleaner

Don't want to put harsh chemicals on Granny's old silver? Make a cleanser that's less harsh than commercial polishes—and one that won't remove all the tarnish from a complicated pattern, a look many silver lovers prefer because it throws a beautiful pattern into stunning relief. Mix cornstarch with water to make a thick paste. Rub it on the silver and let it dry. Buff off with a lint-free cloth to bring up the shine.

cream of tartar

Before the advent of reliable commercial baking powder, cooks made their own with varying mixtures of baking soda and cream of tartar, an acid salt that has many other uses besides making baked goods rise.

Create your own soft scrub

Got a surface that needs gentle cleaning, such as your elderly cast-iron tub or perhaps your brand-new designer sink? Make an effective cleanser that's devoid of harshness by mixing 2 teaspoons white vinegar with 2 teaspoons cream of tartar. Rub and scrub with a sponge, then rinse with warm water and buff dry.

Shine aluminum cookware

Aluminum pots conduct heat beautifully, but woe to the cook who lets acid touch the pan: Aluminum discolors like crazy. Remove discoloration and stains by putting 1 quart water and 2 tablespoons cream of tartar in the pan. Bring to a boil, and as it simmers for 10 minutes, you'll see the stains fade and disappear.

Take stains off tile and tubs

Got a bathtub ring that won't scrub off or stubborn stains on the tile? They're no match for hydrogen peroxide and cream of tartar. Put a few tablespoons of cream of tartar in a cup or jar, then add hydrogen peroxide by the drop to make a thick paste. (If you accidentally add way too much liquid, you may want to dump half the entire cup before stirring in more cream of tartar—otherwise you may find your container empty fast!) Spread on the stain and let it dry. Rinse off with warm water, and the stain should be history.

THE DANGERS OF CREAM OF TARTAR

Today you head out to the grocery store to buy cream of tartar; back in the 19th century you'd head to the druggist if you didn't want any trouble. In 1883, the *New York Times* covered the story of Manhattan grocer Henry V. Fuller, who, along with others, was charged by the City Board of Health "with selling cream of tartar." According to laws of the day, pharmacists sold cream of tartar (which could be used both medicinally and as a food) to ensure it was of the correct chemical makeup. Grocers could get in on the action—but they ran the risk of prosecution. Fuller claimed he bought "pure" cream of tartar at 164 Duane Street to sell as a food only. Interestingly, the street where he committed his "crime," along with its neighbor, Reade Street, became the birthplace of one of today's largest chain of drugstores: Duane Reade.

Repel ants

Sprinkle a thin line of cream of tartar across the path that ants are traveling to come in. Put it across the windowsill or in corners and cracks around the kitchen. As with boric acid, ants won't cross the line—but it's a much safer chemical to have out in your kitchen around foodstuffs and where children might be playing.

flour

You knew flour makes the bread that is our staff of life. But did you know that flour is also endlessly useful all around the house in a wealth of other ways?

Clean copper and brass

Mix 2 tablespoons flour with 2 tablespoons white vinegar and 2 tablespoons regular iodized table salt. Rub the resulting paste thickly on copper or brass (the uncoated kind; not anything with varnish on it) and let it dry. Use a soft, lint-free cloth to buff the dry remains off your metal object, and you'll find a smooth, mellow shine with an unharmed finish.

Buff up a stainless steel sink

Metal sinks look terrific when they go in, but the impact of daily use steadily dulls their luster until they look stained and worn. Bring the shine back to a steel sink by drying it with a dishtowel. Then sprinkle plain white flour over the surface—not too much, just a light coating—and rub it with a soft dry cloth. Rinse with warm water and polish with another dry cloth.

Restore a deck of cards

Your favorite, most winning deck of playing cards will gradually show the wear and tear of all those finger oils from you and your fellow players. You don't have to give them up, however. Put the cards in a ziplock bag and scoop in about a cup of flour. Seal and shake to coat every surface, then let the cards sit for 10 minutes so the flour can absorb the oils from the surface. Remove the cards and shake off the excess flour. You're ready to start clearing all the poker chips off the table again!

ketchup

It's on every table in every diner you've ever visited, and it's hard to find a fridge that doesn't hold a bottle. Ketchup is terrific for lots besides serving as a condiment for your burgers and fries.

Clean detailed silver patterns

Some people like a tiny bit of tarnish left in a complex silver pattern to throw the detail into relief, but if you want your silver to shine, shine, shine, without rubbing and wearing off the pattern, then ketchup is the way to go. The acids in ketchup will quickly remove every last speck of tarnish from an elaborate silver pattern, leaving it gleaming. Smear a few pieces at a time with ketchup and let them sit for several minutes. Rinse a piece to see how it's coming along. If needed, apply more ketchup, but keep checking so you don't do any damage with the acid. When the silver shines to your satisfaction, rinse with warm water and buff with a soft, lint-free cloth.

Banish chlorine green hair

Any blonde—whether natural or not—knows that too much time in the pool can leave a distinct green cast to light-colored locks, not to mention a decided smell of chlorine that builds up after days at the pool. To return your tresses to their rightful color and eradicate the chlorine, massage ketchup into your wet hair while in the shower and leave it for 10 minutes. Rinse well and shampoo as usual. The green will be gone, and you'll smell like nothing but freshly washed hair.

To brighten up copper pots, smear a generous layer of ketchup all over the copper surface you want to clean.

Brighten the copper

While copper details on the exterior of a home look lovely as they take on an aged green patina, copper pots and decorative items inside the house look best when they're gleaming and bright. Rather than donning gloves to apply chemical cleaners, use your hands (or a sponge) to smear a generous layer of ketchup all over the copper surface you want to clean. The acidic coating quickly works to remove every speck of tarnish. Rinse with warm water and buff to a shine to make your brightwork bright again.

Kool-Aid

Powdered drink mixes, especially the Kool-Aid brand, are readily available, even though you might think these envelopes of potent drink mix might have outlived their usefulness in a world of soda pop. You would be wrong, as you'll find in these wide-ranging tips for using Kool-Aid.

Clean concrete

The same acids that make lemonade-flavored Kool-Aid taste good are a potent cleaning solution before you add water and sugar. Mix the contents of a package with 2 tablespoons hot water to make a paste, then rub that paste over rust stains in concrete. Scrub with a stiff cleaning brush and the stains will disappear. Rinse well.

Remove dishwasher rust stains

If you have hard water, the inside of your dishwasher will eventually get dingy, as iron and other minerals build up on the interior walls. Return your appliance to pristine condition by putting a package of lemonade Kool-Aid in the soap dispenser, then run a hot (or "heavy") cycle. The inside will gleam like new again.

Decorate a kid's room

Kids always want to have a say in decorating their own rooms, and here's a way to make their private space highly personal. Let your child choose the color and/or flavor of Kool-Aid he most prefers, and stir one or two packages into a quart of white, water-based paint. The strong dyes result in a distinctive paint that's perfect for brightening a wall of your child's room.

lemon juice

Bottled lemon juice is great for cooking That's just the start. In particular, it's a great cleaner: Rub on gold jewelry or copper pots, and they will glitter! Or mix equal parts lemon juice and water for a handy all-purpose cleaner!

Cook fluffy rice

Add a tablespoon of lemon juice to the water when you're making rice. After it's finished cooking, fluff it with a fork. No more sticky rice!

Crisp up lettuce

Forgot to make a salad for supper the last few nights? Tonight you can redeem yourself, even if that head of lettuce seems soggy and sad. Put a couple tablespoons lemon juice in a bowl of cold water and let the lettuce leaves soak for 20 minutes. They'll be crispy and fresh again.

Remove stains from marble

Marble looks beautiful in the kitchen, whether on the countertop or a board for rolling pastry. If you've lived with marble, though, you'll realize its drawback: It stains. If you have a really stubborn stain, try scrubbing with a paste of lemon and salt. This ought to remove the stain, but don't scrub too hard, and rinse it very well so the acid doesn't damage the stone.

Clean a crusty microwave

Been awhile since you washed down the inside of the microwave? Don't spend ages scrubbing. Mix 2 cups of water with 1/4 cup lemon juice in a microwave-safe glass dish and cook on high for 8 minutes. The steam will loosen food particles on the walls and glass, making it easy to wipe clean with a few swipes.

Replace salt

If you have high blood pressure, omit salt from savory foods and sprinkle with lemon juice instead. This chef's trick really works!

marshmallows

What can you do with a marshmallow besides make a dessert treat from it? Here are some sweet ideas.

Top a cupcake

Anyone can make frosting. Be the coolest mom in school by bringing cupcakes topped with melted marshmallows! Once the timer goes off on your batch of cupcakes, open the oven door and put a single large marshmallow on the top of each cupcake. Return the pan to the hot oven for 1 minute, until the marshmallows soften and melt over the tops. Remove the pan and cool completely. Just before serving, melt 1 cup of chocolate chips in a glass bowl in the microwave for 1 minute on high. Whisk with a fork until smooth, then use the fork to drip a crazy pattern of chocolate stripes all over the surface of each cupcake.

Drip-proof a sugar cone

Kids love ice cream in a cone but they rarely understand that the clock is ticking once you hand it over. Eat it or it's going to melt! Buy little ones some time to enjoy their cone by dropping a mini-marshmallow into a pointed sugar cone and pushing it down into the tip. Put a large marshmallow above it and push it down, too.

WAY BACK WHEN...

Marshmallows Soothed Sore Throats

Today a marshmallow is a spongy treat cooked over campfires. Up until the mid-1800s, marshmallow candy was used medicinally. Doctors extracted juice from the roots of the marshmallow plant and cooked it with egg whites and sugar, then whipped it into a foamy meringue. This hardened and the resulting candy soothed children's sore throats. Eventually, advanced manufacturing processes replaced the root juice with gelatin, which eliminated any healing properties.

You've just created two very effective barriers to the drips that always make their way out of the bottom and all over someone's shirt!

Preserve brown sugar

One day you have a lovely fresh bag of soft brown sugar, and the next time you go to make cookies, you've got a piece of brown granite. It's hard to keep brown sugar fresh, even in a sealed bag, but you can ensure easy scooping by putting two or three very fresh large marshmallows in the sugar bag before you seal it. If you add a few marshmallows *and* seal the whole thing up in a plastic container, you'll be ready to bake cookies at the drop of a hat for months to come.

mayonnaise

Lots of salads are nearly unimaginable without mayonnaise—from slaw to potato to egg—but once you've eaten lunch, you'll find plenty more to do around the house with that jar of mayonnaise.

Take crayon off polished wood

Did the kids color waaaay outside the lines on your varnished maple dining table? No problem— don't scrub it with water or anything scratchy or you'll mar the surface. Just rub on a tablespoon or two of mayo with a paper towel and let it sit. Rub again and, presto, the marks are gone. Don't let your children know how easy it is to repair *that* mistake or they may try it again.

Take sap off auto paint

Parked your new car under a pine tree in spring? You may think you'll never get all those dots of pine sap off the hood. They're utterly impervious to soap and water, and you certainly don't want to scrub with anything abrasive. Mayonnaise is your car's new best friend. Rub a generous

dab directly on each sap deposit and let it sit for 10 minutes. Use a soft, absorbent rag to remove the mayo and sap, then wash the car as usual. This same treatment will also remove road tar that can accumulate on the fenders. Now, don't park under that tree again!

Photo-worthy houseplants

Even a healthy houseplant looks sad and dingy when the leaves are coated with a fine layer of dust. Make the whole house look as verdant as a florist's shop by rubbing each leaf with a paper towel dipped in a little mayonnaise. Polish off with another paper towel and you'll have a gleaming, deep-green shine that will last for months.

Soften ragged cuticles

Housework making your nails look rough and ragged? Don't soak in dishwashing liquid! Put your digits in a dish of mayo for 5 minutes and then wipe off with a paper towel. Trim nails while they're slightly softer from the soak, and use an orange stick to push back raggedy cuticles. Wash with warm water, slather on some lotion, and you just saved yourself the price of a fancy manicure!

Two-for-one hair and skin treatment

Condition your hair and smooth your face at the same time with a mayonnaise treatment. Massage mayo into your dry hair and scalp, then wrap it in a towel or put on a shower cap. While your hair rests in this luxurious treatment, spread a thin layer of mayo over your freshly washed face, avoiding the eye area. Lie down with a couple of damp tea bags or cucumber slices over your eyes for 15 minutes and then step right into the shower to wash it all off. You'll feel like you're just back from the salon.

meat tenderizer

If that jar of meat tenderizer has been sitting on your shelf unused, take it down again. As you'll see here, you can do more with it than simply tenderize a steak.

Take the bite out of a mosquito attack

Got a bite on your face and a meeting in the morning? Make the itchy red bump of a bad mosquito bite disappear by slathering on a paste made by mixing a little meat tenderizer with a few drops of water. You can do this right in your palm and apply directly to your skin with your fingers. Let sit for 5 minutes before washing off. If you apply this paste within minutes of the bite, there will be no mark at all, but even if you do it hours later, you'll still reduce the redness and swelling significantly.

Ease a sting

The same trick works for a wasp or hornet bite, relieving the pain almost instantly and preventing or reducing swelling or hives. If the stinger is still in the skin, gently remove it with tweezers, being very careful not to squeeze it deeper into the wound. Apply the meat tenderizer and water paste and let it remain until it dries and flakes off, 15 minutes or so. The enzymes break down the toxins from the sting.

Soothe your lower back

Moving heavy boxes all day? Your back must be killing you. Mix 1/4 cup meat tenderizer with 2 tablespoons of water, adding a bit more as needed to make a runny paste. Have someone rub this right into the skin over your aching lower back, and ideally cover the area with a washcloth dipped in hot water and squeezed out. After 10 to 15 minutes, you'll feel the muscles start to relax. Rinse off and take it easy.

THE Story Behind...

Adolph's Meat Tenderizer

In 1949, two former GIs, Lloyd Rigler and Larry Deutsch, found a restaurant in Santa Barbara, California, that served tasty *and* inexpensive steak. The chef, Adolph Rempp, explained how he was able to release fine flavors in inexpensive cuts of meat: He sprinkled on a tenderizer of his own creation. One of the main ingredients was papain, an enzyme from papaya. The men saw huge commercial potential—the years after World War II were lean, and meat was expensive. They bought the recipe and Adolph's Meat Tenderizer was born. Rigler toured the country demonstrating the product to food critics. Rave reviews led to windfall sales. After the men retired, they became patrons of the arts. Adolph's Meat Tenderizer is still an artful way to stretch a budget.

Take on tough stains

Hot chocolate, coffee with milk, blood—these types of protein-based stains are usually nearly impossible to remove completely. If the stain is still wet, you've got the best chance. If not, wet the cloth and hope for the best. Sprinkle the area thickly with meat tenderizer, rub it in, and let it rest for an hour. Launder as usual.

milk

More and more dollar stores are carrying a limited selection of fresh items, usually basics such as bread and milk. Many stores already carried powdered milk in their grocery aisles, but whatever type of milk you find there, you'll find here some novel ways to use it.

Shave your face

Use milk in place of shaving foam. Warm full-fat milk and pat it onto your skin. While you shave, continue to pat on more to keep your skin wet.

For men, it's probably an emergency fix, but women shaving their legs may never go back!

Relieve a child's itching skin

Many parents hesitate to put hydrocortisone creams on children, but mild rashes can drive your kid crazy with the scratching. Mix powdered milk with just enough warm water to make it the thickness of heavy cream. Add a tiny pinch of salt and spread it over the affected parts. It will soothe the itch, and it's so mild that you can reapply as often as necessary to bring relief. Rinse off the previous application and slather on a new one.

You're soaking in it!

Cleopatra knew the benefits of a milk bath for the skin, and a couple thousand years later, it's still true. Milk moisturizes and softens the skin. Pour 2 to 3 cups of milk into the bath as the water runs (or use a cup of powdered milk) and add a little scented bath oil, if you like. Soak for at least 10 minutes for best results.

Sweeten fish and corn

When you thaw a block of frozen fish, it can taste disappointingly watery. Avoid that by placing the unwrapped block in a shallow dish of milk and

Sweeten corn by adding 1 cup of milk to the pot of boiling water.

To freshen a recycled bottle, squirt yellow mustard into the bottle, half fill with warm water, and slosh gently.

letting it thaw there—it will taste fresher when cooked. If you have corn on the cob that's been sitting in the fridge for a few days, add 1 cup of milk to the pot of boiling water, and you'll get sweeter corn.

Have a milk massage

If you like to use essential oils for your personal fragrance but don't like the greasy feeling of the carrier oil, use milk instead. Add a few drops to a little milk and spread it on your skin or use it in a bath. Make the solution up fresh when you need it.

mustard

You may find a tin of mustard powder in the food section, or you may be equally lucky and find a jar of prepared mustard. Either way, there are a lot of unexpected things you can do with it besides top a hotdog.

Soothe a chest cold

That awful feeling of congestion has settled right into your chest, and the cough is wearing you out. Sometimes Grandma really did know best, and what you need is an old-fashioned mustard plaster. Smear plain old yellow mustard (not Dijon or any other type) directly on your chest, then rinse a hand towel in hot water, wring it out, and lay it over the mustard. You'll feel that congestion start to break up.

Relax your muscles

Mustard can be very soothing for aching backs and weary muscles. While you run the hot water into the tub, add 3/4 cup yellow prepared mustard to the water and mix it in well. Soak for at least 15 minutes, and feel those tense muscles start to unwind.

Get the skunk out

Get sprayed by skunk? Wash with tomato juice. It's an old wives' tale that's also true. But what if your car runs over a skunk? Dead or alive, the scent can cling, and you can't splash tomato juice all over your car. But you can splash mustard. Mix 1 cup of dry mustard powder with a gallon of warm water, and slosh it all over the tires and underbody to get rid of the smell.

Freshen a recycled bottle

Want to use that nice wine bottle for cold water or that cold cream pot for a homemade cosmetic? That's a great idea, unless you can't get rid of the scent of whatever went before. Squirt yellow mustard into the bottle, half fill with warm water, and slosh gently. Let it sit for 15 minutes, then rinse and wash. The bottle will smell of...nothing.

oatmeal

Yes, you know it's one of the healthier breakfast options when you're starting your day. Now you can turn to oatmeal for help around the house at other times of day as well.

Tighten your pores

Oatmeal makes an extremely soothing face mask that tightens your pores and leaves your skin feeling soft and smooth. Grind 1/4 cup oatmeal to a fine powder in a blender. Add 1 egg white and 2 tablespoons honey. Pulse to combine, then smooth this mixture over your clean face, avoiding the eye area. Wear for 15 minutes, then rinse with warm water, pat dry, and apply a light moisturizer.

Scrub your hands

Been gardening and can't get that dirt scrubbed off your fingertips? Mix oatmeal—either quick-cooking or old-fashioned, but *not* the flavored instant kind—with enough milk to make a thin paste, and scrub your hands well with it. The dirt will come out, and your hands will feel softened and smooth.

Soothe itchy skin

Whether you've got chicken pox or poison ivy, oatmeal is what you need—not to eat, but to soak in. Grind a cup of oatmeal in your blender, food processor, or even a spice or coffee grinder until the oatmeal is a fine powder. Stir this powder into a warm bath and soak for as long as you like. For just a few pennies, this is the exact same thing you're getting when you buy special oatmeal baths at the drugstore. Oatmeal soothes and heals whatever ails you, and it's completely harmless and nonirritating, making it ideal for children with eczema.

Shampoo a shut-in

Oatmeal and baking soda make an excellent and effective dry shampoo that can be very comforting for someone who's bedridden or ill. It soaks up excess oils and neutralizes odors. Grind 1/4 cup oatmeal to a fine powder in a blender or spice grinder, then add 1/4 cup baking soda and pulse to combine. Put a towel around the shoulders of the person to be shampooed and another towel on the lap. Sprinkle a few tablespoons of this mixture over the scalp, working it to the roots with your fingers. Let it sit for 5 minutes, then gently brush it out over the towel.

olive oil

For years you've been hearing that olive oil is one of the most heart-healthy oils you can cook with. With these tips and ideas, you can also benefit from olive oil's goodness even if you're nowhere near the kitchen.

Mediterranean polish

Most modern furniture sprays and polishes are nothing but silicone, which leaves a quick shine but builds up to a sticky dullness over time. For a much more environmentally friendly polish for finished wood surfaces, simply wipe on a dab of pure olive oil with a soft cloth, then buff to a shine.

Rub three times for luck

Is your old baseball mitt in need of new life? Recondition it with olive oil and you'll bring softness and shine to that hard-worn old leather. Pour oil on a rag and then work it into the glove well, rubbing into cracks and crevices. Use a clean rag to buff off any excess, and then fly balls better watch out!

Repair damaged hair

Too much sun, chemicals, blow-drying, and curling can leave hair as dry and brittle as autumn leaves. Put hair in a time machine and undo severe damage with olive oil. Wash hair and rinse with warm water. Heat 1/2 cup of olive oil in a cup in the microwave for about 45 seconds, until it's warm but you can still hold your finger in it. Massage it all through your hair and then cover with an old shower cap or wrap your hair with a sheet of plastic wrap. Cover with a towel and wear it for 30 minutes. Shampoo and rinse well, and your hair will feel thick and silky.

peanut butter

Peanut butter is a cheap and healthy source of protein, and kids love it. But even if you have no intention of eating it on a sandwich, you shouldn't banish peanut butter from your kitchen cupboard, as you'll see from these useful hints.

Help the (pet) medicine go down

You've tried burying your dog's pill in his food but he finds it and spits it out every time. Who's the master here? Outmaneuver him with peanut butter! Take a teaspoon of peanut butter and push the pill into the center, then push the lump off with your finger and hold it out as a tempting treat. Down it goes, and Fido won't be any the wiser!

Catch a mouse

Mice don't want cheese; they want peanut butter. It's the best bait there is to lure the pesky critters into a mousetrap, and it won't dry up and harden like a piece of cheese. (Mice seem to prefer smooth to crunchy, but you can decide since you're serving up their last meal!)

Take off a price tag

Sure, WD-40 is terrific at removing price-tag adhesive, but you don't want to spray it on the outside of your kid's new plastic lunch box or beach ball. So use peanut butter instead. Rub on a dab, let it sit for a few minutes, and then wipe clean with a paper towel. The peanut butter wipes clean in seconds, and so do the remains of the glue.

Foil fried fish's odor

Frying fish can leave a strong odor lingering in the kitchen. Add a dollop of smooth peanut butter to the oil before you fry and it will absorb the smell, letting you enjoy fish for dinner—and not keep smelling it days later.

pepper

Black pepper is the seasoning most of us reach for right after the salt. You may be surprised to find that it has other uses besides perking up your stew. And when you're thinking pepper, don't confine yourself solely to the black stuff. Potent cayenne has lots of off-the-table uses as well.

Relieve arthritis in your hands

If your hands are stiff in the morning, make a warming massage oil to use like lotion: 1 tablespoon neutral oil (such almond oil or olive oil) mixed with 2 drops lavender essential oil and 1/4 teaspoon cayenne (or 2 drops pepper essential oil). Rub gently 'til your joints loosen.

Use peanut butter to remove a price tag. Rub on a dab, let it sit for a few minutes, and then wipe clean with a paper towel.

Fight off a migraine

Migraine sufferers usually know just before an attack is coming on, and some of them swear by this old-fashioned remedy that has averted many a painful headache. Briskly stir up to 1/2 teaspoon of cayenne pepper into half a glass of tepid water. Drink it down and lie down to rest. If you still feel the pain, repeat again in 30 minutes.

Break the grip of a cold

Is your nose stuffed up? Cayenne pepper breaks up sinus congestion swiftly. Heat some chicken stock to boiling and lace it with a teaspoon of cayenne pepper (or less, depending on how much you can bear). Drink it from a mug, and be sure to sniff at the vapors as you sip. Soon that stuffed-up nose will be operating normally again.

Deter deer and groundhogs

Mix 1/4 cup cayenne with warm water in a spray bottle and mist it over the plants that the deer seem to be zeroing in on. If you can find the hole in your yard where that pesky groundhog hides in between eating your flowers, pour a liberal amount of cayenne down the hole (there's usually a second hole, too, that you should find and anoint), and he'll hastily make other habitation plans.

popcorn

You can buy unpopped kernels of popcorn to pop your own fresh at home, or you can sometimes buy ready-popped bags of popcorn in the food aisle, ready to be put to uses besides movie snacking.

Pad a package

If you're shipping a package overseas, popcorn isn't a recommended replacement for foam peanuts, but for domestic shipping, it's ideal. Cheap and environmentally friendly, it's also a terrific shock absorber. Wrap the object you're shipping in paper or plastic, and lay it down on a layer of air-popped popcorn on the bottom. Shake more popcorn all around to cover, then seal it. Ready to ship!

Decorate a tree

The old-fashioned look of a popcorn garland will remind you of childhood holidays at Grandma's house. Let your own kids and grandkids re-create those memories with a big bowl of popcorn and a couple of long strings or pieces of yarn attached to large plastic needlepoint needles.

Make a squirrel-unfriendly bird feeder

A couple loops of popcorn strung on thread and hung from a back porch make a tasty snack that birds can perch on and peck off, but squirrels will find too lightweight and unstable to climb.

potato chips

It's true that most uses of potato chips involve eating them, but there are a handful of useful kitchen tricks that expand the uses of a chip and may have you reaching for them more often.

Top a casserole

Crushed potato chips are a delicious casserole topping to use in place of bread crumbs. And they don't require any additional fat to crisp up. If your macaroni and cheese or green bean casserole looks naked going into the oven, grab a handful of chips out of the bag and crush them between your palms over the top. Bake as usual.

Give fried foods a crispy crunch

Out of bread crumbs to bread your pork chop, chicken fingers, or piece of fish? Roll the item in fine potato chip crumbs and fry as usual. The crust will be crisp, salty, and delicious.

Make a sandwich

In the British Isles, there's a phenomenon known as a "crisp butty" or "crisp sarnie," which is nothing more than two buttered pieces of bread enclosing a handful of salt and vinegar potato chips. Next time you think the larder is nearly bare, give it a try—it's strangely addictive.

Bake some cookies

Use your favorite butter cookie recipe, or the standard recipe for chocolate chip cookies, but instead of chocolate, add crushed, salted potato chips. If you love a mix of sweet and salty in your snack foods, you'll never look back!

salt

When someone is incredibly grounded and full of common sense and essential usefulness, we refer to them as "the salt of the earth." You may say the same about the huge variety of salty uses we've assembled here.

Salvage a pan

Is baked-on or burned food ruining one of your favorite pots or pans? Salt will bring it back into service. Sprinkle salt heavily on the stuck-on food and dampen it with a little water. Let the salt sit until the food lifts right off the pan, then wash.

Clean up a bubble-over

Fruit pies are especially guilty of bubbling all over the bottom of your oven. When you remove the pie, sprinkle salt thickly on the spill while it's still liquid. You can also do this with messy boil-overs on the stovetop. When the salted area cools, wipe it right up with a sponge.

Get dishwasher stains off glassware

Spots on glassware, such as Pyrex dishes or glass mixing bowls or heavy tumblers, can be very stubborn, but they're no match for salt. Mix

Save time... save money!

1 cup salt with 1 quart vinegar and soak the glassware in it overnight. Rub off the stain and wash as usual.

Clean fish more easily

Catching fish is half the battle. Cleaning is the rest! Sprinkle salt liberally on a fish before you start to descale it. You'll find that the scales flick off faster, making the whole job easier.

Polish your griddle

Pour a few tablespoons salt on the cold clean griddle and polish firmly with a paper towel, then discard and wipe before heating. The smoothly polished surface will prevent flapjacks from sticking.

Chase cabbage worms away

Every gardener knows the frustration of cabbage worms gnawing away just as the big heads of cabbage are ready to be harvested. Stop worms in their tracks with a mix of one part salt and two parts flour, dusted around the cabbages every few days as harvest approaches.

Whip cream higher

A tiny pinch of salt added to a bowl of whipping cream will make it whip up higher and fluffier. Same with egg whites and also with eggs you're whisking for scrambled eggs. They'll be fluffier.

Stop a sudsy disaster

Ever put too much soap in a washing machine, or found that your trying-to-help kid used dishwashing liquid in the dishwasher? When the suds start to emerge from the door of the machine, you may think they'll never stop. Put a halt to the proceedings by sprinkling salt over the mountain of bubbles. They'll quickly subside so you can clean up fast.

Kill poison ivy

It's hard to fully destroy this dangerous vine once it takes hold, but salt will do the trick. Dissolve 3 pounds of sidewalk salt in a gallon of water and add a squirt of dish liquid. Saturate the plant and its roots. It will soon be gone.

shortening

Butter makes a tasty piecrust, but the real secret to a flaky one is shortening. Even if you're not making pastry, shortening is the secret to lots of useful household tips.

Make a magic snow shovel

Early snowfall catch you unaware? Before you start the backbreaking labor of digging out your car, smear a generous amount of solid vegetable shortening on your snow shovel. The snow will slide on and off much more quickly and easily, for a faster and more efficient job.

Restore a pair of galoshes

Grownups wear galoshes to keep our feet dry, but kids wear them as a license to walk through every mud puddle they see. And now your daughter's favorite pink princess galoshes are sadly scuffed and dull. Bring back the shine to your little princess's face and her boots by polishing the galoshes with a dab of shortening on a clean rag.

Soften your feet

The active ingredient in fancy foot creams is pretty much the same as the active ingredient in shortening: fat, or grease. That's what softens your skin. So save yourself more than a few bucks and soften with shortening. Before bed, slather it on your soles and put on socks. In the morning, you'll have satiny soft tootsies.

Remove tar from fabric

Is a drip of tar or pine resin ruining your favorite work jeans? Scrape off what you can with the edge of a credit card, then work shortening directly into the stain. Let it sit overnight, then dab up the excess with a paper towel and treat the whole area with a grease remover such as Wisk. Launder as usual.

Shine a pair of galoshes with a dab of shortening on a clean rag.

Tell squirrels to take a hike

Is your standing bird feeder getting raided by hungry squirrels? Grease the pole of the feeder liberally with shortening. Squirrels will soon learn to forage elsewhere, and your favorite birds can return to the table.

soda and cola

When you're watching your sugar intake, you might find that it's best to cut back on your soda consumption. That's okay; there are still plenty of immensely useful things you can do with it besides drinking it.

Take rust off chrome

Got a car old enough to have real chrome on it? Then it's probably got a few rust spots, too. Crush a piece of tinfoil and dip it in cola, then scrub off those little dots of rust with ease.

Speed up a drain

Kitchen sink starting to drain slowly? You've probably got a clog waiting to happen. Make sure it never does by slowly pouring a whole 2-liter bottle of cola down the drain. The potent carbonic acid in cola will get things moving again.

Clean car battery corrosion

If your car battery has corrosion on the terminals, dip a rag in cola and wrap it around the terminals. Let it sit for several minutes and then scrub off the rust deposits and any cola residue with a damp sponge. The same trick works to loosen rusted-on nuts and bolts.

Restore stained porcelain

Got a toilet with a stain ring around the bowl? Pour in 1 1/2 cups of soda and let it sit for an hour. Scrub and flush—good as new.

 ### BAKE A CAKE WITH SODA

Short on eggs and oil but yearning for a piece of cake? If you have soda in the house, you have no worries. Most packaged cake mixes direct you to add 3 eggs and 1/4 cup of oil to the mix. But the thing is, you don't *have* to. Here is a way to bake a cake without either eggs or oil that will result in a cake that is delicious—and lower in fat and cholesterol.

1 Take out your packaged cake mix. Any flavor will work.

2 Grab a can of your favorite soda. Use diet soda for the fewest calories.

3 Ignore the directions on the box—don't add eggs, water, or oil. Just add one can of soda.

4 Bake for the amount of time suggested on the cake mix. You will have a delicious cake—and eat it, too!

Get oil off concrete

Car leaked oil on the garage floor? That's a mess to clean, unless you have some cola. Sprinkle the spot liberally with sawdust or kitty litter, working it in with a broom. Leave for half an hour to soak up the grease, then sweep it up and discard. Pour on enough cola to cover the area, and work it in with a rag. Let sit for half an hour, then mop it up with 2 tablespoons each laundry detergent and bleach mixed with 2 quarts of warm water.

Keep flowers fresher longer

When putting flowers in a vase, add 1/2 cup of a clear soda, such as Sprite or 7-Up, to the water and the flowers will live for days longer than they will in plain water.

Wipe a chunk of Spam across the mirror, then rub it off with a soft cloth; **your mirror won't steam up again for weeks!**

Spam

Spam has passed from being a survival food to a source of humor to simply a cultural icon. And in that time, its uses have expanded far beyond the limits of the kitchen.

Polish wood furniture

Cut off a chunk of Spam, wipe it across your wood tabletop, and polish it off with a soft cloth. You'll get a gleaming shine and no harmful chemicals. Best of all, there's no silicone buildup like most commercial polishes leave behind.

De-mist mirrors

Trying to shave but all the steam in the bathroom keeps thwarting you? Spam is the answer. Wipe a chunk of Spam across the mirror, then rub it off with a soft cloth. The light coating of oil it leaves behind is invisible, but your mirror won't steam up again for weeks!

Catch fish

Sure, worms are tasty, but any catfish or carp fisherman can tell you that what the fish really want is a chunk of Spam. Take along a can of Spam on your next fishing trip and you'll be pulling them into the boat! In fact, take two cans, and you can eat one for breakfast before you start the day.

spices

The selection of spices and dried herbs will vary widely, depending on your dollar store and its current stock. What won't change is all the many uses to which you can put these inexpensive items.

Discourage insects

The pungent fragrances that humans so enjoy in spices are the exact same scents that makes bugs scurry for cover. Keep ants and other insects out of flour and sugar by dropping a bay leaf into the container (the bay fragrance it imparts to your stores will be minimal). Put apple-pie spice into a small square of fabric and tie it tightly with a string. Hang this easy sachet in moist places such as under the bathroom sink or behind the washer to discourage silverfish.

Keep thermoses and storage jars fresh

Ever open a thermos to pour in coffee or soup and been horrified at the stale smell? Make sure it never happens again by dropping a whole clove into the bottom of a container that you usually store closed. Just be sure to discard the clove before using the container.

A sage solution to smelly sneakers

Crumble a bit of dried sage into each shoe before putting it on. Sage is not only gently fragrant, but it actually kills the bacteria that make your teenager's gym shoes smell so bad. Shake out the flecks at night, and add a new leaf the next day.

Keep dark hair glossy

To keep black, brown, and chestnut hair glossy, rinse weekly with an herbal tea of color-enhancing spices and herbs. In three cups of boiling water, steep 1 teaspoon each of dried rosemary, sage, cinnamon, and allspice, along with 1/2 teaspoon ground cloves. Strain through a paper towel–lined sieve or a coffee filter and let cool. Use as the final rinse after washing your hair.

sugar

Sugar makes baked goods tender and food more appealing and is an excellent preservative. It's also full of other completely nonfood uses that you'll be thrilled to try.

Scrub on a healthy glow

You can spend a fortune on a sugar scrub at a salon—or you can mix 1/4 cup olive oil with 1/4 cup granulated sugar and use it like soap in the shower, scrubbing your arms, legs, shoulders, and, gently, your face. Rinse well, pat dry, and moisturize. You'll glow like you just returned from a beach vacation! (This same mix will also safely scrub oil or paint off your hands after a job.)

Get rid of roaches

Toxic chemicals work to get rid of roaches, but particularly if you have children or pets, you don't necessarily want to use commercial roach products in your house. Instead, scatter corners and behind cabinets with a mix of half sugar and half baking soda for a nontoxic and highly effective "poison." The roaches come to eat the sugar, but also eat the baking soda and die. Replace often until the roaches disappear.

Cure a chile burn

Sprinkled on too much hot sauce? Found that salsa a bit hotter than you bargained for? Your next bite should be a spoonful of sugar. The chemical in chiles that burns is capsaicin, which bonds to the pain receptors in your tongue, and all the cold water in the world can't fix that. A taste of sugar, however, breaks those bonds right away.

Keep cheese fresher

Toss a few sugar cubes into the bag when you seal a lump of hard cheese. The sugar helps prevent mold from forming. Also add a few sugar cubes to the container before you seal up a cake or loaf of pumpkin bread, and it will also stay moist for days longer.

Prevent killer worms in the garden

If your garden is about 250 square feet, all you need is a 5-pound bag of sugar to keep nematode worms off all your plants. These microscopic parasites attack roots, destroying the plants and all your hard work. If your area is prone to nematodes, spread the sugar over the soil in the spring when you're preparing the ground, and the nematodes will never get started.

Save a bundle!

Rosebushes love the tannins in tea leaves. **Keep your tea leaves in a compost bowl by your kitchen sink, and dump them around the rosebushes once a week.**

tea

A nice cup of tea will perk you right up. But a nice handful of tea bags or tea leaves has even more uses that you'll be eager to try.

Keep the fridge fresh

An open box of baking soda in the refrigerator is the time-honored way to keep odors down, but did you know that tea bags do an even better job? Put three or four tea bags around the fridge, and odors will be readily absorbed. Change them every few weeks for best results.

Use tea in your smoker

Rip open a few tea bags and sprinkle the tea leaves over the soaked wood chips next time you're smoking fish or meat on the grill. The tea leaves impart a distinctive, unique flavor.

Help heal pinkeye

Children are more susceptible to pinkeye than adults, and they're also more apt to rub at their sore and tender eye while it's infected, making it likely they will spread the bacteria. Help heal pinkeye faster and give your child relief with a soothing tea bag compress. Wet a tea bag, squeeze out the excess, and have the child lie still for 10 minutes with the tea bag on the eyelid. The tannin helps the swelling go right down.

Brighten dark hair

Has summer sun and chlorine made your dark hair rough and dry? Soothe your sun-stressed tresses with a warm rinse of dark tea. Pour a quart through your hair after a mild shampoo. It will bring out highlights and make your hair feel soft again.

Freshen your feet

Sweaty, smelly feet ruining your shoes and your day? Every night, soak your feet in a basin of strong tea for 20 minutes. After a week or two, you should notice a real difference in both the sweat output and the odor.

Clean delicate Oriental rugs

Oriental and Persian rugs must be cleaned carefully to protect their valuable fibers and prevent damage to the patterned weave. Avoid major dirt and dust buildup by periodically cleaning the rug. Empty the contents of six tea bags into a bowl and sprinkle it with 1/2-teaspoon water. Sprinkle these barely damp leaves on the rug, and then brush them off vigorously with a clean broom. The tea leaves will draw out dust and dirt without leaving any stain or color on the rug.

Feed your roses

Rosebushes love the tannins in tea leaves, so if you're a regular tea drinker, keep your tea leaves in a compost bowl by your kitchen sink, and dump them around the rosebushes once a week.

Speed up compost

You're trying to compost your kitchen waste and not throw it all away, but it's not working as well as it should. If your compost pile seems sluggish, pour a few cups of strong brewed tea on it. The acidic tea will jump-start the compost, encouraging the acid-loving bacteria that make the whole thing work.

tomato juice

Canned tomato juice is handy to keep in the refrigerator for breakfast. It's even handier to keep around for any of these uses.

Freshen a fridge

If your power went on the blink while you were out of town, you can have a real mess in your fridge or freezer. Clean it out and get rid of any remaining odor by wiping down the fridge and freezer walls and shelves with undiluted tomato juice on a sponge. Rinse off with warm water and take a sniff. You may need to repeat once, but your major appliance will be saved.

Clean a cooler

You're not the only family that ever forgot a pack of hotdogs in a cooler after you came home from a trip. But you don't have to throw away an expensive item just because of one mistake. Clean it out and pour in a large can of tomato juice, undiluted. Rub it up the sides of the interior and under the lid with a sponge, then close the lid and let it sit in a cool place for a couple of days. Rinse and wash with dish soap and water and dry thoroughly. Sprinkle the inside with a little baking soda before you put it into storage.

Soothe a sore throat

The acids in tomato juice take the sting out of a sore throat. Make a solution of 1/2 cup tomato juice and 1/2 cup water, and add a couple drops of hot sauce. Gargle with this mixture several times, and the burning will subside in your painful throat.

Clean out the fridge and get rid of any remaining odor by **wiping down the shelves and freezer walls with tomato juice.**

vanilla

Pungent and fragrant, vanilla extract is the necessary flavor in so many baked goods. Without it, cookies and cakes can taste flat and dull. But it's also great to have on hand for a variety of uses even when you're not turning on the oven.

Sweeten a microwave

Wiped it down, washed the glass turntable, and yet still your microwave smells like all the dinners you've ever reheated? Vanilla is the answer. Pour a couple tablespoons of vanilla in a glass bowl and microwave on high for 1 minute. Let the vanilla in the bowl cool, then repeat. It will smell as sweet as freshly baked cookies.

Perfume the paint

Stir 1 tablespoon of pure vanilla into a gallon of paint before you start work. You won't completely eradicate the smell of fresh paint as it dries, but you'll make the whole experience a lot pleasanter!

Make a kid-friendly tick repellent

Children playing in long grass in summer are at risk of tick bites, which can lead to dangerous illnesses. Short of dressing them in haz-mat suits, it's hard to keep ticks off. But instead of toxic sprays, you can repel ticks with pure vanilla. Douse a cotton ball with real vanilla extract, and dab it liberally around ankles, wrists, and any uncovered skin on the limbs and trunk. The kids will smell great, too. Reapply as needed.

Sweeten the house

People who are allergic to air fresheners and sprays can still enjoy the benefits of a sweet-smelling house. Wet a cotton ball with vanilla and dab it very lightly on the outside of a regular light bulb (not a halogen bulb) in your lamps. When you turn on the lamp, the bulb heats up and a faint but alluring scent of vanilla drifts out.

vegetable oil

Plain vegetable oil makes a mild salad dressing and it's great for deep-frying and for making baked goods. It's also useful to have on hand for uses that have nothing to do with cooking.

Keep your birdbath operational

In summer, many people have to dump birdbaths after every rain to prevent mosquitoes from breeding in the standing water. But you can have

Stir some vanilla into a gallon of paint before you start work. You won't completely eradicate the smell of fresh paint as it dries, but you'll make the whole experience a lot pleasanter!

your birdbath and keep water in it, too, if you float a few tablespoons of vegetable oil on the surface of the water. Birds don't care, but mosquitoes do. (Do change the water weekly, however, just in case.)

Give yourself a hot-oil treatment

You don't need a spa or special oils for silky hair! Heat half a cup of vegetable oil in the microwave for 20 seconds until it's just warm. Massage into your dry scalp and hair and wrap in a towel for 10 minutes. Wash as usual.

Remove water rings from wood furniture

Forgot to use a coaster yet again? Try this miracle cure: In a small bowl, combine 1 tablespoon each vegetable oil and white vinegar. Rub the mixture with a soft cloth in the direction of the wood grain. Use a soft lint-free cloth to polish the oil and vinegar mixture gently into the ring and you'll see it steadily disappear.

Break apart tumblers without breakage

Who stacked the drinking glasses again? They can stick together as if they're stuck with cement. All you need is a thin drizzle of oil poured all around the top edge of the outside glass. Give it a few minutes to work in, and they'll separate with ease.

vinegar

Along with salt and baking soda, vinegar completes a powerhouse trio that no home should be without. With plain white vinegar and apple cider vinegar, you can perform near miraculous feats of laundry, housecleaning, health care, and more.

Perk up a rug or carpet

Foot traffic, dust, and dirt can wear down a carpet's fibers and dull the pattern and color.

Bring back the life to a carpet with a solution of 1 gallon warm water with 1 cup white vinegar. Dip a clean broom in the mixture and brush it into the rug. Let it dry, and the fibers will stand up and the colors will revive.

Brighten wood paneling

How can wooden panels get dusty and grimy? But they do, and you'll be surprised at how bright they look when you wipe them with this mixture: 2 cups warm water, 1/4 cup white vinegar, and a glug of olive or vegetable oil. Wipe down the whole area, then rub with a dry cloth.

Keep cats out of the sandbox

Don't let the neighborhood cats treat your child's sandbox like a public restroom. After your child is done playing for the day, drizzle a pint of white vinegar over the sand and stir it in with a spade. It will dry overnight, but cats will avoid the place for weeks.

Clean dirt off blinds

Nobody wants to get into the job of cleaning window blinds, but now and then the grime and dust is too much and you have to give it a go. Make your life simpler by using socks and vinegar. Mix half and half water and vinegar, and draw a clean cotton tube sock loosely onto each hand. Dip the socks in the vinegar mixture and pull your hands along individual blinds, clutching top and bottom. The dirt will slip right off onto your socks. Dip them in clean water to rinse the dirt and back in the vinegar again for the next slat.

Protect plants from mildew

Powdery mildew or rust spots on your garden plants? The solution is simple: a quart of water and a tablespoon of apple cider vinegar, sprayed directly on the leaves, preferably in the early morning or evening so the leaves dry before they are hit by full sun.

If you've forgotten to wash a paintbrush, you may be able to revive it by **soaking it overnight in undiluted white vinegar.**

Keep plaster pliable

Plaster dries quickly—so quickly, in fact, that if you're not experienced at plastering, you may find it has seized up before your job is done. Buy yourself some time by stirring a few tablespoons of white vinegar into the plaster as you mix. It will dry more slowly, giving you a few extra minutes to perfect your technique.

Avoid oven odors

When you use a potent chemical cleaner to scrub out your oven, it will emit a strong chemical smell the first time you use it again, no matter how well you rinsed. Avoid this odor, and don't let your baked food carry its taint, by soaking a clean sponge in white vinegar and using it for the final wipe-down after you've finished cleaning the oven. Let the vinegar dry completely before you turn the oven on again.

Fluff sweaters after washing

Wool and acrylic sweaters can look flat and dull after washing, and sometimes a hint of soap lingers in the fibers. Cut the soap and fluff up the fibers by adding 1/2 cup of white vinegar to the final rinse water, whether hand or machine-washing.

Clear the air of grease

It's an old southern trick to prevent a kitchen smelling of grease while chicken is frying: Put a small dish of white vinegar in the kitchen, and the grease will miraculously collect on the surface rather than hanging in the air. Try it and see.

Eradicate a carsick odor

Young riders sometimes become carsick, even riding on the straightest of roads. Once you've cleaned up every trace, you may still find that the odor lingers, making everyone else feel a little carsick, too! Erase the smell overnight by leaving an uncovered bowl of half-full undiluted white vinegar on the floor of the car. In the morning, the odor should be gone.

Make your car gleam

You've got time to wash your car at home yourself, but not the whole afternoon to spend waxing it. Skip the wax step and use vinegar instead. A teaspoon of undiluted white vinegar in the bucket of soapy wash water will help remove road grit and tar from the paint. When you fill the bucket with clean water for rinsing, add another teaspoon of vinegar and pour this blend all over the car. For an added touch, wipe down the windows with vinegar to repel rain and frost.

Treat a cold sore

When you feel a cold sore coming on, get out the apple cider vinegar. Douse a cotton ball and dab your lip three times a day. If you already have the sore, do the same. The pain and swelling will subside, and the vinegar speeds healing.

9 More Nontraditional Ways to Use VINEGAR

1 Bird Poo Voodoo

Have birds used your windshield as a target? Pour vinegar onto a rag and wipe those messes away with ease. Have winged friends left "gifts" on your patios and decks? Pour a little vinegar straight onto the spots and watch them dissolve like magic.

2 So Long Stickers!

Can't get the price tag off that glass vase? Get out some plain white vinegar. Soak the paper of the sticker in the vinegar, then scrape it off with a credit card or the edge of a plastic spoon. Use a dry cloth or paper towel to polish away the remaining glue.

3 Wave Good-bye to Odor

Get rid of smoke or cooking odors quickly and effectively by wetting a cloth in vinegar and waving it around the room you're trying to air. Soon you'll be able to take a big sniff of… nothing, Just like you wanted.

4 Spray It Proud!

Why use commercial cleaner when you can make an all-purpose wash that's cheap, simple, and green to boot? In a spray bottle, mix 2 parts water with 1 part white vinegar. You can spritz it on anything including grease spots, spills, and bathroom surfaces.

5 As Clear as Glass

Why buy a special spray to clean your glasses when you've got vinegar in the cabinet? Spritz your specs with white vinegar and polish with a soft cloth. It will work just as well as that tiny, overpriced bottle of cleaner.

6 Shiny Scissors

It's best not to clean good kitchen shears in water because it can rust the central fastener and dull the blades. Instead, dip a cloth in undiluted white vinegar and wipe the blades well. Dry with a towel.

7 Make Salt Surrender

Winter sidewalks leave unsightly white rings of salt on leather shoes and boots. There is a way to defeat sidewalk salt: Wipe your footwear as soon as you get inside with a cloth dipped in white vinegar. You will not only get rid of the rings, you'll also prevent damage to your shoes.

8 A Cut Above

Fresh-cut flowers are beautiful. Keep your blooms a-bloom for as long as possible by adding the following to the vase: 2 tablespoons apple cider vinegar and 2 tablespoons sugar. Then fill the vase from the tap and your flowers will be "drinking" something a cut above plain water.

9 Keep Water Bottles Fresh

If you're hiking in the heat all day, the water you carry can taste stale. Keep the flavor bright and bacteria down by adding a few drops of apple cider vinegar when you fill your bottle.

HEALTH AND BEAUTY

YOU MAY NOT MAKE A 99 CENT STORE THE first stop for your health and beauty products, but you should. You can find name-brand products for significantly less than at the grocery store or the drugstore and names you may not recognize (but are perfectly good) for a song. And so many of these items have purposes beyond their original intent—baby oil to polish your shoes, cotton balls to light a campfire, toothpaste to fight pimples—that you're bound to find an astonishing number of items that will make your life easier. Just consult the list that follows for endless possibilities.

adhesive bandages

Are adhesive bandages better than tape? In certain situations, you bet they are. How many different ways can *you* use them?

Test for allergies

Are you worried that you might be allergic to a product you just bought? Before you use it, test it on yourself. Put a little bit inside your wrist or elbow, and cover it with an adhesive bandage. Let it sit for 24 hours. Remove the bandage and check your skin; if your skin isn't red or irritated, the product is probably safe to use.

Stick it to your skin

Use adhesive bandages whenever you need to attach something to your skin. For example, you can get rid of a wart by taping a cotton ball soaked in vinegar to the wart for about two hours every day. Tape won't hold the cotton ball—but an adhesive bandage will.

Test your painting power

Have you cleaned your walls sufficiently before painting them? Is your primer a high enough quality for your project? To answer these questions before painting a large area, test your walls with an adhesive bandage. Paint a small, clean, inconspicuous spot with the paint you plan to use, and let it dry for two days. Put a bandage over the area, then strip it off. Did the paint come off? If so, you need to clean the walls more or use a better primer. If not, get to work!

Protect your fingertips

Thimbles save wear and tear on your finger, but they can be too rigid for many sewers. Ditch the thimble and put an adhesive bandage on your fingertip instead. You'll get the protection without the resistance.

antacid tablets

Antacid tablets work wonders for upset stomachs—and for healing and cleaning. Check out the surprising uses for these hard workers here.

Neutralize canker sores

Place an antacid tablet directly on the canker sore, giving it time to dissolve, or simply chew one. The medicine will stop the acids and enzymes in your mouth from attacking the tissue in the sore, and more importantly, it will stop the pain. (Be sure to check the product's label for correct dosage instructions.)

Clean flower vases with antacid tablets. Drop one in a dirty vase filled with fresh water.

Put the fizz to work

Clean your toilet with antacid tablets. As long as they contain sodium bicarbonate, two tablets will do the trick. Dissolve the tablets in the toilet bowl for 20 minutes, then scrub the bowl clean with a toilet brush. Flush and you're done.

Make a hot and cold cleaner

Cleaning out a thermos is always difficult, especially if its contents—generally coffee or tea—have been sitting in it for a while. Instead of trying to wedge your hand into the narrow opening to wipe it out, dump the contents, fill it with water, and dissolve four antacid tablets in it. Let the solution sit for an hour, then rinse and wash as usual. Your thermos will sparkle again!

Say so long to slime

Get rid of the brown and green slimy mess on your flower vase with a common antacid tablet. Drop one into the dirty vase filled with fresh water and give it five minutes to work. Wipe the inside with a sponge or cloth and rinse. Your vase will be ready for a new bouquet.

aspirin

It's hard to believe that one little white pill could have so many alternate uses beyond its original intent. From your face to your feet, aspirin can perform wonders.

Stop acne

Got an outbreak? Try taming it with one or two 325-milligram pills four times per day (after your doctor confirms you can take aspirin regularly). If you prefer a topical treatment, crush one aspirin, mix it with a little water to make a paste, and dab the paste on your pimple. Let it sit for a few minutes, then wash it off with soap and water. Repeat as needed.

Use it this way!

Crush corns

How? Mix five crushed aspirin tablets with 1/2 teaspoon of water and 1/2 teaspoon of lemon juice. Swab the mixture onto the corn. Cover the corn with a patch of plastic wrap, and top that with a hot towel. Let it sit for 10 minutes. Remove the coverings and the mixture, and gently file down the softened corn with a pumice stone.

Make a homemade styptic pencil

Nicked yourself shaving? Ouch! Don't rummage for an old-fashioned styptic pencil to dry up the cut. Just crush a single aspirin, mix with just a few drops of water to make a paste, and dab it on the cut. As the paste dries, the cut will too.

Give your face a day at the spa

An aspirin facial will smooth and exfoliate far better than an expensive preparation. Grind six uncoated aspirin tablets into a coarse powder and combine it with a tablespoon or two of lemon juice if your skin is oily—or olive oil if your skin is dry. Smooth it on and let sit for five minutes, then rinse.

Get rid of athlete's foot

The salicylic acid in aspirin can serve as an antifungal. Crush two or three aspirin to a fine powder and mix with some cornstarch or talc. Sprinkle it on every morning when you put your socks on and your toes will be clear in no time.

baby oil

Baby oil isn't just for babies—and it isn't just for making skin soft or for tanning (which isn't recommended anyway). Instead, use it on your shoes and your ears and many other places you may never have considered.

Stop an earache

Baby your ear when it hurts. How? Hold a bottle of baby oil under hot running water for about a minute to warm its contents. Then place a few drops of the heated baby oil into the affected ear canal to soothe away the pain.

Improve your shoes

Give your shoes new life without spending anything on shoe polish. Dab a few drops of baby oil on your leather shoes, and rub the oil in with a soft clean cloth. You'll soften the leather as well as polish it. You can also use baby oil to freshen other leather and patent leather accessories: purses, belts, briefcases—even jackets! Just be sure to wipe off any excess oil when you're done.

Rip it off the right way

Pulling an adhesive bandage off your child's skin can be tough on both of you. Make it easier by rubbing the bandage with a cotton ball soaked in baby oil. Rub until you can easily pull the bandage off. This trick works well for adults with sensitive skin, too.

Give it a rub

Get rid of stubborn latex paint splatters on your face and hands (and anywhere else you may find them on your skin) by rubbing the area with baby oil. Once you've removed the paint, wash your skin with soap and water.

baby powder

Whether you call it baby powder or talcum powder—baby powder doesn't necessarily contain talc, which talcum powder does—the soft white stuff can work wonders around your house, in your garden, and with your jewelry. See how it can help you!

Squash the squeak

If your hardwood floor squeaks and you can see gaps between the boards, you can fix the problem

Dusting bulbs with baby powder before planting helps keep rot and pests away.

with a dusting of powder. Sprinkle the powder in the cracks—or use a plastic ketchup bottle filled with talcum to aim the powder directly into the gap. Place a towel over the boards and work the powder into the cracks with your foot. Clean up the excess powder with the towel. Your room will seem very quiet!

Baby your bulbs

Put 3 tablespoons of medicated baby powder and five or six flower bulbs in a plastic bag, seal it, and shake. Dusting the bulbs before planting helps keep rot and pests away.

Clean your carpet overnight

Whether your carpet smells dank and musty because of a pet, a smoker, or a season of rain, take the odor out with baby powder. Using a flour sifter, spread the powder generously over the carpet. Let it sit overnight—a few hours will suffice, but overnight is better—and vacuum up the powder and the smells in the morning.

Undo a knot

It may seem as soft as a newborn, but never underestimate the strength of baby powder! It can undo the toughest knot in a jewelry chain. Just cover the knot with a light dusting of powder, then pry the knot apart with a straight pin. Wash the chain with a mild soap, rinse it, dry it, and wear it!

baby shampoo

Baby shampoo was designed to be gentle on babies' eyes, and its gentleness is a godsend for adult eyes, too. Here are several alternate ways to use this kind solution.

Baby your eyes

Don't let conjunctivitis get you down! Soak a cotton ball in a mixture of 1 part baby shampoo

THE HISTORY OF JOHNSON'S BABY POWDER

The original Johnson's Baby Powder owes its existence to medicated plasters (bandages) that caused skin irritation. Johnson's sold these plasters with a container of talcum powder meant to eliminate friction and keep covered skin comfortable. The question arose: Could talc use be expanded? The answer came in 1893, when Johnson's Baby Powder, made with talc, became available in a metal tin that declared: "For Toilet and Nursery." The tins were a mainstay in baby's room until 1963, when plastic bottles arrived. Today, many pediatricians don't recommend talc; Johnson's also offers a cornstarch formula.

and 10 parts warm water, then simply use it to wash the crud out of your eyelashes.

Wet your dry hair

Dump those expensive shampoos and conditioners promising a quick fix for dry hair right down the drain, and wash your hair with ordinary baby shampoo instead. Baby shampoo is cheaper and may be even less drying than its more expensive cousins.

Wash your eyelids, along with your hair

If you get sties more than occasionally, you may want to take preventive steps to stop them in their tracks. The secret? Wash your closed eyelids once a day with a solution of warm water and no-tears baby shampoo.

Remove eye makeup

Stop spending money on expensive, less-than-sensitive eye makeup remover. If you have baby shampoo in your house, you already have the perfect solution for taking off your face at night. Dab a bit of baby shampoo on a damp cotton ball, wipe off your makeup, and rinse your face. It's gentle on your face *and* on your wallet.

baby wipes

Considering all the unusual uses for baby wipes, it's hard to believe that they were originally intended for the younger set. You can use them for cleaning carpets and cars and so much more. Even the container is handy!

Wipe it off with a wipe

Did a little one use your skirt as a napkin? If so, you can get the food off by blotting the area with a paper towel, then rubbing it gently with a baby wipe.

Stop it before it sets

Did baby (or someone who should have known better) spill on your carpet? If so, use a damp baby wipe to blot up the fresh mess.

Wipes for windows

Grime and dead bugs can quickly build up on your car's windshield, particularly when you don't have time to find a bottle of glass cleaner and a clean cloth. A more practical solution: Keep a container of baby wipes in your glove compartment, and use one every now and then to clean your car windows.

Dash away the dregs

Use baby wipes to clean sticky stuff off your dashboard—greasy handprints, spots of misdirected hand lotion, drips from juice boxes, and anything else that has found its way to the front of your car. If you really want your dashboard to shine, buff it with a little baby oil.

Take a swipe at your shoes

Don't let unpolished leather shoes turn your bright day dull. Use a baby wipe to quickly shine your shoes and brighten your day.

bath oil

Bath oil is an essential ingredient in a calming, luxurious bath—and, apparently, an essential ingredient for cleaning messes and repelling bugs. Who knew? You will, when you see the tips below.

Leave shower doors sparkling

Soap scum on glass shower doors can build up fast when you shower every day. If you never have time for a long, hot soak in the bathtub, you may

Keep your patent leather shoes sharp. Moisten a clean, soft cloth with a few drops of bath oil, and gently rub the oil on to the shoe.

as well put your bath oil to good use cleaning off the scum. Pour a little bath oil straight on a sponge and swipe it over the glass. The scum will wipe right off. Rinse the sponge and wipe the doors lightly.

Tell insects to buzz off

You don't need a particular brand of bath oil to act as a repellent for flies, mosquitoes, and other biting insects. A strongly scented oil, especially one with citrus, can do the same job. Rub it on exposed skin (if you have sensitive skin, test it on a small area first) and flying pests will look elsewhere.

Use oil to clean off oil

Maybe you got grease or oil on your hands from trying to fix the chain on your bicycle, or maybe you were solving a problem under the hood of your car. Maybe you don't know how the grease got there! But you can get the goo off easily by rubbing a little bath oil into your hands, then washing your hands in warm water with soap.

Protect your patent leather

Keep your patent leather shoes and purse looking sharp by getting rid of scuff marks. Just moisten a clean, soft cloth with a few drops of bath oil, and gently rub the oil into the patent leather. (A towel works well, too.) Polish the area with another dry cloth or towel, and you'll see new life in your old accessories!

bubble bath

What liquid can you use to clean your car, your plants, and your hands? Bubble bath! (And you can take a really fun bath with it, too.)

Give your car a bath

Stop buying all those fancy and expensive products for washing your car. You can give your

Smart savings!

car a luxurious bath—and a beautiful shine—by washing it with bubble bath instead. Add one or two capfuls to a bucket of water and wash away.

Shine on!

Bubble baths aren't just for kids—or adults. They can be for plants, too! Dilute a little bubble bath in water. Wash your plant's leaves with a clean cloth dipped in the bubble bath solution. The leaves will shine, and the plant will look healthier.

Replace your hand soap

Don't relegate bubble bath to the tub—use it at the sink as well. Pour it into liquid hand soap containers that need to be refilled. Bubble bath is an effective, inexpensive replacement for your regular soap.

calamine lotion

Calamine lotion is a lifesaver for skin problems well beyond poison ivy—though it's a lifesaver for poison ivy, too. You can even use it to disguise your skin at Halloween! Here's how.

A new use for an old remedy

You may think of the pink stuff to soothe poison ivy, but it also provides great relief for heat rash. Slather it on and feel the itching and irritation ease.

Pond's Cold Cream

In the 1840s Theron T. Pond, a pharmacist from Utica, New York, observed Native Americans treat small cuts and other ailments with tea made from witch hazel. He founded the T. T. Pond Company and used an extract from this plant to produce a general heal-all cream called Golden Treasure, later renamed Pond's Extract. It was the first commercial use of witch hazel. In 1905, Pond's Cold Cream—specifically made for the face and still containing witch hazel—was introduced. Cold cream had been around since ancient times, but Pond's created ad campaigns featuring celebrities and royalty, and soon Pond's became *the* brand to buy for face care.

As débutante ... *and Today*

"I ADORE THESE CREAMS EVEN MORE TODAY"
...MRS. ALAN HARRIMAN

Get relief from hives

It's a good idea to take an antihistamine to get relief from hives, but don't forget that you can get even more relief from itching by slathering the hives with calamine lotion.

Beat back blisters

Dab a healthy dose of calamine lotion onto blisters to dry them out. The lotion draws the moisture out of the blisters as it dries.

Think pink for Halloween

Going as a ghost to this year's Halloween party? Dab a few layers of calamine lotion on your face with a cotton ball to achieve a ghostly white pallor. Be sure to apply it evenly; you don't want to end up as a ghost with splotchy pink skin!

chest rub

It prevents and treats bug bites, relieves sore feet, and makes you feel so much better when you're sick. Is it a bird? Is it a plane? Is it chest rub? You bet it is!

Kick the cough!

Buy a chest rub containing camphor or menthol, and spread it over your chest and throat. Along with relieving the pain in your chest caused by coughing, it will help stop the cough itself. (Don't take it internally.)

Steam away your stuffiness

Add a teaspoon of vaporizing chest rub to a pot of water, and bring it to a boil. Remove the pot from the stove. Lean over the pot—keeping your face about 18 inches from the water—and place a towel over your head and shoulders so that it forms a dome over the water. Breathe in the air trapped by the towel. Your sinuses should feel better shortly.

Chest rub for your feet

Maybe you danced a little too much last night. Maybe you walked a little too far. Whatever the reason, pamper your sore feet with chest rub at night. Cover them with the goo, put on a pair of socks to protect your sheets, and go to bed as usual. You'll have happy dogs in the morning!

Tick off ticks (and other pesky bugs)

Don't give ticks, gnats, and mosquitoes a chance to bother you next time you venture into the great outdoors. Slather a healthy dose of chest rub on your legs and pants to repel the bugs. Like many humans, they want to stay far away from that smell!

cold cream

Cold cream, sour cream, heavy cream—which is the most versatile? Try these ideas for using cold cream, and then you'll know.

Remove bumper stickers, not just makeup

Is that bumper sticker from the last election starting to look silly on your car? Cover it with a thick layer of cold cream. Let it sit for 3 or 4 minutes, then scrape it off with a dull table knife or a credit card.

Take off temporary tattoos

Street fairs, carnivals, and parties are fun for your kids, especially when they get temporary tattoos—but removing them isn't fun for you. Make it easier on yourself by slathering cold cream on the tattoo and then gently rubbing it with a clean cloth until it comes off.

Kiss that stain good-bye

If you got a lipstick stain on your blouse as well as on your glass, remove it the way you remove makeup. Rub cold cream into the fabric (try it in an inconspicuous corner of the fabric first), then wash with washing soda, an alkaline compound used to remove stubborn stains from laundry. The stain should disappear.

comb

A comb seems so ordinary that it could have only one use—to comb your hair. Right? Wrong! Here are some fun ideas for using a surprisingly useful tool.

The hair of the dog

Consider buying a new comb, even if you already have one—just put it to a different use. Your dog or cat will thank you for the new belly-scratching tool (even though it's really designed for your locks)!

Comb more than your hair

Don't despair if you have an itchy back and no back scratcher (and no way to reach the itch). Rubbing your comb across the affected area will help relieve the problem quickly and easily. It's effective on other itchy parts of your body, too!

Be creative and frugal!

Thwart thieves

Use an ordinary comb to foil pickpockets. How? Fold your wallet in half, and put your comb in the middle of the wallet, with the teeth sticking out. Secure the comb to the wallet with a rubber band, running it around the wallet and through the teeth of the comb. Now put the wallet in your pocket. If anybody tries to steal the wallet, the comb will catch on your pocket so it will be harder to remove—and you'll know exactly what's happening.

Hold a nail

Stop hitting your fingers every time you hammer a nail in place. Use the teeth of an ordinary comb to hold the nail while you hammer.

Protect your shirt

Cutting a button off a shirt without cutting the shirt can be tricky. Make it easy by sliding a comb under the button, then cutting through the button's thread with a razor.

cotton balls

Liberate cotton balls from the linen closet—even from the house—and let them work at a campsite, on a plane, in a car, and many other places. Let them show you what they can do!

Light my fire

You may have heard of using lint from the dryer to start a campfire, but what about cotton balls? Rub petroleum jelly over a bunch of cotton balls—making sure they're completely covered—and store them in a ziplock bag. Take the bag with you on your camping trip, along with a lighter or waterproof matches. When it's time to light the fire, pull a few strands of fiber out of the cotton ball, place the ball into your pile of tinder and wood, and light the cotton ball. Instant fire starter!

Calming cotton balls

Take a little of the misery out of air travel by packing in your carry-on luggage some cotton balls designed to bring the stress down a notch. Before you leave for your trip, dribble lavender oil or clary sage onto a few cotton balls, then place them in a small ziplock bag. Take them out during the flight for instant tension release.

The fresh express

Take the stale stink out of your car with cotton balls. Soak a few in eucalyptus oil, tea tree oil, or vanilla extract, and transport them to your car in a plastic bag. Take a few out in the car—you can hide them in the cup holder or any other storage container—to refresh your ride.

Squash bugs with cotton balls

You may not need insect repellent when you travel, so you don't want to bring a bottle of it—but then again, you might need it. Leave the cans and bottles at home and instead bring a ziplock plastic bag containing a few cotton balls soaked in the repellent. Dab the cotton ball on your skin when you sense trouble. The small bag is easier to carry, and you'll avoid any potential spills in your luggage.

Have a ball with bleach

Forget about using elbow grease! Tackle mildew in crevices in your bathroom with cotton balls soaked in bleach. Put them in areas you can't normally reach—behind faucets, for example—and let them sit for a few hours. When their job is done, remove them and rinse the area with warm water.

cotton swab

Think of a cotton swab as a tool you can use around the house as well as in your beauty regime. These little swabs have big ambitions, as you'll see.

Simplify your makeup routine

Use one less makeup brush—substitute a cotton swab for an eye shadow applicator. It's even better than the real thing, capable of smoothing on the shadow, softening eyeliner, and smudging colors into each other. It's disposable, too!

Splint a bent stem

Push a cotton swab into the garden's dirt to make a splint for a bent flower stem. Wrap transparent tape loosely around the swab and the plant to hold the stem in place.

Use as a tiny duster

Crevices, cracks, and small spaces are a challenge for anyone trying to keep a home dust-free. Use your regular dust cloth for big and medium surfaces and cotton swabs for the tight spots: between the number keys on a phone, on the inside of photo frames, and all around a computer keyboard. Don't forget that swabs work equally well with household cleaners to clean difficult spots, such as on and around oven knobs and the base of the hot and cold faucets.

Swab your way to a professional look

Use cotton swabs the next time you give yourself a manicure or pedicure, and bump your technique up to a professional level. Use swabs with nail polish remover to get rid of the old nail polish wedged into your cuticles, and use them to wipe the new polish off the skin that borders your nails.

dental floss

Even if you don't floss daily as your dentist recommends, you should still buy dental floss to use in the kitchen, in your purse, and on a picnic. You may even want to buy it in bulk!

It cuts like a knife

Dental floss, that is. Hold it taut to cut butter, brownies, cakes, soft cheeses, and many other soft foods. Move it side to side to make a clean cut. Now you don't have to worry if you forget to bring a knife to your next picnic!

Use one less makeup brush—substitute a cotton swab for an eye shadow applicator.

Make a lifeline for your keys

Stop fishing around your purse for your house keys every time you need them. Make them readily accessible by tying them into your handbag with dental floss. Measure the distance from the bottom of your purse to the bottom of your purse handle. Add 6 inches, and cut that length of dental floss. Tie your keys to one end with a tight knot, and tie the other end to the bottom of the purse handle, again with a tight knot. Now you can easily retrieve your keys by pulling on the line!

Get crafty

Don't spring for specialty beading wire or string the next time you feel the urge to create a beaded masterpiece. Just use dental floss (two strands for extra strength) for your bracelet or necklace—you'll save money and a trip to the craft store.

WAY BACK WHEN...

The Ballpoint Pen Inspired Ban Roll-On

An anonymous inventor from Philadelphia trademarked the first commercial deodorant in 1888. Called Mum (an acronym for "Morning Until Midnight"), it was a cream that you applied with your fingers. Deodorant application didn't evolve until Helen Barnett Diserens joined Mum's production team. She developed an applicator based on the ballpoint pen. It was tested in 1952 and marketed under the name Ban Roll-On. This was a fantastic innovation, and today Ban is still a bestselling roll-on deodorant. Incredibly, the world would have to wait until 1965 for antiperspirants to enter the picture.

Button, button, who's got the button?

Sometimes it feels like buttons disappear as often as socks disappear from a dryer! Stop buttons from fleeing by sewing them on with ultra-durable dental floss, rather than ordinary thread. Use dental floss on coat and jacket buttons for a particularly strong bond.

deodorant

Get rid of bug bites and moist feet along with body odor the next time you buy deodorant. It's more useful than you thought!

Protect your feet

Roll or spray a little deodorant—specifically, an antiperspirant—on your feet for a change. Why? You'll keep them dry and keep blisters at bay.

Banish bug bites

Apply a dab of deodorant onto a bug bite to reduce itching and irritation. Many deodorants contain ingredients designed to reduce skin irritation. Yours may do the trick!

Say good-bye to sweaty palms

Whether you have an important business meeting or a big date, you don't want to have sweaty palms. Rub some antiperspirant into your palms, and don't sweat it.

emery board

Whether you buy an emery board by itself or a nail file as part of a manicure or pedicure set, you'll find plenty of new uses here for what you normally use on your nails.

Erase the eraser

Rub away smudges and scuffs on your pencil eraser with an emery board. Lightly rub it over the eraser until the mark is gone.

File seeds before planting

Rub off the hard coating on seeds using an emery board before you put them in the ground. They'll absorb moisture better and get a head start sprouting.

Steam away stains on suede

Whether you discover a stain on your suede shoes or your suede jacket, you won't be happy. Bring a smile back to your face quickly by rubbing the stain gently with the fine side of an emery board, then holding the suede item over steam from a pan. The stain will disappear! You can use the emery board again to freshen the nap.

Get to the point

Knives get dull. Scissors get dull. Even needles get dull. Make your needle sharp again by rubbing it against an emery board.

epsom salt

Sweat, splinters, raccoons, and roses—what do they have in common? Epsom salt! This product will amaze you with its many uses.

Salt your bathwater

Why? To get rid of rough patches of skin. Add 2 cups of Epsom salt to a tub filled with warm water, soak for a few minutes, then finish the job by rubbing additional salt on the rough spots. You'll be a smoother person when you emerge from your bath!

Season your toes

You know Epsom salt can relieve sore feet, but did you know it can also help prevent foot odor? Just add 2 cups of Epson salt to 2 gallons of warm water in a suitable container (a bucket or tub), then soak your feet in the solution twice a day, 15 minutes each time. You'll find your feet sweating less and smelling less.

Ditch the itch

Got a case of poison ivy? Soak in a tub of warm water and Epsom salt to dry out the rash. Check the label for soaking instructions.

Stop splinters

Make a paste of Epsom salt and water and apply it to the area harboring a splinter. The paste will pull the splinter to the surface of the skin in about 10 minutes. It will pull insect stingers out of your skin, too. A luxurious bath in Epsom salt will also help draw out the splinter or stinger.

Rub off the hard coating on seeds using an emery board before you put them in the ground.

Relish your roses

Sprinkle half a cup of Epsom salt around the base of your rose bush in early spring and in the fall for healthier roses. After the leaves appear and again when the roses appear, spray them with a mixture of 1 tablespoon Epsom salt per gallon of water. Gardeners in the know swear by it!

Rid yourself of raccoons

If those cute but annoying nighttime pests are getting at your garbage, sprinkle a few tablespoons of Epsom salt around your trash cans to drive them away. Remember to do it again after it rains.

foot powder

You may not be looking for foot powder when you visit a 99 cent store, but you should grab a container of it to keep around the house. Why? See below.

Power to foot powder!

You find a dark puddle on your garage floor and realize that oil is leaking from your engine, but you don't know the exact source of the leak.

Count your pennies!

Clean the engine with WD-40, then cover the sides and bottom of the engine with spray-on foot powder. You'll see the leak when it turns white.

Give fleas the boot

Sprinkle a light dusting of foot powder around the edges of each room and outside the doors leading into your house to get rid of fleas. If you have fleas in your yard, sprinkle some there, too. (But make sure no one in your house is allergic to the powder before using it, and don't use it if you have small children in the house. They may try to eat it.)

hairbrush

Whether it's a round styling brush, a flat brush, or a pocket brush, hairbrushes are one of those things that we take for granted. But there are so many more uses for them than just doing the obvious!

Brush the cat

The kinds of women's hairbrushes you find at 99 cent stores are ideal for your hair—and for your cat. In fact, brushes with round-tipped plastic bristles work better on cats than the soft (and expensive) kind sold in pet stores.

Scratch your back

Can't reach that itch square in the middle of your back? Rubbing your back against a door frame may help, but using your brush as a back scratcher is more efficient. You'll be able to zero in on the offending spot faster.

Scrub a stainless steel sink

Stainless steel may be the material of choice when it comes to kitchen sinks, but it's also easily scratched. A 99 cent store hairbrush is perfect for gently lifting grime off the surface without scratching it.

Find a hair conditioner that contains lanolin, and **use it to wash your car.**

hair conditioner

Stretch your thinking about hair conditioner, and you'll find that it has many uses (other than conditioning hair) in the bathroom—and far outside of it. Can you use it on cars and tools? Why not?

Keep conditioning all day

Super-dry hair requires more than a casual rinse with conditioner in the shower. Spray wet hair—or dry hair slightly dampened—with a mixture of half hair conditioner and half water. Leave the conditioner in for the rest of the day.

Skip the shaving cream

Use hair conditioner for a smooth, clean shave—on your legs, under your arms, and (for men) even on your face. The conditioner will pamper your skin as well as your hair! You can also use hair conditioner as a soothing agent for legs irritated by shaving.

Condition with care

Keep your tools in tip-top shape by stopping rust before it starts. How? Rub hair conditioner onto screwdrivers, saws, and other tools before a problem erupts.

Wash and wax

Find a hair conditioner that contains lanolin, and use it to wash your car. You'll get a nicely waxed car—and one that will repel the rain.

hair spray

Hair spray has so many uses beyond its original purpose that you may think it was designed to help you all over the house, not just on your hair. Use it in the laundry room and in the kitchen, as well as in the bathroom. You may even forget why you originally bought it!

Preserve your bouquet

Spray the undersides of your cut flowers—leaves and petals—with hair spray to prolong their life. Be sure to stand about a foot away when you spray them for best results.

Stop static cling

If your pants or skirts or dresses are getting a little too friendly, spritz the underside of the garment with hair spray to stop it from clinging. You can also spray some hair spray on a paper towel, and then rub the paper towel on the inside of your clothes.

A DIFFERENT Solution

9 More Nontraditional Ways to Use
HAIR SPRAY

1 Banish Bites
If a mosquito bite doesn't itch, it's almost like it isn't there. You have the power to make bug bites less irritating with a squirt of hair spray. One shot and the stinging feeling will subside.

2 No Running!
Having even a tiny run in your panty hose can spoil your outfit—especially if you don't have a spare pair. You can't make it vanish, but you can stop a run in its tracks by spraying it with hair spray.

3 Carpet Saver
If you spill nail polish on the carpet, take quick action to clean the mess by spraying it with water and then squirting on some hair spray. After a few squirts, the polish will get tacky, and you can blot it off your rug with a paper towel.

4 Zap Bugs
Don't panic if you discover you've run out of bug spray just as a winged insect is buzzing its way through your home. Grab a can of hair spray and take aim. You'll find it kills most bugs.

5 Glue Glitter
If your child is making a project and doesn't have glue to add a touch of glitter, you can save the day with hair spray. Spray the surface that will be sprinkled, and the glitter will stick like magic.

6 Preserve Polish
Here's a neat trick: After you polish your leather shoes, spray them lightly with hair spray. The shine will last longer.

7 Faux Dye
Want to add a shocking color to your hair for a holiday? A temporary and inexpensive way is to pick a powdered drink mix (like Kool-Aid) in a shade that suits your mood, sprinkle it over your hair, then moisten and hold it in place with hair spray.

8 Fur Fix
No time to vacuum? A quick way to remove pet hair from furniture is to spray a tissue with hair spray and then wipe. The hair will cling to the tissue, and you can toss the furry mess into the trash.

9 Chalk It Up
If you've carefully marked chalk lines for a home improvement, don't let them get smudged accidentally—spray them with hair spray. You can easily wash everything away when you want to, but until you do, that chalk won't disappear.

Zip it shut

Does your zipper refuse to stay shut? Show it who's boss! Put the item on, zip the zipper shut, then coat the teeth with hair spray, applying it with a cotton swab. The hair spray will act like invisible glue.

Remove the stink and the ink

If a pen leaked on your shirt or your child autographed you as well as her artwork, just spray the offending mark with hair spray and launder as usual (making sure the ink has disappeared before you dry the item).

Thread a needle

If you have trouble threading a needle, try spritzing the end of the thread with hair spray. It will stiffen the end and make it easier to push through the needle.

hemorrhoid cream

You may not think of your face when you buy hemorrhoid cream, but that may be the most logical place to use it. Rethink the purpose of your purchase, and make your face the beneficiary.

The eyes have it

Puffy, wrinkly eyes need help, and they can get it from expensive eye cream—or common hemorrhoid cream. Oddly enough, the hemorrhoid cream tightens the puffiness and the wrinkles and makes eyes look brighter and more alert. Mix scented lotion into it before applying it to your face if you're bothered by the smell. Rub it under your eyes, let it sit for 20 minutes, then wash the cream off gently and pat the area dry. And be sure to keep it out of your eyes.

Reduce swelling from pimples

Rub a dab of hemorrhoid cream into pimples to relieve the swelling that accompanies a breakout. You won't get rid of the redness, but you will get rid of the inflammation. The blemishes will look less obvious.

Laugh away facial lines

Apply a little hemorrhoid cream to laugh lines, frown lines, and worry lines on your face. The cream will help tighten those areas and soften the lines and wrinkles.

Remove a stuck ring

Warm outside? Retaining water and your wedding band is stuck? Simply massage your ring-bearing finger with hemorrhoid cream and wait 3 minutes. The ring should slip right off.

hydrogen peroxide

Heal and clean yourself with the hydrogen peroxide that you buy at a 99 cent store. It's one of the store's most useful bargains!

Stop bad breath

Kill the bacteria that cause bad breath by storing your toothbrush in hydrogen peroxide. Stick it head down in a plastic container filled with the liquid, rinsing it thoroughly before every use. Your friends and family will thank you!

Banish body odor

Don't despair if you suddenly run out of deodorant. Simply swipe a little hydrogen peroxide under your arms instead. You'll kill the bacteria that cause odors. Rubbing alcohol and vinegar work, too!

End ear pain

Use hydrogen peroxide to stop an earache in its tracks. Check the label to make sure you have 3 percent commercial-grade hydrogen peroxide, then place 3, 4, or 5 drops into the ear canal every 3 to 4 hours. The pain and inflammation will subside. Be careful not to let it drip on your clothes because it will remove color from fabric.

Tame a toothache

If you have a toothache, a fever, and a bad taste in your mouth, you'll benefit from a hydrogen peroxide rinse. Simply use 3 percent hydrogen peroxide as mouthwash to kill bacteria and temporarily provide relief from the toothache. Spit out the solution and rinse repeatedly with water. Be sure to see your dentist as soon as possible—you likely have an infection.

ice pack

Ice packs help keep cold food cold and frozen items frozen. They are also surprisingly helpful when it comes to noses and mouths, as you'll discover.

Solve an inside problem from the outside

If your gums are swollen and painful, try treating the problem with an ice pack. Wrap it in a cloth and apply it to your cheek where the gums hurt. It's a twofer: The cold will both numb the pain and reduce the swelling.

Stop the flow

Don't let a nosebleed get you down. Stop the bleeding by placing an ice pack on the problem nostril. The blood vessels in your nose will react by narrowing, and the flow of blood will slow and eventually stop.

Numb your eyebrows

Make plucking your eyebrows much less painful by putting an ice pack on them until they're uncomfortably cold. At that point your skin will be numb enough to begin plucking. You won't even feel the tug!

How to Stock Your MEDICINE CABINET

...THE 99 CENT WAY

Every medicine cabinet we know is filled with similar items: cotton balls, aspirin, Q-tips. But here is a quick roundup of (some surprising) must-haves that will make your bathroom storage work better for you and your family.

1 Baby Oil
It does everything from staving off an earache to making bandage removal painless.

2 Bubble Bath
Hand soap too drying? Decant bubble bath into a container, and keep it on the sink.

3 Chest Rub
Massage into your tired feet for a quick pick-me-up.

4 Cotton Balls
Soak them in bleach and clean out the gunky crevices in your bathroom and kitchen.

5 Cotton Swab
Substitute a swab for an eye shadow applicator.

6 Deodorant
Sweaty palms? Rub some antiperspirant into your hands and never be nervous again.

7 Hair Spray
Mosquito bites giving you an itch? One quick blast of hair spray will kill the sting.

8 Lip Balm
Dry nose? Rub a dab of lip balm on it the way mountain climbers do, and you'll feel better.

9 Mouthwash
Wash your toothbrushes instead, by soaking them for a few minutes every day.

10 Toothbrush
Bushy eyebrows? Spritz a spare toothbrush with hair spray and use it to tame them.

lip balm

Your lips may be the last thing you touch with your lip balm after reading the tips below. Who knew lip balm could be so versatile? (And lipstick is as well—here's a tip for that, too!)

Tame the wild beast

If your wayward eyebrows or mustache make you look like you belong in a zoo, apply a little lip balm to calm them down. It's clear, waxy, and able to groom wild hair.

Lip balm for your hands

Hand lotion is a necessity in the winter, but it isn't always a miracle worker. If your hands still get chapped—particularly between your fingers—rub some lip balm on them at night before bed. You'll treat the rough spots and contribute to overall moisturizing.

A bright idea

Prevent lightbulbs in outdoor fixtures—floodlights, porch lights, and motion detector lights—from rusting and resisting removal by coating the threads with lip balm. Apply the lip balm before you screw in the lightbulb and you'll have less trouble removing it when you need to replace it.

A faux finish

Don't let a chipped nail ruin your dinner date. Temporarily solve the problem by applying lipstick or lip pencil to the chipped area. Reapply as necessary until you can properly fix it.

Take the ouch out of shaving

Nick yourself while shaving? Lip balm is a pain-free alternative to styptic pencil. Just dab a bit on your cut and you'll be good to go.

lotion

Hand and body lotion was designed to moisturize your hands and your body (surprise, surprise). Here are alternate uses for the lotion. Some still involve your hands and your body, but with a twist.

Hand lotion for your hair

If you're having a particularly bad hair day because of dry hair, try rubbing your hands with lotion, then running your hands through your hair.

Shine your shoes

Give your shoes a quick polish with hand cream. Rub a little into your shoes and then briefly buff them. They'll look like they have a new life!

It's not so shocking

Slather yourself with body lotion in the morning and continue putting hand lotion on during the

Give your shoes a quick polish with hand cream. Rub a little into your shoes and then briefly buff them.

day, and you'll be less likely to receive those annoying static electricity shocks that often happen over the course of the winter.

Stop hanging out with hangnails

Get rid of annoying hangnails by rubbing hand or body lotion into your cuticles daily. The lotion will keep those troublesome areas soft and help prevent future hangnails.

maxi pads

Put those maxi pads that you bought at the 99 cent store to good use around your house. Here are some unusual ways to make them work.

A maximum idea

If you run out of window washing fluid in your car, you can wash your windshield without it—as long as you use a feminine hygiene maxi pad. Keep the sticky side next to your hand, and rub the windshield with the padded side. You might want to keep a box in the trunk if you're prone to running out of the fluid.

Feminine first aid

Suppose you cut your arm and an adhesive bandage isn't substantial enough to stop the bleeding. What's a good alternative? Try putting a maxi pad on your arm and wrapping it with an ace bandage. It will staunch the bleeding, and no one will be the wiser!

Quick-thinking solution

Your toilet starts to overflow and the only towels you have on hand are your good bath towels. What can you use to stop the overflow from flowing all over your bathroom? Maxi pads! Grab a bunch from under the sink (or wherever you store them in or near the bathroom) and stop the water in its tracks.

mirror

Remember "Mirror, mirror, on the wall?" One big mirror hanging on the wall is so old school. Try these ideas with mirrors to enlarge and brighten your world.

See yourself in a newly decorated room

You know a large mirror can enlarge and enhance a small room, but have you ever thought about using a collection of small mirrors to accomplish the same effect? Buy several small inexpensive mirrors, preferably in different shapes and sizes, and mount them on a single wall. (Experiment with various arrangements by using masking tape to mark the position of the mirrors before you mount them.) You'll suddenly have more space!

Add sparkle to your garden

Give your plants what they want—light—*and* add interest—dancing sunshine—to your shady garden by hanging a mirror on a fence or wall.

Think like a dentist

You know how your dentist uses a tool with a tiny mirror on the end to help see into the recesses of your mouth? Like your dentist, you can use a mirror to help see under the siding on your house when you're caulking cracks and gaps between your siding and your foundation.

Look into your reflection

Create a warm centerpiece by grouping different size and color candles on top of a mirror. (Use candleholders as usual.) The mirror will reflect the light from the candles, warming the atmosphere in your room.

mouthwash

Healing, cleaning, soothing feet—who knew mouthwash could do so much more than clean your breath? You will, after you read the tips below!

Give your toothbrush a bath

Kill viruses that lurk on toothbrushes by giving your toothbrush a daily bath in mouthwash. Your immune system will thank you. (Your mouth will too!)

Bite your tongue!

In fact, if you do bite your tongue, rinse your mouth with mouthwash. It won't help your tongue heal faster, but it will help keep infection at bay.

Refresh tired feet

Take this tip from marathon runners, who know that a ten-minute soak in a sugarless mouthwash will take your tootsies from tired to terrific. Alcohol invigorates and mint will make them smell sweet again.

Help heal a bruise

When you bump your arm or leg and you feel a bruise coming on, alleviate the pain and cut

Refresh your feet with a ten-minute soak in sugarless mouthwash.

down on the discoloration by rubbing the surface of the skin with a splash of an alcohol-based mouthwash.

Rinse away skin problems

Help your dog or cat recover from minor skin troubles with mouthwash. Dab a mouthwash-moistened cotton ball onto cuts and scrapes—even boils. The mouthwash will clean out the wounds and cool down the boils.

nail polish

You probably know to use nail polish to stop a run in your stockings, but did you know you can use it to fix a scratch on your car? This little bottle of varnish is worth its weight in gold, as you'll see below.

Mark keys

Don't fumble for your keys on a dark doorstep. Mark your front-door key or other important keys with a colorful dot of bright nail polish so you can pick it out of the bunch in a hurry.

Banish the green meanies

Have you ever had a beautiful piece of costume jewelry turn your skin an ugly shade of green? Try painting the inside of the next piece you buy with clear nail polish. Once you've covered the part that touches your skin, you'll eliminate the chance of green fingers, neck, and wrist.

Ditch the ding

If you find a scratch on your car, rub your fingers over it to determine its depth. If you can feel the indentation, you'll need to camouflage the scratch—with nail polish. Find a color that matches the color of your car, and carefully apply the nail polish to the scratch. Let it dry, and drive off in your shiny looks-as-good-as-new car. (If you make a mistake, remove the polish with a cotton swab dipped in nail polish remover. Let the area dry and start again.)

Tag a toothbrush

Will your kids use a toothbrush of any color, so long as it's purple? You can keep the peace by dabbing different colored nail polish on the end of each brush for easy identification.

nail polish remover

Superglue, gum, sap, and more—remove more than just nail polish with this super substance. Check out how much you can really do with nail polish remover.

Remove pain with polish remover

Don't let pain from shingles get you down. Mix two crushed aspirin with 3 tablespoons of nail polish remover, and stir until the aspirin disappears. Apply the concoction directly to shingles blisters with a cotton ball. Let air-dry.

Stop being sappy

Did your tree- and bush-trimming shears get covered with sap last time you worked in the yard? Get rid of the stubborn sap with nail polish remover. Put some on a clean cloth, and rub the sap off the tool.

Carefully clean chrome

First the caveat: Keep it away from the paint on your car. Now the solution: Clean chrome with a clean cloth moistened with nail polish remover. It works wonders!

Take the "super" out of superglue

Superglue is a great invention—until you can't get it off your hands. Don't rub it until you hurt your skin. Instead, thoroughly wet a cotton ball

Vaseline

During an on-site visit to an oil well, Robert A. Chesebrough, a chemist born in London and raised in New York, noticed workers smearing the cuts on their skin with a residue wiped from their drills. Chesebrough experimented with the substance, and from it he extracted petroleum jelly. He patented it in 1872 and marketed it under the name Vaseline. Then he traveled his home state, injuring his skin in front of audiences and covering his wounds with petroleum jelly. People may have been horrified—he'd burn himself over an open fire—but they were also impressed. By the late 1880s, Vaseline was sold nationwide. Chesebrough lived to be 96 years old and credited his longevity to one simple fact: He ate a spoonful of Vaseline every day.

with nail polish remover (make sure it contains acetone), and hold the cotton ball against the superglue until it dissolves.

petroleum jelly

Petroleum jelly, how do I love thee? Let me count the ways—and let me count the different ways to use it! Here are a few to get you going.

Petroleum jelly spells relief!

You already know that petroleum jelly relieves chapped lips; now try putting some under your nose to relieve allergies. The goo will trap the pollen before it enters your nostrils, stopping an allergy attack before it can even start.

Paint perfectly

Coat door hinges and handles with petroleum jelly next time you paint a door. You won't have to remove the fixtures, and the paint won't stick—so your paint job will look great! Just wipe off the jelly when you're done painting.

Sometimes glue works *too* well

If you've ever had the cap of glue—wood glue, school glue, or any other type of glue—get stuck on the container of glue, just apply a thin veneer of petroleum jelly to the cap's threads, and you won't have trouble opening it again.

Protect cuts and scrapes

Apply a layer of petroleum jelly to your cut. It will soften the scab so you won't even *think* about picking at it. It protects the scraped skin, too.

Seal the deal

If you think your plunger isn't working up to its normal standard, try covering the rim with a thick coating of petroleum jelly. You'll get a tighter seal and better suction.

shampoo

You can always use shampoo to wash that man right out of your hair—or you can use it for really practical purposes that have nothing to do with hair. Here are some different ways to use shampoo.

Get rid of ring around the collar

Rub a little shampoo into shirt collars with an old toothbrush. (Shampoos containing ammonium lauryl sulfate work best.) Let the shirts sit for half an hour, then launder as you normally would. The rings will disappear.

Wash away hair spray

Your hairdo may look better with hair spray, but your vinyl floor doesn't. Mop your floor with a cleaner consisting of one gallon of warm water and a squirt of shampoo. Rinse with a damp mop.

Shampoo your silk

You can feel comfortable hand washing silk in cool water and a protein-based shampoo. Not only will the shampoo not destroy the silk, but it will actually give the silk more body and a longer life.

Forget about the fog

Driving with a foggy windshield is annoying and potentially dangerous. If the inside of your windshield tends to fog up in the winter, wipe it with a clean cloth moistened with shampoo. You'll clear out the fog and clean the glass at the same time!

Say good-bye to sap

Whether you're working in your yard or bringing in the annual Christmas tree, chances are good that you'll end up with sap on your hands. Zap the sap by washing your hands with shampoo.

shaving cream

Shaving cream has long been used by mischief-makers on Halloween, but you know there are much better alternative uses for it. Try the tips that follow instead—you're more likely to stay out of trouble!

Shave away the stain

Find a fresh stain on your carpeting? Blot up as much as you can, pat it with a damp cloth or sponge, then shoot shaving cream (the non-gel variety) onto it. Wipe the shaving cream and the stain away with a clean damp cloth or sponge.

Color it gone

If you find crayon markings on your wall, don't get mad—get shaving cream. Spray the shaving cream directly onto the offending artwork, and scrub it off with a toothbrush or scrub brush.

Stop soap scum

Spray shaving cream directly onto glass shower doors, then wipe it off with a clean dry cloth to prevent a buildup of soap scum. A bonus: The shaving cream creates a thin film that prevents the shower door from fogging.

Cut through the fog

Foggy glasses—which can happen when you come in from the cold or lean over a pot of boiling water—are both irritating and potentially dangerous. You need to be able to see! Prevent this problem by occasionally cleaning your glasses with white foamy shaving cream. It covers the lenses with a thin, invisible coating that repels water (also known as fog).

See clearly once again

Don't panic if you've accidentally sprayed your glasses as well as your hair with hair spray. Add some shaving cream to the mess, rub the lenses and frames gently with a clean cloth, and then wipe it all off.

shoe polish

Use shoe polish on your skin, your furniture, your picture frames, and your blinds—not just your shoes. In fact, forget about your shoes and try these tips instead!

Dash your rash

If you have poison ivy but no calamine lotion handy, dab a little liquid white shoe polish on your rash. The pipe clay (found in the old-fashioned bottle of liquid shoe polish) is cousin to one of calamine's main ingredients. You'll stop the itch.

Shine away the scratches

Hide light scratches in your wood flooring with shoe polish. Find a shoe polish color that closely matches the color of your floor, and use a soft clean cloth to apply it. Let the polish dry. Use a clean, damp cloth to buff it, and your secret is safe!

 **THE TRUTH ABOUT SHINOLA**

For many years, the American Mining & Manufacturing Co. in Rochester, New York, supplied the world with Shinola shoe polish. Trademarked in 1929, the brand went out of business in the middle of the 20th century, but the name is immortalized in the saying: You don't know...poop...from Shinola. The original alliteration implied a person fooled by appearances. Shinola might have looked like a sidewalk gift from a canine—but between the two substances, only one would be advantageous on shoes, and the wise person would know which. Many people today have heard the phrase yet have no idea it was once the name of a shoe polish.

Picture this

Polish a new wooden picture frame for an antique look. How? Sand the frame, then apply a thin coat of brown or reddish-brown shoe polish. Lightly buff the frame. New will look old!

Polish your blinds

Venetian blinds are notoriously difficult to clean and, to make matters worse, easily soiled. Spruce up dirty spots on your white blinds with liquid white shoe polish.

shower cap

Though you should feel free to use a shower cap in the shower, you'll find even better uses for it outside the bathroom. Try it on your bike, in your suitcase, and on your kitchen counter.

Cover your camera

If you're planning to take pictures in the rain— even a slight drizzle—wrap your camera in a shower cap. Let the lens peek out through the opening in the cap. If the shower cap isn't clear, cut a small hole in it so you can look through the viewfinder or see the LCD monitor.

Don't leave home without it

Shoes can be a problem to pack, particularly if the soles aren't brand spanking new. Protect your clothes from your shoes next time you travel by encasing your shoes in shower caps.

Be ready for an unexpected shower

If you've parked your bike for a few minutes in threatening weather while you run into a store, cover your bicycle seat with a shower cap. You'll have a dry place to sit on your ride home if it rains!

Keep out dust—not just water

Cover the kitchen appliances you keep on your counter—your stand mixer, your food processor, and your bread machine—with shower caps to keep them free of dust.

Create a makeshift saucer

Does your hanging plant have a saucer beneath it to catch drips and protect your floor? If not, slip a shower cap across the bottom of the plant when you water it.

soap

Bars of soap are inexpensive—especially so at a 99 cent store—and can be used well beyond the kitchen or bathroom sink. So think beyond the sink!

Wash away your door troubles

If wooden doors in your house tend to swell and stick in humid weather, try rubbing their edges with a common bar of soap. The thin coating of hand soap will help the door open and close with ease.

These teeth have no bite!

If your zipper looks fine but doesn't zip up or down smoothly, try rubbing the teeth with a dry bar of hand soap. You'll be zipping up and down in no time.

Save your stockings

Stop a run in your stockings with soap if you don't have a bottle of nail polish handy. Rub a wet bar of soap—or dab some liquid soap—on the end of the run. The run will stop running when the soap dries.

Stop sewing snafus

Sewing on a button? Make tangles and knots easier to unravel by running the thread over a bar of soap before you even thread the needle.

toothbrush

Teeth and toothbrushes don't really have to go together, since toothbrushes have so many other uses. Here are a few of the best.

Put a toothbrush to grate use!

Use an old, hard-bristled toothbrush to clean cheese (or lemon zest or anything else) from the cheese grater. Scrub the grater with the wet toothbrush, then rinse the grater and the toothbrush and you're done. No muss, no fuss, and you haven't destroyed a sponge or cloth in the process.

Spruce up dirty spots on your white blinds with liquid white shoe polish.

Tame those brows

If your eyebrows go every which way, bring them under control with the tool for your teeth. Spray a new soft toothbrush with a light coating of hair spray, and brush your brows into shape.

Get dirt out of the grout

Use commercial grout cleaner to clean your grout—but with a twist. Apply the cleaner, let it sit for a few minutes, then use an old toothbrush to remove the cleaner and the dirt.

Brush *before* you eat

Clean craggy vegetables with a soft toothbrush before you cook them. Brush mushrooms, asparagus, and peppers before throwing them in a pot. You'll get rid of dirt that won't normally just wash off the vegetables.

toothpaste

Toothpaste does everything from clean jewelry to fix glass coffee tables. It's so versatile that it's undoubtedly one of the most valuable products in your 99 cent store. Buy a tube and try the tips below for yourself!

Gently rub toothpaste on your jewelry with a tissue if you don't have any jewelry cleaner handy.

Clean your jewelry

If it can make your teeth sparkle...it can make your jewelry sparkle, too! Gently rub toothpaste on your jewelry with a tissue if you don't have any jewelry cleaner handy. Rinse under water and wear.

Brush away water rings on wood surfaces

Put a bit of white non-gel toothpaste on a clean rag, and rub away the water ring—gently, and in the direction of the wood grain. Though it may take some time, the ring will disappear. Let it dry, then apply furniture polish.

Make your glass gleam

If you discover small scratches in your glass coffee table, rub plain, white toothpaste into the glass top with your fingertip or a soft cotton cloth. (The "extra-whitening" kind is recommended.) Be sure to rub in a circle for best results. Let dry, then rub the area gently with a clean lint-free cloth to clean completely.

Soothe minor burns in the kitchen

Grabbed a hot pot handle or touched the edge of a baking sheet fresh from the oven? Keep a tube of white, minty toothpaste nearby to soothe a minor burn. First, run cold water over the burn, then gently pat dry and spread on a layer of toothpaste. The pain will quickly fade.

9 More Uses for WHITE, NON-GEL TOOTHPASTE

A DIFFERENT Solution

1 End Itches
Putting toothpaste over bug bites—including those from mosquitoes, fleas, and ants—will quickly lessen the itch. This method also helps to cool down burns on your skin.

2 Clean Sinks
If you've run out of bathroom cleaner and company is on the way, you may have a sinking feeling. Never fear! Use toothpaste instead and your basin will be sparkling clean in no time. Bonus: The toothpaste will kill any odors emanating from the drain trap.

3 Magic Mirrors
Write a message to a loved one on the bathroom mirror using toothpaste. Then wipe it off. After your sweetie steps out of the shower, the message will appear outlined by the fog that covers the rest of the mirror—it will seem like magic.

4 Clean Piano Keys
Clean them up with toothpaste and a toothbrush, then wipe down with a damp cloth. Makes sense, since ivory is essentially elephant teeth. However, toothpaste will work just as well on modern pianos that usually have keys covered with plastic rather than real ivory.

5 Clear up Pimples
Dab a bit of non-gel, non-whitening toothpaste on the offending spot, and it should be dried up by morning. The toothpaste dehydrates the pimple and absorbs the oil. This remedy works best on pimples that have come to a head. Caution: This remedy may be irritating to sensitive skin.

6 Remove Scratches from Smartphones
Rub toothpaste on the front or back of your phone (wherever there are scratches). The toothpaste will work to reduce the look of the scratches and make your phone screen look much better. Use masking tape to cover parts of the screen and phone not needing the paste rub.

7 Water Views
If you want to prevent "fog" in your swimming goggles, smear them with toothpaste and then wipe them clean with a dry cloth. When you dive into the pool you'll see clearly underwater.

8 Illuminate Your Ride
Plastic headlight and taillight covers start to look dull over time, but can be revived by rubbing a pea-sized drop of paste on a clean rag and polishing in circular motion for 2 to 5 minutes. Wipe away the toothpaste, then use a clean cloth to rapidly buff the surface to shine.

9 Brighten Shoes
Squeeze toothpaste on a brush to clean and whiten the rubber on your sneakers. After scrubbing, wipe with a damp cloth. A little toothpaste does an amazing job of removing scuffs from leather shoes also. Squirt a dab on the scuffed area and rub with a soft cloth. Wipe clean with a damp cloth.

AISLE 3

GARDENING AND OUTDOORS

THE GREAT OUTDOORS HOLDS SO MANY possibilities—gardening, camping, barbecuing, and sports—and a number of responsibilities, too, including taking care of pets and cars. Your local dollar store has supplies for both the possibilities and the responsibilities. You'll find flowerpots for gardening, matches for camping, charcoal briquettes for barbecuing, golf tees for sports, cat litter for pets, and ice scrapers for cars. And best of all, each of the outdoor items listed here can be used for a wide variety of other practical purposes, too. So start digging into this chapter right away for innovative ways to stretch your gardening and outdoor dollars!

bandannas

Bandannas are part of every camper's arsenal. They're used for keeping your hair out of your face (particularly if you haven't had a shower in a few days), as a washcloth, a towel—even an emergency bandage. But bandannas aren't just for camping anymore. See where else they're handy!

Cure a headache

Stop a headache in its tracks with a bandanna. Tie one around your forehead, tightening it until you feel pressure at several points around your head. The bandanna will reduce the flow of blood to your scalp, which in turn will reduce the pain you feel from swollen blood vessels. For extra benefit, soak the bandanna in vinegar. You may not like the smell, but you'll like the added relief.

Wipe your mouth

Stop wasting money on expensive fabric napkins and use dollar store bandannas at casual meals instead. They're affordable and less likely to show stains than their fancy counterparts.

Wrap presents

Turn your wrapping paper into an additional present by using a brightly colored bandanna as the giftwrap. The recipient will love getting two gifts in one!

Turn it into a carryall

Keep a bandanna with you whenever you travel. You never know when you'll need a container—made by tying together the corners of the bandanna—to collect shells on the beach or pinecones in the forest.

Get a good night's sleep

If light at night stops you from sleeping, tie a bandanna around your eyes. You'll block out the bothersome rays until you're ready to see the morning light.

Make a bib

No need to run out to the store to buy a bib when young children visit. Just turn a bandanna into a bib with a clothespin.

buckets

Buckets have a reputation for being outdoor carryalls. They're perfect for collecting weeds, filling with water for cleaning the car, and toting around gardening tools. Give them a chance to do more, however, and they shine. Check out what they can do below.

Clean your room

Before you start the hard work of cleaning a room—dusting, vacuuming, and so on—you need to get rid of the clutter. Clear out the mess by walking around with a bucket, filling it with items you need to move to other rooms or sort through when you're done cleaning.

Soak dirty laundry

Rather than commandeering the sink for soaking dirty clothes, put the clothes, water, and detergent in a small bucket. You can simply remove the bucket when someone else needs to wash their hands, brush their teeth, or otherwise use the sink.

Make a container pot

Container gardening is all the rage, and container pots come in all shapes, sizes, and colors—and often with serious price tags. Skip the garden store and buy a few 5-gallon plastic buckets at the dollar store instead. Poke drainage holes in the bottom of each bucket with a hammer and a large nail. You can even decorate the buckets with enamel paint to give them a little pizzazz.

Keep car clutter to a minimum

Store a bucket in the back seat of your car to act as a catch-all for directions, magazines, loose change, and anything else that finds its way into your car but never seems to leave. Cleaning out the car will be a cinch—just take the bucket out and empty it—and your passengers will always have room for a ride.

Tote your tools
Climbing a ladder? Carrying your hammer and screwdriver up the steps with you is dangerous. Put all the tools in a bucket, then attach a long rope to the bucket. Take the free end of the rope up the ladder with you—and simply haul the bucket and tools to your level when you're ready.

Organize an extension cord
Does the extension cord that you use outside get tangled every time you store it? If so, a plastic bucket can save the day. Drill a hole a little larger than the size of the cord's plug at the bottom of a 5-gallon bucket. Run the plug through the hole—from the inside to the outside—and pull a foot of the cord outside the bucket. Now coil the remainder of the extension cord inside the bucket and store it in its usual spot. All you have to do to use it is pull as much of the extension cord as you need out of the bucket—no tangles! When you're done, coil it back in the bucket.

Stop magazine clutter
Nothing makes a house look messier than hordes of magazines scattered across a prominent coffee table. Get rid of the clutter by storing rolled-up magazines in a bucket. You'll still have access to your favorites, and your house will immediately look cleaner.

Help your Christmas tree stand tall
Store-bought Christmas tree stands can be surprisingly annoying to use—screws that don't turn, water that sloshes out of the base—but the solution can be found in a bucket. Make your own Christmas tree stand by partially filling a bucket with sand or gravel and lowering the tree trunk into it. Now fill the bucket with more sand or gravel, then pour water on it to prevent the needles from dropping. Keep the bucket contents moist as long as the tree stands.

bungee cords
No longer only for thrill-seekers, bungee cords entered the mainstream a while ago. But they never really proved their worth to people who weren't interested in jumping off bridges. Here, though, they show exactly what they can do.

Protect food storage containers
Keeping containers of food that you bought on sale or at a warehouse store on open shelves in your pantry is smart; you saved money and probably extra trips to the grocery store. But all that food will go to waste if the containers topple

Hold appliances, chairs, and tables together with bungee cords while you make necessary repairs.

off your pantry shelves and break open. Save yourself a headache by stretching a bungee cord across each shelf to corral the containers.

Use cords as clamps

Hold appliances, chairs, and tables together with bungee cords while you make necessary repairs. Attach several cords to each other to make one large clamp, and wrap a long cord several times around the item you're repairing to make a smaller one.

Keep trash cans covered

Stop raccoons and other hungry animals from opening your trash can and spreading garbage all over your lawn with the help of a bungee cord. Just attach the cord to the can's two handles and stretch it across the top of the can. Your lawn will stay clean.

burlap

A staple of gardeners everywhere, burlap protects new lawns and baby flowers and vegetables. But it's a lot tougher than you might think—it's even strong enough to move heavy objects!

Keep soil in pots

Prevent dirt from escaping from repotted houseplants by covering the drainage hole of each pot with burlap before you fill the pot with soil.

Create necklaces and bracelets

Tease out several threads from the burlap and weave them or braid them into unique pieces of jewelry. Add beads for an even greater special effect.

Store root vegetables

Turn a sheet of burlap into a burlap bag and use the bag to store potatoes and onions. The burlap lets the vegetables breathe.

Move heavy objects

Use a sheet of burlap to transfer heavy items like container plants from place to place in your yard or on your patio. The heavy weave makes it a solid workhorse.

candles

Whether you're repelling mosquitoes with a candle designed to keep your barbecue free of insects or illuminating the dark with a candle on a camping trip, you'll probably want to buy a few of these lights at the dollar store. Here's how to light up your life in even more ways with those dollar store candles.

Wax your windows

Do your double-hung windows have a bumpy ride every time you open or close them? If your windows don't slide up and down with ease, let a candle help them. Clean the insides of the window frame where the sashes travel, then rub the same area with a candle. The windows will have a much smoother journey.

Unstick dresser drawers

If your dresser drawers won't cooperate when you want to open or close them, take them out of the dresser and see if they move on wooden runners. If they do, turn the drawer upside down, and remove any dirt or other obstructions in the wooden tracks that hold the runners. Rub a white candle on the runners and, if possible, on the tracks. Return the drawer to its upright position, and put it back in the dresser. It will move with ease.

Silence sliced onions

Try burning a candle the next time you chop onions. It will burn off some of the fumes emitted from sliced onions and make for a more tear-free chore.

Mask a dusty room

Don't panic if you don't have time to dust before your last-minute guests arrive. Just turn down the lights in the dining room and living room and set out candles on side tables, windowsills, the mantel, a coffee table, and so on. The dim—but atmospheric—lighting will hide any housekeeping faux pas.

Save a stuck zipper

Have dirt and lint gummed up the teeth of your zipper? If so, you need to take two steps to get your zipper working again. First, get rid of the dirt and lint by brushing the teeth with a dry toothbrush. Second, lightly rub the clean teeth with the end of a beeswax candle. Your zipper will return to its usual ups and downs.

Test for drafts

Close the front door, back door, side door, and any other doors to the outside, then place a lit candle near them to see if a draft makes the flame move. If it does, consider installing a door sweep or weather stripping to stop the air from coming inside.

Protect mailing labels from rain

And sleet and snow, for that matter. Rub a white candle over the label you've addressed with a marker. The label will remain legible on its journey through the mail.

Make a home for pins

Don't let lost pins and needles put you on pins and needles! Make a pincushion out of a wide candle. Not only will the wax trap these pointy objects, it will also help them move more easily through fabric.

Squelch squeaks

Does opening and shutting a door hurt your ears? Take the door off its hinges and rub a candle over the hinge and other metal surfaces that touch it. Replace the door and enjoy the quiet.

Decorate Easter eggs

Before you dip your Easter egg in dye, use a candle to draw designs on it. The wax from the candle will repel the dye. You'll end up with a design in white. For a multicolored design, draw on the egg with the candle after each color dye. The candle will save the most recent color from disappearing.

car wax and polish

Who knew there were so many alternate uses for car wax and car polish? Maybe the dollar store did, because they stock a lot of them. You might want to stock up and use them for all these different purposes.

Clean window frames

Get rid of oxidation deposits on the frames of your aluminum windows by cleaning them with one of three things you can usually find in your house: a mild detergent, a light abrasive cleaner, or fine steel wool. Once the window frames are

Armor All

Car wax defends the outside of your car; the inside of your auto found its champion in 1962 when Joe Palcher (a polymer chemist) created a formula to protect rubber, plastic, and vinyl. He sold it as "Tri-don" ("no dirt" spelled backward). Marketing expert Alan Rypinski redubbed the product Armor All Protectant, a name that is now internationally recognized.

clean, polish them with car paste wax. Keep them looking spiffy by reapplying the wax every year.

Spruce up patio furniture

If you have aluminum furniture on your patio (or if some of your patio furniture sports aluminum parts), make it look better by scrubbing it with detergent and water, then drying it with a soft absorbent cloth. Weatherproof it by coating it with car wax.

Keep dust off blinds

Venetian blinds are never a pleasure to clean, so a trick to keep them clean is a trick worth knowing. Here's what to do: Clean the blinds as you normally would, then apply a thin coating of car wax to the blinds. The wax will repel dirt and dust, so your next cleaning will be easier.

Stop a CD from skipping

How? Use car wax. Put some wax on a clean, 100 percent cotton cloth and wipe the CD. When the wax has dried, buff the disc with another clean cotton cloth. Be sure to buff it in straight lines from the center of the disc to the outside edges, not in a circular motion. Rinse the disc in water, let it air-dry, then enjoy your tunes again.

Hide countertop scratches

If you find superficial scratches on your laminate countertop, you can camouflage them with car polish. Follow the directions on the car polish container to apply it, then buff it with a soft cotton cloth.

Polish your refrigerator

Forget about fingerprints and other smudges on your white refrigerator and freezer. Wash and wipe the appliance dry, then apply a coating of car paste wax. Finally, buff it with a clean soft cloth. Your fridge will have a glossier finish and a smudge-free shine.

Wax your snow shovel

Shoveling snow is a big enough headache without snow sticking to your shovel. Stop the sticking by applying two thick coats of car wax to the shovel (but not the handle, obviously) before you start working. And don't forget to lift with your knees, not your back!

Keep tools rust-free

Prevent rust from attacking the tools you store in your garage—particularly if your garage is damp—by coating them with a light application of car wax. Petroleum jelly works, too.

Work away wood scratches

Does your dining room table have a high-gloss lacquer finish? Does it seem to scratch easily? Get rid of those small scratches with car wax. Once you've tested the wax on an inconspicuous section of the table (confirming that it won't hurt the finish), polish the table with a soft cloth dipped in it. Work in a circular motion for best results.

Rub away rust rings

Metal cans—containing vegetables, tomato sauce, shaving cream, or hairspray—are essential items in the kitchen and bathroom, but can leave nasty rings on countertops. Get rid of these rings by rubbing them away with car wax.

See clearly in the morning

Prevent fog from forming on your bathroom mirror when you take a hot shower. Before you step into the shower, rub a little bit of car wax on the mirror. Let it dry, then buff it with a soft cloth. You'll no longer be in a fog in the morning.

Buff out scorch marks

If you've accidentally scorched your laminate countertop—and who would harm it on purpose?—let car wax help you fix it. Assuming the burn is superficial, put some car wax on a clean cloth and buff the counter until the mark is gone. Don't use abrasive cleanser because it may remove the finish as well as the mark.

cat litter

Cat litter can be used for so much more than cats. And in so many different ways! Make your home smell better, your garage cleaner, and your car ride safer, all with a little kitty litter.

Save a cell phone

If you've ever dropped a cell phone in water, you know your heart sinks, too. But don't stand there. Whip the phone out, remove the battery and pat both dry. Wrap in a dish towel and push this lumpy package down into a clean new bag of litter. In three days, take it out and plug it in. You should be good to go.

Make your garage floor sparkle

Let kitty litter help you clean your garage. If you find a puddle of oil on your concrete garage floor, pour paint thinner over it, and then cover the area with kitty litter. (Make sure that the garage is well ventilated by keeping the garage door open, and don't let anyone smoke or strike matches anywhere near the affected area—and keep the cats away.) The kitty litter will absorb the oil. Just sweep up the mess and you're done.

Refresh your books

If, when cleaning your bookshelves, you find a book that has a musty smell, put it in a paper bag with some clean kitty litter and leave it in the bag for about a week. When you take it out, brush off any litter—and the musty smell.

Dry long-stemmed flowers

Most dried flower arrangements look better when they include long-stemmed flowers, as well as shorter versions. Here's a handy way to dry statice, snapdragons, and more: Fill a long airtight container about halfway with cat litter. Place the flowers on top of the litter, leaving some space between them. Put the lid on the container and put it away for a week to 10 days. Open the container and find the flowers dried and ready to arrange.

Scare off unwelcome rodents

This is a great use for *used* cat litter, something that rarely gets recycled! Pour it down the holes of burrowing rodents such as groundhogs or moles. The scent of predatory urine frightens them away!

Take the stink out of the garbage can

Pour about a cup of cat litter into the bottom of your garbage can before you toss in bags of garbage. Replace it every week or when it is damp. Your cans will stop smelling like trash.

Use as an air freshener

Does your closet smell musty? Or your entire basement? Get rid of that unpleasant odor by filling shallow boxes or aluminum pans with kitty litter and placing them in the closet or around the room. The air will smell fresher!

Dispose of paint

Chances are your garbage collectors no longer pick up cans of paint. If you need to get rid of latex or water-based paint, do it with kitty litter. Simply fill a paper bag with cat litter and pour the paint into the bag. Let the kitty litter absorb the paint, then toss the bag out with the trash. (Don't use this method to dispose of oil-based paint.)

charcoal briquettes

What can you do with charcoal briquettes other than start up your grill? Even Santa preferred coal over them! But Santa apparently never saw the multitude of alternate uses for this barbecue staple. Here's what he missed.

Get rid of refrigerator odors

You already know that baking soda will prevent bad smells in your fridge, and even absorb some odors already there. But what to do if you have strong, sour smells? Simple. Place a few charcoal briquettes on a dish—don't cover it up—and put the dish in the fridge for a few days. The odor will disappear.

Keep silver tarnish at bay

Since polishing silver is probably not your favorite way to pass the time, consider a novel way to delay the inevitable tarnish. Put a few charcoal briquettes—which absorb moisture—into your silver drawer or cabinet. You can go the extra distance by putting a briquette inside a silver teapot to prevent a build-up of moisture.

Lock rust out of your toolbox

Place a few charcoal briquettes in your toolbox to keep rust away from your tools. Chalk and silica gel packs (those small white packages that inevitably accompany a new pair of shoes) work well, too.

Stop bathroom smells

Place a few charcoal briquettes in clever spots in your bathroom—in a decorative vase, behind the toilet, or hidden in a corner—to stop moisture and odors. Don't forget where you put them, and replace them every few months. Your bathroom will smell fresher.

Protect your books

If you keep your books in a bookcase with glass doors, they may be more susceptible to mold and must because the doors keep moisture in. Get rid of the moisture—and the musty smell and the mold—by placing a piece of charcoal inside the bookcase. The books will stay dry and your problem is solved.

dustpan

Take the brush away from the dustpan and you're left with...just a dustpan, right? Wrong! You're left with a snow shovel and a craft tool and a toy picker-upper.

Shovel a little snow

Let young children shovel snow alongside you—they'll learn how to do it and may really help you when they're older—with a mini shovel. Give them a dustpan and show them just how much fun shoveling can be.

Clean up crafts

Pom-poms, sequins, and beads are all-important ingredients in many craft projects, but they can also be a headache to put away when the project is done. Use a clean dustpan to scoop up these little pieces and pour them into their containers. You'll save time and a trip to the medicine cabinet for aspirin.

Pick up tiny toys

Little army men, doll accessories, and games like jacks can be annoying and potentially dangerous underfoot. Clean them up in one fell swoop using a dustpan. Drop the toys in the toy chest and admire the clean room.

flowerpot

You may think a flowerpot is a pot in which to plant flowers. That's true. But it's also true that flowerpots can be incredibly versatile tools in the garden *and* in the house—and in ways you might not have considered. Consider these!

Trap slugs

At night, put a piece of orange or grapefruit rind inside a flowerpot, then place the pot on its side in your garden. The slugs will enter the pot overnight, and you can get rid of them in the morning.

Plant a pot in a pot

Save yourself the expense of filling a large container pot with potting soil if you're planting shallow-rooted plants. Instead, turn a smaller flowerpot upside down at the bottom of the container pot—it will take up the space usually reserved for the soil.

Clean up small toys in one fell swoop using a dustpan.

Protect basil from the sun

Whether you're planting basil seeds or transplanting seedlings into your garden, you need to protect these babies from the strong sun. Water the seedlings well, then cover them with an upside-down flowerpot. Remove the pot after a few days—when the plants can handle the sun—and watch the basil grow.

Attract toads to your garden

Insects eat garden plants, and toads eat insects—so you'll want to make your garden into a happy home for toads. Give them water by placing a pan filled with rocks and water in the soil, and place a flowerpot—with a broken edge, so the toads can and come and go—upside down in the shade for shelter.

Kill off ants

If you find an entire colony of ants in or near your garden, you'll want to get rid of it. How? Cover the anthill with an upside down flowerpot. Pour boiling water through the hole in the bottom of the pot. You'll get rid of all the ants at once.

flowerpot saucers

Count on plastic flowerpot saucers to catch more than water from an over-watered plant. They can catch ketchup and cocktails and even hamburger meat. Give the saucers a chance to astonish you.

Stop sticky shelves

Keep refrigerator shelves clean by placing plastic flowerpot saucers under salad dressings, condiments, and other containers that can become sticky. Even if the container is a mess, your shelves will stay pristine.

Create coasters

Who ever has enough coasters for a party? Protect your wooden tabletops the next time you have many guests by using plastic flowerpot saucers as coasters. You'll keep your tables safe and have a conversation piece at the same time.

Freeze individual portions

Plan ahead for your next barbecue by creating your burgers now. Place each one in a small, shallow plastic flowerpot saucer, then stack the saucers on top of each other. Put the stack in a freezer bag and stick it in the freezer. You'll be able to separate the burgers easily when you're ready to grill.

Frisbee

The Frisbee is the ultimate toy—and an ultimate sport (called Ultimate Frisbee)—even if it started its life as a pie plate. So what can you do with it other than toss it or use it for pies? The ultimate answers are here.

Feed Fido on the road

Whether you're traveling with your pet or simply on an outing to the park, use a Frisbee as a dog food dish or a water dish for your pet. It's easy to carry and easy to clean.

Keep paper plates steady

Take several Frisbees on your next camping trip and use them as paper plate holders. Better yet, take an assortment of colors and assign each camper a color for the trip. No more soggy, floppy plates.

Create a paint palette

A Frisbee is the perfect paint palette. Flipped upside down, it has room for individual dabs of paint and room for mixing different colors together. The lip around the edge even keeps the paints in the palette, rather than dripping on your canvas.

Make a soap dish

Don't let your soap slide around your campsite. Give it a home on an upside-down Frisbee.

7 More Nontraditional Ways to Use FLOWERPOTS

1 Candy Garden

A plastic or terra-cotta pot can be made into a unique gift. Place a square of florist's foam into the bottom of the pot and stick lollipops (or any favorite candy on a stick) into the foam. Cover this base with green shredded paper. Your gift will look like a garden, and after the treat is gone the pot can be put to use!

2 Wind Chimes

Gather several terra-cotta pots in descending sizes. Thread a piece of nylon rope through the drain holes, starting with the largest pot on top; the progressively smaller pots should hang below. All the flowerpots must hang upside down. At the end of the rope, tie some beads to serve as the chime. This is a lovely way to add some "music" to your garden.

3 Fowl Fun

Two clay pots and a saucer can make a bath that will please backyard birds. Use pots that are around 18 or 20 inches in size, and a similar sized saucer. Glue the bottoms of the pots together, then glue the saucer to the top (smaller) pot to hold the water. It is best to coat the saucer in polyurethane before attaching it to the pots.

4 Hit the Beach

Plastic pots come in many sizes and work great as molds to build castles in the sand—either at the beach or in a sandbox.

5 Basket-less Gift

Make a flowerpot an integral part of a gift's presentation. Fill a terra-cotta pot with gloves, bulbs, seed packets—everything you know your favorite gardener will love.

6 Outside Ashtray

A way to ensure that cigarette butts end up in the proper place is to make ashtrays for your garden parties. You can do this on the cheap by taking terra-cotta pots, covering their drainage holes with duct tape, and filling the pots with sand.

7 Interior Decoration

Who says inexpensive terra-cotta pots can only be used outdoors? Paint them in shades to match your home décor using acrylic paints. Try special finishes like silver or copper. When your paint is dry, use a clear polyurethane sealer, inside and out. You can use your one-of-a-kind pot for plants or dried flowers.

gardening gloves

What do blinds, knickknacks, and chandeliers have in common? Gardening gloves! See what other kooky uses they have here.

Stop the swelling

Do you have stiff, swollen hands when you wake up in the morning because of arthritis? If so, try wearing form-fitting garden gloves to bed at night. They'll help reduce the swelling.

Dust your tiny treasures

Find a pair of soft fabric gloves and put them on the next time you dust your knickknacks. Clean your treasures with your fingers. You'll have more control over the cleaning—meaning you'll be less likely to knock over a knickknack and damage it.

Wear two pairs of gloves

If you suffer from eczema, you may have noticed that your condition gets worse—or at least doesn't get any better—when you wash dishes. Protect your hands by wearing rubber gloves over a pair of thin gardening gloves (but don't choose latex gloves because the latex may make your eczema worse).

Protect your nails

Do you have dry, brittle fingernails? If so, you can strengthen them by rubbing petroleum jelly or a thick hand cream into your nails at bedtime, then covering your hands with a pair of thin cotton garden gloves before you turn in for the night. The petroleum jelly or hand cream moisturizes the areas around and under your nails, and the gloves retain the moisture. Repeat as needed.

Wash slatted blinds

Overcome your dislike of cleaning blinds with a combination of a garden glove and fabric softener. Fill a small bowl with fabric softener, and put the glove on your power hand. Dip your gloved fingers into the fabric softener, then rub your first two fingers over the top, then bottom, of each slat. The fabric softener will not only clean the blinds but will also help keep dust at bay.

Clean houseplants

Put on old cloth garden gloves and run your fingers over the tops and bottoms of each leaf simultaneously. You'll have dusted the entire plant in no time!

Fool your fingers

Whether you scratch at night because of eczema or out of habit, you can trick yourself by covering your hands with garden gloves. You'll stop scratching in your sleep.

Give a chandelier new life

Soak a pair of cloth gardening gloves in window cleaner, put them on and wipe away any mess you find. Your chandelier will sparkle again.

WAY BACK WHEN...

Golf Balls

Small, round, white, dimpled—these are images that may come to mind when one thinks of golf balls. However, the first golf balls, dating to the 1500s, were made of wood. By the 1600s, golf balls were made of goose feathers tightly packed into a small pocket of animal hide that would dry into a ball shape. If you wanted one, you asked for a "feathery." Imagine the misery if modern golfers were faced with such a thing today!

Place golf balls at the bottom of a pot or container before adding the soil and the plants to help the water drain.

golf balls

Fore! Well, actually here are three alternate uses for golf balls. If you've given up the game and have golf balls lying around the house or just bought some at the dollar store on a whim, you can put them to good use with these suggestions.

Enjoy a warm bath

Don't let a missing tub plug stop you from luxuriating in a warm bath. Use a golf ball in place of the plug. It will keep the water in the tub—and you in heaven.

Drain potted plants properly

Place golf balls at the bottom of a pot or container before adding the soil and the plants. The golf balls will help the water drain—and the flowers grow.

Give yourself a hand massage

Place a golf ball in one palm, then place your other palm over it and interlock your fingers loosely. Now roll the golf ball around your hands, pressing your palms together at the same time. The tension in your hands will ease. Roll your bare feet over a golf ball for a few minutes for a soothing foot massage, too.

golf tees

Both golfers and non-golfers will want to buy golf tees to use in these creative ways—off the course, of course.

T marks the spot

A golf tee, that is. If flowers that normally bloom in the spring don't show up, mark the bald spots with golf tees. In the fall, plant new bulbs beneath the tees. You'll have a full complement of flowers next spring.

Fill an empty hole

If you're replacing a screw in a hole that's gotten too big for it, let a golf tee help you. Simply dip the tip of the tee into yellow carpenter's glue, then insert the tee into the too-big hole. If some of the tee juts out of the hole, trim it with a utility knife. Let the glue dry. Now drill a new hole for the screw and screw it in.

Organize your ties

Make a tie rack out of golf tees! Grab a piece of pine board. Sand it, paint it, and drill 1/8-inch holes every 2 inches. Find a corresponding number of golf tees, and dip their tips into yellow carpenter's glue. Insert each tee in a hole, securing it with a hammer. Let the glue dry. Hang the tie rack on the inside of a closet door or on the closet wall, and watch your favorite golfer smile.

TOP 10 GARDENING TOOLS

One of the things that constantly boggles the minds of our editors is the uselessness of so much expensive specialty stuff that's out there on the market. Instead, we scoured the aisles of our local 99 cent store.

1
Trowel
This ancient tool is our go-to favorite for planting perennials, potting plants, and burying bulbs.

2
Watering Can
Pick up an inexpensive plastic watering can for spot-watering delicate seedlings.

3
Pruners
You'll use them for everything from pruning shrubs and roses to the odd tree.

4
Scissors
Pick up a package of children's school scissors for cutting stems or removing dead flower heads.

5
Meat Fork
A meat fork will help you lift out the roots of established perennials or divide overgrown plants.

6
Transplanting Spade
Long, narrow, and super-useful, this tool doubles as a great bulb planter.

7
Trug
This big, plastic barrel drags dug-up weeds into the woods, or newspapers out to the recycling bin.

8
Wheelbarrow
Spend a few extra bills for one that is solid and doesn't teeter on its wheel. You'll use it forever.

9
Soaker Hose
A few good soaker hoses will save your roses. Hook them up, and watch your garden smile.

10
Gloves
Rubber gloves are great for weed pulling, but we prefer soft leather for everything else.

holiday lights

From protecting a plant to making your stairs safer, holiday lights have many uses far beyond the Christmas season. So turn your ho, ho, hos into oh, oh, ohs with these merry ideas for holiday lights.

Protect your plant from frost

Don't let an early frost damage a large plant you may have in a container outdoors. Save it with Christmas lights! Weave the lights around the plant, then cover it with a sheet. Turn on the lights. Your plant will not only look festive, it will also stay warm.

Light stairs for safety

String white holiday lights on the banister going up the stairs. Along with looking pretty, the lights serve as a night-light for the steps.

Outline walkways

Use bright white holiday lights to illuminate the border of a walkway at night. Guests will appreciate being able to find their way to their cars easily when they leave your party.

Make your own Christmas tree

Don't have room for a Christmas tree in your house or apartment? Make a two-dimensional one out of holiday lights! Outline the shape of a Christmas tree on a wall with a pencil, then place nails at each angle in the tree. String the lights around the nails, and a festive Christmas tree is born.

ice scraper

Bring your windshield scraper in out of the ice and snow and cold. Reward it for a job well done outside, and let it show you all the good it can do inside!

Level your floors

If you're filling small indentations in your wood floors with wood filler but worry that your floors will end up uneven, rest assured that no worry is necessary—if you have an ice scraper. Just pack wood filler into each gouge, then use an ice scraper to smooth out the work. Your floor will look as good as new!

Clean a gas stovetop

Food baked onto the top of a gas range can be a challenge to remove. Make your job easier by using a car's ice scraper. First and most importantly, turn off the pilot lights and burners. Next, spray the baked-on mess with WD-40, and give it a few minutes to work its magic. Then scrape the food off easily with a plastic ice scraper. To finish the job, wash the stovetop with hot soapy water and wipe it dry.

Replace a spatula

Have you ever had a spatula break in the middle of preparing a dish in a nonstick pan? Replace it pronto with a plastic ice scraper and calmly finish cooking.

Scrape off paint splatters

Don't fret if you've splattered paint on your acrylic bathtub while you painted your bathroom. Remove it easily and quickly—and without scratching the surface of the tub—with an ice scraper.

Wipe away baking messes

Whether you're making cookies or baking bread, you'll probably end up with some dough stuck to your work surface—no matter how much flour you've used to keep it from sticking. Use an ice scraper to clean off any gummy residue.

Remove ice inside

An ice scraper can work as well on a freezer as it can on a car window. If you don't feel like defrosting your freezer but want to get rid of some of the ice and frost, gently chip away at it with an ice scraper until you're happy with the space you've created.

kneeling pad

Kneeling pads were designed to make gardening a little more comfortable for people who spend a lot of time planting and weeding. But maybe kneeling pad designers had more ideas like this in mind.

Bring your plants to their knees

Protect your floor and tables from scratches caused by flowerpots by putting the pots on top of garden kneeling pads. The pads will keep your floors and furniture looking spiffy.

Kneel comfortably at bath time

Bathing a child in a tub can mean bubbles and giggles, but it can also mean sore knees. Give your knees a break by using a garden kneeling pad the next time you enter your child's soapy world.

Protect your wood floors

Cut a garden kneeling pad into small pieces and superglue each piece to the bottom leg of a chair or table. These tiny pads will keep your wood and other hard-surface floors free from scratches caused by tables and chairs.

leaf bags

Paper leaf bags are more than grocery bags on steroids. They're gentle with your sweaters and protective of your car's windshield. They're versatile and useful, and you should always have some on hand. Here's why.

Make a temporary cover

Don't stop ironing just because the ironing board cover is useless. Make a new one by opening up a leaf bag or two, dampening the bags, and laying them over your ironing board. The bags will work as a temporary cover until you have time to buy a new one.

Protect your steering wheel

Actually, protect your hands from the steering wheel on a hot summer day. Cut a leaf bag in half, and place the bottom half—the half that still looks like a bag—over your steering wheel when you park the car. It will keep the steering wheel from overheating and hurting your hands.

Wrap a large present

Don't waste money on rolls and rolls of wrapping paper just because you need to wrap a large gift. Cut a leaf bag along one of the seams so that it opens out into a flat sheet of paper, and make sure that any printing faces you. Put your present on top of the bag and wrap it as you would wrap

Use a garden kneeling pad the next time you give your child a bath.

any gift. Decorate the brown paper with markers or tie it with a particularly colorful ribbon.

Stop snow on your windshield

Keep snow and ice off your windshield with leaf bags. If snow is forecast, get in your car and turn on the wipers. Turn the car off when the wipers are practically vertical. Place leaf bags that you've split open under the wipers and wait for the snow. Once the snow has stopped, simply remove the leaf bags—and the snow. (Be sure to remove the bags and the snow before you turn the car back on to avoid damaging the wipers.)

Reshape sweaters

Before you wash your favorite wool sweater, trace its shape onto a leaf bag—cut the bag along one seam and open it up if you need more room. After washing the sweater, place it on the outline to stretch it back into its original shape.

Keep spray paint in the bag

If you need to spray paint a small to medium-sized item but don't want to make a mess, reach for a leaf bag. Place the item in the bag, spray it as needed, let it dry, take it, out and toss the bag. You mess will be contained!

lighter fluid

Dollar stores sell lighter fluid with their barbecue supplies, but it can be used all around the house. Keep a bottle on hand, even if you never grill. (However, be sure to use it in a well-ventilated area. Don't use it near an open flame, and don't smoke around it because it is highly flammable. And of course, do not inhale or ingest it.)

Wipe away heel marks

Black heels marks on light-colored floors—or any colored floor, really—are a jarring sight. Get rid

Save big!

of them easily by rubbing them with a paper towel dipped in lighter fluid. The marks will quickly disappear.

Get rid of rust

Have rust spots sprouted on your stainless steel sink? If so, use lighter fluid to make them disappear. Rub the rust spots with a drop of lighter fluid, then wash it off with a combination of nonabrasive scouring powder and water.

Correct cooking-oil stains

Cooking oil belongs in the pan, not on your clothes—but accidents happen. If you discover a cooking-oil stain that didn't come out of a garment the first time you washed it, pour a capful of lighter fluid directly onto the stain before tossing it in the wash again. Kiss that stain good-bye!

Let labels go

Sometimes labels don't want to part from their friends—books, drinking glasses, or anything else that's individually marked in a store. And the thrill of buying a nice new item is significantly lessened if you can't get rid of the gummy adhesive that remains after you take off the price tag. Get the thrill back by removing the adhesive with a little bit of lighter fluid.

matches

Matches and matchbooks or boxes are an essential ingredient in barbecuing and camping. But your plants and your car and your knives can use them, too. Here's how.

Fix your lipstick

Throwing away a broken lipstick is like throwing away money. Fix it instead by using a match to warm the bottom of the broken piece (don't melt it completely) and the top of the piece that stayed in the tube. Put the two pieces together and slightly melt the edges of the break together with a new match. Put the lipstick in the refrigerator until it has completely cooled, then return it to your purse.

Unfreeze a lock

Does your car door or your front door freeze closed in the winter? Thaw out the lock by holding your key over a lit match, then putting the key in the lock. The lock should open.

Repair a hole

If you have a nail that won't fit back into its hole because the hole has gotten too big, get some matches to help. Break the tips off several matches and properly dispose of them. Stuff the remaining matchsticks one by one into the hole, until you can't fit in any more. Now hammer the nail back into its hole. It should stay snugly in place.

Smooth rough nails

Whether you break a nail barbecuing or realize while grilling that your nail is snagged, use a box or book of matches to smooth out the problem. Instead of striking a match against the emery-board-like strip, rub your nail on it.

Feed acid-loving plants

Make your hydrangeas, azaleas, impatiens, and gardenias happy by adding sulfur to the soil (to lower the pH). Place matches torn from matchbooks into the holes before you plant these acid-lovers. They'll pay you back with vivid colors and bright whites later.

Sharpen knives

Bring a dull utility or craft knife back to life by rubbing its blade repeatedly on the strip of a matchbook that normally serves to light matches. Don't forget to sharpen both sides of the blade.

seeds

Vegetable and flower seeds may not have much of a life beyond the garden—unless you plan to use them in crafts—but the colorful seed packets can live on in unusual and exciting ways. Here are some to consider.

Make labels for your garden

Don't discard the seed packets you've bought for your vegetable garden once you've planted the

Make your azaleas happy by adding sulfur from matches to the soil (to lower the pH).

seeds. In fact, plan to keep them for labels before you even put the seeds in the ground. Open the packet from the bottom—this way the packet will stand right side up in the garden—then plant the seeds as you usually would. Cover the packets with small, clear plastic bags, and attach them to Popsicle sticks or twigs that you stick in the soil. You'll always know what you've planted where!

File garden information

Use seed packets as mini files that contain everything you need to know about what you planted when and where. Keep a file—a seed packet—for each kind of plant, and you'll never be at a loss for detailed garden information again.

Create homemade greeting cards

The photos of flowers and vegetables on seed packets can be stunning. Cut off the front of a seed packet and glue it onto good–quality card stock (or even construction paper) to make a unique, old-fashioned–looking card.

spatula

Take the spatula away from the grill and it takes on a whole new life as a tool that protects and removes and repairs. Who knew such a simple tool had such a complex alter ego?

Remove old finish

Look no further than a spatula the next time you need help stripping finish off a piece of furniture. Hold the spatula by the blade—but upside down—and push it firmly and repeatedly in a straight motion. You'll be finished with the finish before you know it.

Pull nails out gently

If you're planning to pull a nail out of wood but worry that the hammerhead will hurt the grain, protect the wood before using the hammer.

How? Slip a plastic spatula under the head of the hammer before you start the job.

Repair plaster

Use a small rubber spatula to fill an indentation or hole in a plaster wall. You'll find it more flexible than a putty knife—and, as a result, easier to use.

Scoop up unmentionables

Sometimes, it happens—especially if you have a young puppy or kitten running around your house. Buy one spatula and put it aside as your go-to tool if your pooch or kitty has an accident. Much easier than paper towels, and you only have to buy it once.

squeeze bottles

Plastic squeeze bottles are sold as containers for ketchup and mustard—perfect for an outdoor barbecue. But they're perfect in other jobs, too. Give them a chance to strut their stuff, and maybe they'll give you a friendly squeeze in return.

Pretreat your laundry

Pour your liquid laundry detergent into a plastic ketchup or mustard squeeze bottle. It will make pretreating spots easier—you'll control the amount of detergent you use, plus you'll be able to hit the stain on the spot.

Ration real maple syrup

Does it make your frugal heart constrict when your kids take that pricey bottle of Vermont maple syrup and upend half over a plate of French toast? Transfer that free-running syrup to a squeeze bottle to slow down their consumption. The portion you save may be your own!

> Fill a clean plastic mustard or ketchup squeeze bottle with icing, and use it to decorate your cake.

Fill your iron

The hole you're supposed to use in your steam iron can seem impossibly small when you're using a measuring cup or drinking glass to pour in the water. Make your life easier by loading up a clean mustard or ketchup squeeze bottle with water and using it to fill your steam iron.

Decorate a cake

Fill a clean plastic mustard or ketchup squeeze bottle with icing, and use it to decorate your cake. You'll find that creating flowers, flags, balloons, and piping is much easier, and your words made of icing will be much clearer.

Keep vinegar in the shower

Vinegar enthusiasts swear by apple cider vinegar instead of soap and shampoo for washing sensitive skin and rinsing chemical buildup from hair. Put a bottle of undiluted apple cider vinegar in the shower and see if it works for you, too.

Adorn soups and desserts

Use a squeeze bottle the next time you cook to make your dishes extra fancy. Fill one with pesto or sour cream, and create squiggles on top of soups. Fill another with chocolate, and decorate the dessert you've just made or the plate you plan to present it on for a special effect.

Make a masterpiece in the snow

If you're not a big fan of snowball fights, try redirecting your children toward a different kind of snow play. Arm them with several squeeze bottles filled with water and a few drops of food coloring. They'll get a kick out of squirting colorful designs into the snow.

Think outside the squeeze bottle

Squeeze bottles can be used for so much more than ketchup and mustard. Fill some with honey, mayonnaise, and salad dressing. You'll save space—and sticky messes—in your refrigerator, and your dishwasher won't have to work so hard (no knives!).

Water your kids in the summer

Give your children a few squeeze bottles filled with water on a hot summer day and send them outside to play. They'll have a blast squirting each other, and they'll keep cool, too.

Make perfect pancakes

A squeeze bottle filled with pancake batter is the perfect tool for squeezing out silver dollar-size pancakes onto a griddle. If the nozzle is too small to let the batter flow, use scissors to snip off a bit. For camping, add a bottle half filled with dry pancake mix to the food pack. At breakfast time, add water, shake, and squeeze into the pan.

string

String is so versatile that it can be hard to remember why you bought it in the first place. Maybe you bought it to tie something together—or maybe you were so smart that you knew it had a bunch of different uses. Here are a few of the best.

Bundle kindling

Got string and pieces of twig and dried grasses? Then you've got the makings of little kindling bundles that will help get a cheerful fire started in no time. Toss one in the fireplace, prop a few small logs over it, and set it alight. You can make a basket of these to keep next to the fireplace, or give a basket to a friend as a welcome winter gift.

Trim a long hedge

Create a guide for trimming a hedge to the desired height by using two stakes and a piece of string. Drive one stake into the ground at each end of the hedge, then run the string between the two at the height you want for your hedge. Now trim your hedge down to the string. The top of the hedge will be level from end to end.

Truss a chicken

You don't need butcher's twine or fancy linen string to truss a turkey or chicken before roasting.

A length of clean cotton string off a fresh roll will do the job perfectly. For the most straightforward truss, wrap the string around the drumsticks, which will hold any stuffing in place and help the bird keep its shape during roasting.

tennis balls

Tennis balls help you park and sand and even get a good night's sleep. Forget about bouncing them around on a tennis court— they're much too valuable elsewhere!

Relieve sore feet

Take a load off your aching feet and give them a treat. Put a tennis ball on the floor. Remove your shoes, and place your foot on top of the tennis ball. Now roll the ball around with your foot. You'll end up with a feel-good—and good for you—massage.

Massage your back, too

Drop a few tennis balls into a long tube sock and tie the end shut. Now pretend the tube sock is a towel, and move it across your back the way you would if you were drying off after a shower. Forget about getting dry—you'll get a relaxing back massage instead!

Cut a slit in a tennis ball, and squeeze it to widen the slit. Toss in some nails, then stop squeezing the ball to close your new toolbox.

Make a mini toolbox

Cut a slit in a tennis ball, and squeeze it to widen the slit. Toss in some nails, then stop squeezing the ball to close your toolbox. Carry it with you around the house or in the yard and squeeze it open any time you need a nail.

Fluff up feathers

Throw one or two tennis balls into the dryer the next time you dry down-filled items like pillows, comforters, and jackets. They'll ditch the flat look they get from the washing machine and puff up again with pride.

Save your socks

Don't toss your sock just because it has a small hole in the toe or the heel. Place a tennis ball in the toe or heel—wherever it needs to be mended. The tennis ball will stretch out the surface of the sock so that sewing it will be easier.

Keep your bike level

Help your bicycle's kickstand do its job—keeping your bike standing—and prevent it from sinking

Instant savings!

into the grass or mud by using a tennis ball. How? Cut a slit in the ball and slip it over the end of the kickstand. If you ever find yourself at the beach with your bike, this trick will stop the kickstand from sinking into the sand, too.

Open bottles with ease

Twist-off bottle caps never seem to twist off the way they should. Let a tennis ball help them do their job. Cut a ball in half, then cover the bottle cap with one half and twist it off without a problem.

Soften the hammer's blow

Whether you need to gently nudge some woodwork back into place or tap a nail into soft wood, place a tennis ball with a slit in the middle over your hammer. The tennis ball will treat your job gently.

Park perfectly

Parking your car in the garage is an art: You have to pull only so far forward—but far enough!—and only so close to each wall—but not too close! Take the guesswork out of the equation by hanging a tennis ball on a string from the ceiling or rafters of the garage so that it hits the center of your windshield when you park correctly. You'll never have to guess again exactly where the car goes.

Sand curvy furniture

Voluptuous furniture is pretty, but refinishing it can be an ugly job. Make it easier by covering a tennis ball in sandpaper and using the ball to sand the curves.

Stop snoring

People who snore tend to do so more often when they sleep on their backs. But how can you prevent someone from sleeping that way? Easily. Attach a tennis ball to the back of the person's pajama top by safety-pinning a sock onto the pj's and inserting a tennis ball. (Sewing a pocket in the back of the pajama top works, too.) When the snorer turns onto his back, the tennis ball will prevent him from getting comfortable, and he'll return to his side—where he'll snore less.

twine

Twine is one of those handy-dandy items that you can use all around the house. Use it to tie up newspapers for recycling or tie up packages for shipping. Better yet, use it in these unusual ways.

Go fishing in your drain

Dropping a metal object—a fork or a ring, for example—down a drain is annoying because you can't retrieve it, and it's potentially dangerous if you have a garbage disposer. Get rid of your annoyance and danger by attaching a magnet to a long piece of stiff twine, and use the twine as a fishing line. You should be able to retrieve your belongings.

Close doors quietly

Don't let slamming doors give you a headache. Stop the slamming by tying a piece of twine to the inside doorknob, running it across the edge of the door, and tying it to the outside doorknob. The twine will slow the door down as it shuts, and prevent it from slamming.

Make a hanging planter

Cut two same-size pieces of twine. Cross the two pieces in the middle, then place a container where they cross and glue the container onto the twine. Fill the container with colorful plants, and use the four ends of the twine to hang it on a tree branch or a stake outside.

Create earthy jewelry

Braided twine can make unique natural-looking bracelets and necklaces. Add some beads for a stunning accessory to go with casual clothes.

Fix accessories

Did your shoelace break? Did your belt take a vacation without telling you? Show your accessories who's boss. Replace them with hardworking twine. The twine will keep your pants up and your shoes on.

Stop doors from slamming by tying a piece of twine to the inside doorknob, running it across the edge of the door, and tying it to the outside doorknob.

6 More Nontraditional Ways to Use
TWINE

1 Ribbon Replacement

If you've run out of ribbon, don't dash to the store—use twine! It looks rustic, like raffia, and will contrast nicely with wrapping paper.

2 Stack 'Em

Balls of twine have a very textural, organic appearance. You can make modern-looking holiday ornaments by stacking twine balls three in a row to create snowmen. Add arms with pipe cleaners, facial elements with beads, and you'll have a truly unique display.

3 Knit and Purl

You can knit twine! You wouldn't want to make a sweater, surely, but what about a utilitarian object—like place mats to be used when you are camping? They would definitely be conversation starters!

4 Modern Lighting

You've seen those ultramodern-looking string lamps. They're round and cool looking—and generally pricey. Why buy one expensively when you can make one cheaply? All you need is twine, craft glue, and a balloon or beach ball of the appropriate size. Blow up your round base. Dip twine in your craft glue and paste it crisscross all over the base. Allow the glue to dry, then pop and remove the interior. You'll be left with a hip lamp. A quick trip to the hardware store for a lighting kit will complete your creation.

5 On the Ball

Do you like those decorative balls in home-décor stores? You know the kind—made of twigs or colored sea grass? There is a simple way to make them yourself using twine, Styrofoam balls, and a glue gun. Take a ball and put a dab of glue on the top. Fasten the twine to the ball and then begin tightly coiling it around the ball, adding glue as you go. You will be amazed how expensive looking the finished product is! If you want something more colorful than natural twine, apply spray paint after the ball has dried.

6 Dress Up a Planter

Wrap an entire run-of-the-mill plastic planter with twine for an industrial look, or cover only a portion to give your decorative planters a modern edge. Twine is also easily painted, so consider adding a colorful stripe to the middle section of twine with spray paint for an extra pop of color, or group pots together with assorted colors to accent your other outdoor decor. The only limitation to any planter is to ensure that the size of the planter matches the size of the plants you want to display.

twist ties

Garden twist ties look so little and defenseless—but they act like they're big and powerful. And they are, judging by all the different, practical ways you can use them around your house.

Save time... save money!

Keep your zipper up

Some pants have zippers that won't stay up, and you might not realize it until you take them off that night. If you have pants with a zipper that's a repeat offender, bring a twist tie to the rescue. Loop it through the zipper pull and twist it. When you zip up your pants, twist the tie around the button or snap and *then* fasten the button. An invisible repair!

Organize your keys

Quick: Which key on your key chain fits your back door? If you have several keys that look alike, differentiate them with different colored twist ties. Simply loop a colored twist tie through the hole in each key and you'll never go searching for the right key again.

Hold your place while knitting

If nobody will touch your knitting until you return to it, stop reading. But if you have kids, cats, dogs, or even a meddling spouse, push a twist tie through your last stitch and twist. You won't find your work undone when you return.

Reset a screw

If an unanchored screw in the wall has loosened significantly, the hole it's in has probably grown and you need to make it smaller. How? Bunch up several twist ties, then shove the ties into the hole. Once the hole is filled, reset the screw. It will stay in place.

Tie on a button

Help! A button popped off your shirt and you don't have the time or the supplies to sew it back on. What to do? Grab a twist tie, peel off the paper or plastic covering, then use the wire to attach the button. Push it from the inside of your shirt up through the hole made by the original thread, through one hole in the button, back down through another hole in the button, and then finally down through the second hole in your shirt. Twist the tie ends together so that the button stays in place, and bend them so they lie flat on the inside of your shirt. Done!

Make a fake shoelace

Shoelaces have a tendency to break at the most inopportune times—usually when you don't have another one on hand. Make a temporary replacement with a series of twist ties. Use one tie for each pair of eyelets, and twist it shut. Your shoes will stay on as you run to the store for new shoelaces.

Fix your glasses

The tiny screw that holds your eyeglass frames together has a very big job—but it seems to fall down on the job a lot. If the screw has fallen out and your glasses have fallen off, replace the screw with a twist tie. Tear or cut off the edges of the tie so that only the wire is left. Thread the wire through the screw's hole, twist it shut, then trim off the excess wire. You're good to go!

CLEANING AND HOME SUPPLIES

IF YOU TALLIED THE COST OF ALL THE cleaning supplies and home supplies—like tissues, toilet paper, plastic bags, and toothpicks—that you had bought over the years, you would probably be horrified by the amount you had spent. But think about this: If you used those same products for uses you (and the manufacturers) never considered, you wouldn't be so horrified. And if you bought those products at a 99 cent store, you might even come out ahead! Check out the many different ways you can use what you once thought were expensive, one-shot deals.

aluminum foil

You'll run into foil again in an upcoming chapter. But in this case, forget about using it for leftovers. Instead, think about foil in terms of trees, seeds, couches, grills, and more.

Create a Halloween costume

Homemade costumes are always more fun than store-bought ones. Help your child wrap a large box in foil. Attach shoulder straps to the top and decorate with construction paper to make a robot costume. Or dress your kid with a little padding and cover him in foil. Poof! He's a baked potato.

Bug-proof a container

Wooden tea chests used to be lined with metal to keep insects out. Plastic has taken over in the kitchen, but you can still line boxes with foil before storing clothes or books.

Reflect heat on your grill

Grilling food such as a whole chicken or a roast requires a low and slow heat. Bounce all the heat upward by lining your clean, empty charcoal grill with foil, shiny side up, before you build your fire.

Make individual grill packs

On a square of foil, mound a handful of thin-sliced veggies. Top with herbs and butter, salt and pepper, and a little chicken broth or wine. Fold the packets over tightly and cook on the back of the grill rack until tender.

Scouring power

Backyard grilling and campsite grilling can be thrilling—until it comes time to clean the grill. If you forgot a scouring pad (or don't have one at home), just ball up some foil and use it to scrape grime off the grill.

Fill a stripped screwhole

If the screw keeps turning and turning in a piece of wood, push a bit of foil loosely in the hole and try again. It will grab tight.

Protect decorative buttons

Never risk losing a pricey button again! Before you send an item of dressy clothing to the cleaners, cover any decorative or engraved buttons with foil. They'll be protected during the cleaning process and won't get damaged.

Line storage boxes with aluminum foil before storing clothes or books to keep insects out.

ammonia

Ammonia is one of those incredibly versatile cleaning products. It cleans more in your house than you could ever imagine—but it has a number of uses outdoors, too. Here are several ways you can use this miracle solution, inside and out.

Take it outside

Ammonia is a miracle worker in the house: It cleans almost everything, almost every time. But it can work wonders on your car, too. Mix 1/4 cup ammonia with 1 quart of cold water and use the solution to clean your windshield wiper blades. Lift each blade, wiping it with a soft cloth or paper towel that you've dipped into the mixture. Dry the blades with a clean dry cloth, and put them back in their place.

Whiten your sneakers

Mix a 50-50 solution of ammonia and water, dip a clean cloth into the solution, then rub your tennis shoes with the cloth. You can use this approach to cleaning any white shoes. (Be sure to test the ammonia mixture on an inconspicuous part of the shoe first.)

Water your lilacs

Lilacs, clematis, and hydrangeas are alkaline-loving flowering plants, and as such would love to be watered with ammonia. Mix 1/4 cup of ammonia into 1 gallon of water, and water them as usual. Cucumbers like this treatment, too!

Stop the itch

Don't let mosquito bites drive you crazy—even if you have more bites than anyone else at the picnic. Stop the itch with one or two drops of ammonia applied directly to the bite (unless you've already scratched the bite, in which case this is a painful remedy!).

Save big!

Clean out your vegetable garden

Soak several sponges in ammonia and place them strategically in your vegetable garden to keep animals away. The animals may love the taste of your ripening vegetables, but they'll hate the smell of the ammonia more.

antistatic fabric spray

You probably use antistatic fabric spray to—not surprisingly—get rid of static that attaches your clothing to you. But when it comes to antistatic spray, stop thinking of clothing and start thinking of everything from your computer to your Christmas tree.

Prevent dusty blinds

Clean your blinds as you normally would, then spritz an antistatic spray on the blinds to keep dust at bay. You won't have to clean your blinds nearly as often.

Comb away scary hair

Save frightful looking hair caused by static electricity for Halloween. Get rid of it every other day by spritzing your comb with antistatic spray and combing your hair. You'll look less ghoulish immediately.

Clorox Bleach

The Electro-Alkaline Company was founded in Oakland, California, to make bleach using electrolysis and brine from the salt ponds of San Francisco Bay. The resulting product—Clorox—was sold locally to businesses, but when a less concentrated household version debuted, the company really took off. Butch, an animated glass bottle, became famous nationwide as a "spokesperson" for the renamed Clorox Chemical Company, but he met his demise in the 1960s when plastic containers arrived.

CLOROX GETS **OUT** DIRT THAT SUDS LEAVE **IN** . . .

actually dissolves suds-proof dirt that makes clothes gray!

Clorox gets out dirt detergents leave in!
Weak bleaches can't do it!

Clorox bleach gives you the *only* kind of cleaning power that breaks up suds-proof dirt and cleans it out! No other bleach, liquid or dry, bleaches clothes cleaner, whiter than Clorox.

Tame tinsel

Does the tinsel on your Christmas tree have a tendency to attack you? If so, spray it with antistatic spray, and it will stay in its place.

Protect your electronic equipment

Spritz antistatic spray on the carpeting around your TV, computer, and other electronic equipment to protect them from static electricity. Be careful, though, not to spray any of your electronics directly.

Get rid of pet hair

If your cat has left a trail of hair on your pants, spray your slacks with antistatic spray. Let the spray work for a few minutes, then simply brush off the loose hair.

bleach

Like ammonia, bleach is a miracle worker around the house. And like ammonia, it has uses far beyond the interior of your house. Think outside the box—and outside your house—when you think about using bleach.

Clean and green

Odd as it sounds, you can make cut flowers last longer with bleach. Add 3 drops of bleach and 1 teaspoon of sugar to 1 quart of water. Pour the mixture into a vase to extend the good look and smell of your bouquet. If you don't have sugar handy, just add 1/4 teaspoon of bleach to a quart of water for the same effect.

The kindest cut

You're doing your trees and shrubs a favor by cutting off dead and dying branches, but you won't be helping them if you spread disease from one plant to another. Stop viral and fungal diseases in their tracks by dipping the blades of your pruning shears in a bucket of undiluted bleach each time you cut an obviously diseased branch. Better yet, use the bleach if you even suspect the plant has health problems.

Give plastics a bleach bath

Tomato sauce can stain your plastic containers quickly and—it seems—permanently. Fill the offending container with water and one capful of chlorine bleach. Let the bleach bath sit for at least an hour. Rinse with water, and reclaim your clean container! This trick works for white plastic spatulas, too.

Make glass sparkle

Whether you're washing drinking glasses or glass plates, give them an extra shine with bleach. Add a teaspoon of bleach to your soapy dishwater, and wash as usual. Rinse the glasses and plates well—you don't want bleach to be part of your next meal!—and dry with a soft towel.

Kill that moss

Moss and algae can make patios and walkways slippery and can create dangerous conditions for you and your guests. Make your home safe again by getting rid of the moss and algae on brick, stone, and concrete with bleach. Mix 3/4 cup bleach with 1 gallon of water and scrub hard (keeping the solution away from grass and flowers). Rinse well.

cedar chips

Cedar shavings and chips have come out of the cedar closet, and they're showing us how multitalented they are. Consider these new bug-related ways to use them.

Caterpillars, snails, and slugs, oh my!

If your garden is a haven for insects, caterpillars, snails, and slugs, spread a mulch made from cedar shavings and chips over it to repel these pests.

Repel fleas with cedar

Keep fleas out of your house by adding cedar chips to the stuffing in your pet's bedding. Keep them out of your dog's house, too, by hanging or nailing a cedar ring inside the doghouse.

Make a sachet

Wrap cedar chips in a piece of tulle, and keep it shut with a twist tie. You can use it in drawers or—using the twist tie—attach it to a hanger and use it in your closet. Your clothes will smell nice, and you'll repel moths, too!

Keep fleas out of your house by adding cedar chips to the stuffing in your pet's bedding.

clothespins

Clothespins are so popular that they can appear in more than one aisle...and they do. In this case, clothespins are doing just the opposite of ammonia and bleach—they're coming indoors! You can still use them outside in both their original and new ways, but you'll find several helpful hints here on how to use them indoors in ways you may not have considered.

Relief for a bloody nose

Give your fingers a break the next time you use the tried and true remedy for a bloody nose (pinching it shut). Sit up straight and tilt your head forward. Pinch the tip of your nose with a clothespin, and use it to hold your nose shut for at least 10 minutes. The flow should stop shortly.

Make garlic chips

Plain potato chips just don't satisfy sometimes. If you crave chips with a kick, put a peeled garlic clove in a bag of unflavored chips. Shut the bag with a clothespin, and stay away from it for 6 to 8 hours (though you can return occasionally to shake the bag to distribute the garlicky flavor). Open and enjoy.

Put a clothesline in your closet

Clothespins aren't handy just for an outdoor clothesline; they can do double duty in your indoor closet. Use them to secure tops and dresses with spaghetti straps to their wire hangers.

Keep your side mirrors clear

No more worrying about icy side mirrors on your car on cold winter nights. Cover the mirrors with plastic bags and hold them shut with clothespins. Take the bags off in the morning. No ice!

Clip shut drapes

Privacy can take a back seat at hotels when draperies won't shut tightly. Make sure you have lightweight plastic clothespins with you when you travel—you can use them to hold drapes shut (which will help keep out light when you're trying to sleep, too).

Make a mitten clothesline

Run a piece of string along the lower inside of your coat closet door and attach clothespins. Let your kids hang their mittens from the string—no more missing mittens!

A new kind of pin

Hemming a skirt made of loosely woven fabric can be a challenge: The stitches are more likely to show and the pins used to keep the hem in place while you're working are more likely to slip out. A better solution? Use clothespins rather than straight pins to hold the hem as you sew.

contractor bags

Contractor bags are multi-aisle players, too; they can often show up anywhere from housewares to tools. Nevertheless, they earn their keep around the house. They do the dirty jobs and lots of other jobs, too. See here what they can do.

Toss a gigantic salad

Throw the ingredients into a small new garbage bag as you cut them, close the bag with a twist tie, and shake to mix your salad. Best of all, you can toss the bag into the refrigerator until you're ready to serve your salad.

Wash your oven rack in a bag

Cleaning a greasy tub after you've soaked your oven rack in it is a nasty job, and one you don't have to do. You can still use the tub for the job, but instead of putting the rack directly in the tub, put it in a heavy-duty trash bag with 1/3 cup dishwashing liquid, 1 cup white vinegar, and lots of hot water. Put the sealed bag in the tub (that you've filled with warm water) and let it sit for an hour. Take the rack out of the bag, give it a good scrubbing, rinse it, and let it air-dry. You'll have a clean rack *and* a clean tub!

Create compost

Fill a large black plastic trash bag with autumn leaves, a small bucketful of soil, a handful of 10-10-10 fertilizer, and wet the leaves thoroughly. Close the bag with a twist tie, and scramble the contents a few times. Store the bag over the winter in a sunny spot. Open the bag in the spring and you'll find rich compost.

Protect your car

Stash trash bags in the trunk of your car and pull them out to protect your upholstery and floor mats when necessary. Muddy kids and dogs need a ride? Cover the seats and carpet with trash bags, and you're ready to roll.

Keep clothes dust-free

You know you won't wear your linen dress for several months, and you don't want it to attract dust and dirt while it sits undisturbed in your closet. Protect it from harm with a new trash bag. Cut a slit in the top for the hanger, and push the hanger—holding your dress—through. Hang it in your closet with complete confidence that it will stay clean.

dishwashing liquid

Dishwashing liquid isn't just for washing dishes anymore. It's for killing weeds and ants and washing air conditioner filters and your hair. It's enough to make you feel sorry for the dishes!

Dishwashing liquid is cool

Clean your foam or metal mesh air conditioner filters once a month during the summer—or whenever you routinely use your AC—with dishwashing liquid. Soak the filter in a bath of warm water and dish soap, then scrub it gently with a toothbrush. Once you've removed any debris, rinse it and dry it completely. Put it back in the air conditioner, and enjoy a sweat-free day.

Kill weeds kindly

Be kind to the environment—not so much to weeds—by using a natural weed killer rather than harmful herbicides. Mix 1 teaspoon of dishwashing liquid with 1 cup of salt and 1 gallon of white vinegar. Pour the solution on weeds sprouting in the cracks and crevices of sidewalks, front walks, and patio pavers.

Wash away ants

Outdoor ants can be just as annoying as indoor ants, particularly if they've invaded the crevices in your patio where you eat. Get rid of them with a simple 50/50 solution of water and white vinegar with a dash of dishwashing liquid. (You can substitute glass cleaner for the vinegar if you want.) Spray the affected area with the mix, wait a few minutes, then happily return to your picnic.

Water your lawn with household liquids

Fill the reservoir of a 10- or 20-gallon hose-end sprayer with water and a 12-ounce can of beer or non-diet cola, 1 cup of corn syrup or molasses or household ammonia, or 1/2 cup mouthwash—*and* 1 cup of dishwashing liquid. The dishwashing liquid helps spread the concoction more evenly across your lawn, and as an added bonus, helps it stick to individual blades of grass. Water your lawn approximately every three weeks, and watch your neighbors turn green with envy—like your lawn.

7 Nontradtional Ways to Use DAWN DISHWASHING LIQUID

1 Launder Delicates

You don't need special detergent to hand wash clothes. Mix 1 teaspoon of dishwashing liquid into a gallon of water and let your delicate items soak. Then rinse with cold water. (Do not try this on items marked Dry Clean Only!)

2 Sparkling Shower

Getting soap film off of your glass shower door just got easier. Use dishwashing liquid, and you will be amazed at how quickly and easily the gunk comes off.

3 Vanishing Spots

Out of stain stick and ready to do a load of laundry? Don't worry—grab your dishwashing liquid and get to work. Gently rub the liquid on the stained fabric, let it sit, and then machine wash the item as usual. You'll find stains will disappear.

4 Foil a Rash

A poison ivy rash is diabolical in that scratching can make it worse. To find relief, rub exposed skin with cotton balls soaked in dishwashing liquid. It will strip the plant oils that cause the itchy rash—and cut down your suffering nicely.

5 Farewell Fleas

If you are combing fleas off of your dog or cat, keep a pan of water filled with dishwashing liquid at your side. Drop any fleas you find into the mixture, and they will quickly meet their demise.

6 Shiny Stove

Is there grease buildup on your stovetop or range hood? Squirt a little dishwashing liquid on a sponge and wipe it away with ease.

7 Patrol Pests

To rid your garden of pests without using harsh chemicals, make your own insecticidal soap by mixing 1 1/2 teaspoons of dishwashing detergent in one quart of water. Spray this on your plants and you will get rid of mites, whiteflies, and aphids.

Degrease your hair

If your locks aren't looking so lovely, try mixing a dollop of dishwashing liquid into your shampoo. It fights grease in hair, as well as on dishes!

Clean your blender

Forget about taking your blender apart to wash it thoroughly. Instead, fill it partway with warm water and dishwashing detergent, cover it, and run it for a few seconds. Empty it, rinse it, air-dry it, and call it a day.

dishwasher detergent

Dishwasher detergent is trying to get in on the "I can do lots of other things, too" act—and has succeeded! Add dishwasher detergent to your list of cleaning supplies to buy and use in new and different ways.

Wash your dishes—and your shower

Make the tiles in your shower sparkle with dishwasher detergent (either liquid or powder). Dissolve 1/4 cup of dishwasher detergent in warm water in a spray bottle. Cover the shower walls and floor with the mixture. Let it stand for several hours, then scrub with a sponge and rinse.

Clean screens and dishes

Window screens need to be thoroughly washed once or twice a year, and it's not a fun job. Make it easier on yourself by removing the screens from the window and washing them outside on a nice day. Scrub each side of the screen with a broad, soft brush and a mixture of hot water and lemon-scented dishwashing detergent. Rinse the screen with a hose and let the screen dry completely before putting it back in the window.

Use it this way!

Banish burn marks

You try to make your pants look better by ironing them, but instead you end up scorching them with the iron. Don't get frustrated—get some powdered dishwasher detergent. Mix it with water to make a paste, and apply the paste to the scorched area. (Test it in an inconspicuous place on the fabric first.) Put your pants out in the sun to bleach away the mark. Launder as usual.

Get out grease stains

Soak garments stained with grease overnight in a solution of water and 1 cup of powdered dishwasher detergent. Wash the next day as usual, and watch the stains disappear. The dishwasher detergent boosts the cleaning power of your regular laundry detergent.

dryer sheets

A fabric softener dryer sheet does a great job reducing static cling as your clothes tumble around in the dryer. But it does a great job in other situations, too.

Save your soil

Houseplants generally aren't messy, but if soil escapes from the bottom of the pot through the drain hole when you water your plant, you have

Stinky shoes? Place a dryer sheet in each shoe when you're not wearing them.

a dirty problem. Solve it by placing a used dryer sheet in the bottom of the pot the next time you repot a plant.

Solve stinky problems

Smelly hamper? Put a dryer sheet at the bottom of it, and change it every week. Stinky shoes? Place a dryer sheet in each shoe when you're not wearing them. Need to hold your nose near your wastebasket? Same solution: Keep a dryer sheet at the bottom, beneath the bag holding the trash. Your whole house will smell better, one dryer sheet at a time!

Stuff handbags for storage

If you save all your used dryer sheets, over the course of a few weeks of laundry you may well find you have plenty to fill a purse for storage. Bunched-up dryer sheets will not only keep a bag in shape but will also leave it smelling fresh, not musty, when you use it again.

Take dryer sheets on your travels

A hotel room with a musty air conditioner is not the most comfortable place for sleeping. Carry a dryer sheet in your suitcase. While you're traveling, it helps make clothes smell fresh. Once in the hotel, put it in front of the AC's vent to blow a better scent into the air.

Unpack packing peanuts

Opening a box filled with packing peanuts can be a trial at best. They leap out and attach themselves to you, your carpet, and your furniture. And they cling to your hands like magnets, preventing you from finding the contents of the package. Stop the madness by rubbing your hands with a dryer sheet before you open the box. The packing peanuts will stay away!

Stop knots in their tracks

Rub a fabric softener dryer sheet along your thread the next time you sew. It will help prevent knots and snarls. Soap works well, too.

fabric softener

Take fabric softener out of the laundry room, and see what it can accomplish in other rooms. You'll be amazed by its wide range of abilities, once you set it free.

A sterling solution to tarnish

Sterling silver jewelry is spectacular when it sparkles and dull when it is tarnished. Return dull jewelry to its former luster with fabric softener. Heat 4 cups of water in a pot on the stove, then turn off the heat. Dissolve 4 teaspoons of salt in the water. Mix in fabric softener until the solution becomes cloudy. Add the jewelry (unless it has stones set in it), and let it sit for an hour. Remove the silver, rinse it with warm water, and gently rub it with a clean dry cloth. Your silver should sparkle again.

Run away from runs

Add a drop or two of fabric softener to the water the next time you rinse out your panty hose to avoid future runs. The fabric softener helps the nylons stretch more easily, so you're less likely to run them the next time you pull them taut. Roll them in a towel to dry.

Banish burned-on food

Liquid fabric softener is your best friend when it comes time to scrub pots and pans soiled by your worst enemy, baked-on grime. Soak the offending vessel in water and a squirt of fabric softener. Let it sit for an hour. Wash and rinse it all away.

Free your walls from wallpaper

Whether you're painting or re-papering your walls, you need to get rid of the wallpaper already there—no matter how awful the job. Make your life easier by adding a capful of liquid fabric softener to a quart of water, and cover the wallpaper with it using a sponge. (Be sure to gently score the wallpaper with a wire-bristle brush or razor blade if it has a water-resistant covering.) Let it work its magic for 20 minutes, then simply scrape the old stuff off the wall.

Ready your brushes for their next job

Keep your paintbrushes soft and pliable and ready for the next can of paint coming their way. Clean them as you normally would, but rinse them in a quart of water that contains a drop of fabric softener. Swish the brush around, then wipe the bristles dry. Your brushes are ready to go!

Smart savings!

furniture polish

Polish off a few additional household chores with furniture polish. Once you use it for things other than tables, chairs, and sofas, you'll want to add it to your stable of very versatile cleaning supplies.

Polish your shower door

Prevent soap scum buildup on your shower door with furniture polish. Clean your shower door, then apply lemon oil furniture polish to it with a soft cloth. Let it sit for two minutes. Using a clean dry cloth, gently rub off the excess polish. The oil from the furniture polish will keep soap scum away, shower after shower.

Make your bicycle sparkle

Unless you like to spend your free time polishing the nooks and crannies of your clean bike with liquid or paste wax, consider taking the easy way out. Simply spray your bicycle with a coat of furniture polish that contains wax. It will shine like new!

Oil squeaky hinges

Spray a little oil-based furniture polish on a squeaky door hinge, then open and shut the door several times to work the lubricant into the hinge.

The furniture polish is a lot cleaner than the oil you'd usually use for a noisy hinge, and it works just as well to silence the squeak.

Shine your hubcaps

Furniture polish works well outdoors, too. Spray some on your car's hubcaps and other chrome features, and rub them well with a soft clean cloth. You'll make your car's details shine.

gallon bags

Big plastic bags are particularly helpful in the kitchen, but they can take on big jobs all over the house, too. Use gallon-size plastic bags (or gallon-size freezer bags) to do a wide range of duties.

Save a little paint

You finished painting a room, and have a small amount of paint left over that you want to save for future touch-ups. What's the best way to store less than half a can? Pour the paint into a ziplock plastic food bag, seal the bag (getting rid of the air inside as you go), then place the paint bag back into the paint can. Seal the can, and mark it with the color of the paint, where you used the paint, and when you bought it. If paint has obscured the paint's color and number on the outside of the can, add that too. Your paint will be fresh the next time you need it.

Protect your feet

It's only November and you haven't had time to buy snow boots—and you're faced with a winter wonderland. How can you keep your feet dry? Cover your feet with socks first and plastic bags second, then put your shoes on. If you have time, use duct tape to fasten the tops of the bags to the tops of your socks so that the bags don't slip down into your shoes. Now you're ready for snow!

Have bags, will travel

Pack your belongings in plastic bags the next time you take a trip. If you're traveling by plane, the bags let airport inspectors see your possessions without trawling through them. And no matter your method of transportation, they help you keep your clothing organized and easy to find in your suitcase.

Marinate without a mess

Forget about using a bowl or pan to marinate your next barbecue meal. Instead, marinate the meat in a ziplock plastic bag. Put the seasonings and liquids in first—close the bag and shake it to blend the ingredients—then add the meat. Close the bag, and shake it again. Stash it in the refrigerator, turning upside down occasionally to mix the liquids, for as long as the recipe requires. Then grill and enjoy!

Keep your cookbook clean

Though spills on cookbook pages may bring back fond memories of special meals, they may also make reading the recipe a little too difficult. Keep cookbook pages spotless by covering the open book with a plastic bag or two. You'll protect the book and be able to easily wipe off any splatters.

glass cleaner

Glass cleaner can do so much more than just clean windows (though, thankfully, it does its primary job really well). In fact, it's a pro when it comes to jewelry, hardwood floors, bug bites—even your face.

Help for your hardwood floor

Has hairspray hit on your hardwood floor? Has furniture polish left it cloudy or peeling? Help has arrived—in the form of window cleaner! Wipe

Dry out pimples

Assuming you will keep the window cleaner out of your eyes and have no allergies to the ingredients (which include ammonia, detergents, solvents, and alcohol), spritzing window cleaner on your pimples is a good way to dry them out and make them disappear.

Free your finger

If you thought your ring fit a little too snugly and it turns out that you were right—you can't get it off your finger—spray some glass cleaner on your finger, twist the ring several times, and slide it off.

Spruce up your shoes

If you need to shine your patent leather shoes before you step out for the evening, try spraying them with glass cleaner. They'll look spiffy in a hurry! Use glass cleaner on patent leather purses, too. Wipe dry with a paper towel.

the floor with a clean damp cloth, then apply ammonia-free window cleaner to remove any remaining blemishes.

Make stones sparkle

If the gems in your jewelry have turned dull, revive their sparkle with window cleaner. Dampen a clean, lint-free cloth with glass cleaner, and gently wipe your jewelry. A bonus: The solution will also clean the metal surrounding the gems. (Don't use glass cleaner on opaque stones like opal or turquoise or on pearl or coral because it might discolor them.)

Relieve a bee sting

After taking out the stinger, spray the area with ammonia window cleaner. It will help reduce the swelling and soothe the pain. (Just never use a concentrated product.)

lint roller

It's the perfect stocking stuffer and the perfect lint-picker-upper—and it achieves perfection in lots of other ways, too. Check out the range of a lint roller's abilities below.

Pick up pet hair

Brush your lint roller over couches, chairs, beds, and anywhere else pet hair tends to accumulate in your home. Toss the sheets once they're full, and admire your clean house!

Clean up crafts

Whether you've accidentally spilled glitter all over the craft table or need a way to easily pick up loose beads that didn't quite make it onto your necklace, a lint roller can be your best friend. Just roll it over whatever needs to be picked up and call it a day.

Get rid of bugs

Bring a lint roller on your next hiking trip and use it at the end of your hike to get bugs—specifically ticks—off your pants and shirt. Use it all over your clothing, including your socks, for best results.

Clean your bathroom floor

Roll your lint roller over your bathroom floor to pick up stray hair that the hair dryer has blown onto the tiles. Do this between your regular cleanings and your bathroom will look cleaner longer.

mothballs

Mothballs and moth crystals can repel so much more than moths, but we've all been trained to believe that mothballs are for...moths. Here are some ideas that prove otherwise.

Dash their dreams of dinner

There's no such thing as a free lunch for squirrels, chipmunks, and mice anymore if you protect your flower bulbs from them. Plant your bulbs as you normally would, but add a few moth crystals over them to spoil their predators' meal.

Kill potted plant pests

Get rid of bugs on houseplants using a dry cleaning bag and mothballs. Encase the plant—including the saucer—in the clear plastic bag, water the plant, add 5 or 6 mothballs, and close the bag tightly. Move it to a bright spot (though keep it out of direct sunlight). Remove the plant after a week. You and your plant will be rid of the bugs (and moths for a while, too!).

Protect your vegetable garden

Rodents and (obviously) insects can't stand mothballs, so use them to your advantage when growing vegetables. Hang a mesh bag filled with mothballs from a trellis or a fence to keep the critters and pests away. (Don't put them directly on the soil or in shallow containers that could be knocked over; the chemicals in the mothballs can contaminate the soil.)

Give woolens a final rinse

Mothballs will protect your woolens from moths—it's a given. But did you know that by dissolving a few mothballs in the rinse cycle as you're washing the items you plan to store, you'll provide even more protection for your winter sweaters? Just

Hang a mesh bag filled with mothballs from a trellis or a fence to keep the critters and pests away from your vegetable garden.

make sure you do this the last time you wash your woolens before you put them away.

Drive bats batty

Chances are you think bats won't get into your house—until they do. Keep them away by leaving mothballs around the floor of the attic.

oven cleaner

Cleaning an oven is never a fun job, but if you bought oven cleaner, you really should use it—and now you can use it on a whole lot more than your oven! Here are several really useful ways to put off cleaning your oven.

Clean bricks like an oven

If the bricks on your fireplace, your front walk, or anywhere else sport dingy spots, you need to think outside the box—and into your oven. Spray a coating of oven cleaner on the bricks, and let it sit for 15 minutes. Attack the spots with a scrub brush. Repeat the process, then clean the area with water.

WHO KNEW? MOTHBALLS MORPH AS THEY WORK

Mothballs are pesticides that come in a solid form but change into a gas. In the United States they contain one of two active ingredients: naphthalene or paradichlorobenzene, both of which are toxic. If you have children or pets in the home, there are chemical-free ways to thwart moths: cloves, eucalyptus, lavender, cinnamon sticks, and bay leaves can keep your clothing safe. Simply wrap whichever one appeals most to you in a cheesecloth sachet, and store them along with your clothing.

Help your hubcaps

Clean your hubcaps the easy way—with oven cleaner! Spray it directly onto each hubcap to remove any and all accumulated dirt and debris. Let the cleaner stand for a minute, then spray it off with a hose. Just be sure not to use it on painted hubcaps; it may remove the paint as well as the grime.

Wash whitewalls

If your whitewall tires are looking tired, spray them with oven cleaner. Rinse them with a hose, and see your tires shimmer!

Remove burnt stains from non-aluminum cookware

Drips of food or oil can get cooked to a black, resinous finish on the base or sides of a pan, and it won't scrub off no matter how much elbow grease you apply. Instead, turn the pot upside down on a newspaper, and spray the outside with oven cleaner. Let sit for an hour, then scrub and rinse.

Clean caked-on window grime

Windows that haven't been washed for a long time can be very difficult to clean. When you've scrubbed off most of the dirt but can't get through the worst stains, bring on some oven cleaner. Spray the window lightly and let sit for a few minutes, then wipe away. The sun will shine through at last!

paper bags

Paper bags are hard workers that get little credit. But they should get lots of extra credit for all the extra jobs they do, like these here.

Iron your wood floor

If you accidentally dripped candle wax on your wood floor—or if your child colored on it on purpose—you need to remove the stain pronto.

How? Place an ordinary brown paper bag over the offending mark, and run a warm iron over the bag until it soaks up the stain. The same strategy will work to remove wax stains on carpet, as long as you scrape off as much wax as possible before you start.

Sow paper bags

Protect your seedlings from the wind by planting them in paper bags partially filled with soil. Dig a hole in your garden for each paper bag. Place the bag in the hole, but leave about 2 inches of the bag sticking out of the ground. The paper will protect your plant and will disintegrate as the plant grows, letting the roots unfurl into your garden's soil.

Hide the snap trap

If you have a mouse problem but the sight of a dead mouse gives you the heebie-jeebies, set the trap inside an open paper bag. Once you've caught the mouse, simply close up the bag and throw it—and what's inside it—in the trash.

Breathe better with a paper bag

Hiccups? Stop them before you start to hurt. Breathe in and out of a paper bag for a few minutes. You'll create a build-up of carbon dioxide in your lungs, which helps relax your diaphragm—whose involuntary tightening causes the hiccups in the first place. This trick works if you're hyperventilating, too.

Tame a toothache

Cut a piece from a brown paper bag and soak it in vinegar. Sprinkle black pepper on one side, and hold that side to your cheek. Your cheek will feel nicely warm—which may pull your attention from the pain in your tooth. Of course, call your dentist as soon as you can to get rid of the pain permanently.

Instant savings!

paper towels

Paper towels sound so fragile—how can towels of paper be strong? But strong they are. In fact, they're so strong that they can plug leaks and stop hiccups. Here's how.

Brighten the white

If your white porcelain enamel sink is looking a little down on its luck, bring back its shine with paper towels. Line the sink with them, then douse them with bleach. Leave the bleach-soaked paper towels in place for half an hour, then throw them away. Rinse away any residue with running water. Stand back and admire your sparkling sink. (Don't try this on colored porcelain, though; it may fade the color.)

Halt the hiccups

Put a stop to annoying—and occasionally painful—hiccups with a paper towel. Place it over the top of a glass of water, and take a few swigs through it. Your diaphragm—the villain causing the hiccups—will have to work harder to pull the water out of the glass, and the extra work may stop the diaphragm's involuntary muscle movements.

9 Nontradtional Ways to Use PAPER TOWEL TUBES

1 Baby Your Tomatoes

Keep cutworms away from your tomato plants by slitting a paper towel tube so that you can use it as a "collar." Depending on the height of your plants, you could get several collars from each tube. The cardboard is biodegradable, so you won't need to remove it.

2 Cord Storage

For neater, easier storage, fold your extension cords to the length of a paper towel tube and slide them in. You can label the tube with magic marker, indicating where the cord is generally used.

3 Bag It

If your kitchen is overflowing with plastic grocery bags, here's a way to get a handle on the situation. Stuff those bags into a paper towel tube and toss the whole thing in a drawer. It is a handy (and free!) way to get organized.

4 Happy Hamsters

You can thrill hamsters by placing paper towel tubes in their cage. They enjoy running through them and shredding the cardboard. When the tube is demolished, you can replace it with a fresh one.

5 Protect Paperwork

To store important paperwork, be it a marriage certificate or a treasured child's drawing, use a paper towel tube. Roll the document carefully and slide it inside to keep it from getting creased or torn. Before storing, you can write the name of the document on the paper tube for easy identification.

6 Have a Ball

Yarn is useless if it's in a tangle. Cut a paper towel tube in thirds and notch each end of the pieces. Secure one end of your loose yarn in a notch and wrap it tightly around the tube. Secure the other end in the second notch. You will have one neat ball; make two more with the rest of the tube.

7 Banish Creases

Don't buy padded hangers. Instead, make a cut down the length of a paper towel tube, then slip it over a plain wire hanger, and it will protect your pants from getting sharp creases.

8 Hair Bands

Don't search all over for your hair bands; wrap them around a cardboard paper towel tube. Toss the tube in a drawer, and you'll always know where to find them.

9 Boot Shaper

Before storing your boots for the season, slide a few paper towel tubes inside each boot. This will keep the tops from flopping over and causing creases in the ankle area.

Line your crisper drawer

If you want the vegetables in your refrigerator's crisper drawer to truly be crispy, line it with paper towels. They will absorb the moisture in the fridge that can turn carrots, broccoli, and beans soggy. Replace the towels when they're damp.

Plug a leak around a window

If you detect a drafty window in the middle of winter, try to find the source of the leak—it's a good bet you'll find it along the top of the lower sash. If that's the case, put two paper towels together, and fold them up from the bottom, one inch at a time. Once you've made a thick inch-wide strip, place it over the leak and tape it down on all sides. You'll stop the leak—and high heating bills.

Clean out your ears (of corn)

Picking individual strands of silk from husked ears of corn is as time-consuming as it is annoying. Get your time and your pleasing temperament back by easily wiping away the silk. Dampen a paper towel and rub it gently across the corn. The paper towel will quickly and calmly pick up the silk.

rubber gloves

Rubber gloves are a staple in your cleaning supply cabinet, but they actually can do a whole lot more than protect your hands while you do the dishes or the floors. Here are some of the other jobs rubber gloves can do.

Give the jar a hand

No more banging a jar on the floor to loosen a tight lid. No more running it under hot water. And no more fancy tools designed to do the trick—that somehow don't work. Just put on a pair of rubber gloves, and open the jar with ease.

Lend your broom a hand

Actually, lend your broom and your mop a finger from your rubber gloves. Cut off two fingers and put one over the end of the broom handle and one over the mop handle. They won't slip across the floor the next time you need to stand them up against a wall.

Handle hot potatoes

Don your rubber gloves if you need to take a hot potato out of the oven, move a roasted chicken from the pan to the serving dish, or handle prickly foods like pineapple. You'll protect your hands, and you won't drop your food!

Line your refrigerator's crisper drawer with paper towels. They will absorb the moisture in the fridge that can turn carrots, broccoli, and beans soggy.

Avoid creepy crawlies

Next time you have to clean up a cobweb or pick up a dead ant, put your rubber gloves on first. You won't be as creeped out by the bugs if your skin doesn't get anywhere near them.

Pick off pet hair

Dog and cat hair on a couch or chair can make your house look messy—or dirty—even when it isn't. Whip your house back into shape by getting rid of the omnipresent pet hair. Put a rubber glove on one hand, and rub your gloved fingers across your sofa, back and forth until a ball of pet hair forms. Just pick up the ball and continue on to your chairs.

Some like it hot

Make your own hot-water bottle out of a heavy-duty rubber glove. Fill the glove with hot water, seal it with a strong rubber band, and wrap it in a towel. You'll stay toasty warm!

rubbing alcohol

Like bleach and ammonia, rubbing alcohol is one of those amazing liquids that has a wide range of alternate uses around the house. Here are some that may help you.

Make mincemeat of mealybugs

If you find mealybugs on your houseplants, simply rub them away with rubbing alcohol. Dip a cotton swab in rubbing alcohol, and dab the swab on the bugs. You'll get rid of these common pests pronto.

Stretch your shoes

Help your feet adjust to your new leather shoes by stretching out tight spots with rubbing alcohol. Put your shoes on. Moisten a clean cloth with rubbing alcohol, and dab it on the areas that grip your feet too hard. You'll need to wear your shoes for a full day for the rubbing alcohol to soften the leather (which works best with the heat from your feet). If you can't wear them all day, stuff your shoes with socks to mold them as your feet would.

Care for your car

You've carried the most beautiful Christmas tree you've ever found home on top of your car—and you've carried the sap home, too. If you find sap on your car and can't get it off, apply a few drops of rubbing alcohol directly on the sap. Rub it into the finish with your fingers. The marks will magically disappear!

Rub out a rash

Work fast to prevent a poison ivy rash from developing if you know you've been exposed to the plant. Soak a washcloth in a bowl of rubbing alcohol. Wring out the washcloth, then use it to scrub the area you think may erupt into a rash. Don't be gentle: scrub hard. Take these steps immediately after being exposed. If you wait until the rash develops, this solution won't work.

Keep ice off your wiper blades

Getting in a cold car isn't the worst part of keeping your car outside in cold weather—frozen windshield wiper blades may take that award. Prevent ice by washing blades with a soft clean cloth doused in rubbing alcohol.

sponge

The lowly sponge can actually play several important roles around the house. Here is a range of ways you can use a sponge for more than just doing dishes.

Go natural with houseplants

Skip leaf shine products and wax when cleaning houseplants—instead, just use water and a wet sponge. The waxy store products can clog leaf pores and tend to make the plants look fake.

Wash away a fever

Take a break from washing dishes when you have a fever, and use the sponge on yourself to bring your fever down. Apply a sponge rinsed in cool water to the high-heat spots on your body: your armpits, wrists, neck, groin, and so on. Your body will cool—and your temperature will fall—as the water evaporates.

Soap-dish sponge

Forget about using a traditional soap dish to store your bar of soap—it turns your soap into a gloppy mess that you really don't want to use to clean your hands (or anything else!). Instead, rest your soap on a sponge. It wicks away moisture and leaves your soap clean and ready to use.

Keep your veggies crunchy

The point of a crisper drawer in the refrigerator is to keep your vegetables crisp. Help your fridge out by placing a few new kitchen sponges with the vegetables in the drawer. Squeeze them out when they absorb the excess moisture.

Wipe off pet hair

Clothing and upholstered furniture can be magnets for pet hair. Remove the hair easily by rubbing sofas, chairs, pants, and dresses with a slightly damp sponge.

Stand umbrellas on a sponge

Place a sponge at the bottom of an umbrella stand (or bucket or other type of makeshift umbrella stand) and let your umbrellas rest on it. The sponge will keep water from pooling in the stand. Best of all, you can take the sponge out and squeeze it dry when needed.

Perfect your pedicure

Keep your toes away from each other as you paint your toenails—you don't want the nail polish to smudge. Cut a sponge into small triangles and use the pieces to separate your toes.

Make mini ice packs

Regular-sized ice packs can be too big for bumps and bruises on children. Cut a sponge into a few pieces, soak the pieces in water, and freeze them to make child-sized ice packs for kids.

spray bottles

At first glance, a spray bottle seems to have limited uses. But on second or third glance, a whole new world of possibilities opens up. What can you spray with it? Where can you use it? Here are some intriguing answers.

Spray bugs with vodka

Pour some inexpensive vodka in a clean spray bottle and take it with you on your next picnic. When mosquitoes start biting, spray them—

and yourself—with the vodka. You'll kill the bugs and protect yourself from the bites.

Save money greasing your pans

Stay away from expensive nonstick cooking sprays and use olive oil in a clean spray bottle instead. You'll probably save calories as well as dollars!

Keep your counters cat-free

If you want to keep kitty off your kitchen counter, just spray her gently with water in a spray bottle. She won't like it: In fact, you'll eventually be able to just show her the bottle, and she'll jump off quickly!

Spritz your car windows clean

Keep a spray bottle filled with glass cleaner in the trunk of your car so you'll be ready to clean your car's windows, mirrors, and headlights at a moment's notice. (Be sure to throw a roll of paper towels in the trunk as well.) Add 1/2 teaspoon antifreeze to the cleaner in the winter—it will melt the ice on your windows and mirrors.

Water your pants

A spray bottle is always welcome in a laundry room. Use it to mist your clothes as you iron them, or use it as a container for stain removers. Once you start spraying rather than pouring on your stain remover, you can stop blotting the excess liquid from your clothes.

Spray your way to better baking

Use a spray bottle to lightly spritz your homemade bread with heavily salted water as it bakes. You'll end up with a deliciously crisp, salted crust. You can also use it to squirt a liqueur on a cake.

spray starch

Spray starch is the perfect example of a cleaning item that seems limited in its possibilities—to make pressed garments stiff and crisp—and a cost that you might consider giving up. But wait—you might need it for its other jobs!

Keep your walls clean

Whether you just painted your walls or simply want to keep the paint job you have looking fresh, try lightly coating your walls in busy areas with spray starch. You'll have an easier time getting rid of fingerprints, smudges, and other grime.

Protect your sneakers

Help your canvas or nylon sneakers stay dirt- and stain-free by coating them lightly with spray starch. They'll look cleaner longer.

Frame needlepoint more easily

Give your work of art a light coating of spray starch before framing, and it will hold up better than if you just frame it.

steel wool

It's strong enough to polish metal, yet gentle enough to clean dishes. This multi-aisle favorite can show up in more than one place in a 99 cent store because it's so versatile. Here are several other ways to use it.

Shine your car's chrome

Take a damp pad of ultrafine steel wool (grade 0000) and squeeze it into a bowl containing a little baking soda, mixing with the steel wool until a paste forms. Scrub the chrome trim, rims, and bumpers on your car with the steel wool, making small circles. Rinse the metal and wipe it dry with a clean soft cloth.

Keep mice out

Block small passages—in basement cracks or holes in kitchen cabinets, for example—with steel wool to keep mice out of your house. They won't even try to get around it.

Silence the squeak

Don't come unhinged if you've oiled a door hinge but it continues to make noise. It may just need a thorough cleaning. Prop the door closed with a book or a brick and remove the hinge pin. Scrub it with fine-grade steel wool—be sure to remove any rust and dirt that you can see—and blow off the debris and wayward steel threads. Rub it with oil, and replace it. Swing your door open in silence!

A ring you don't want

Get rid of water rings on a wood table with steel wool. Dip extra-fine steel wool (grade 0000) in lemon oil, and gently rub the ring. Once it disappears, polish the wood with more lemon oil and buff with a soft clean cloth.

Prevent a pet hair clog

Stuff some steel wool in your bathtub drain the next time you wash Fido. It will prevent your dog's hair from clogging the drain. Just make sure that you don't press the steel wool too far down; you'll want to remove it when you're done.

storage bags

Sandwich bags aren't just for sandwiches (though it's always a good idea to keep a few on hand for lunches). These little bags have big ambitions, and they fulfill them every day.

Clean a showerhead

When you're looking forward to a nice, warm shower, nothing is more frustrating than facing a weak trickle of water. If a buildup of lime and mineral scale have reduced your shower to a fading stream and you to tears, fix the problem with vinegar, a plastic sandwich bag, and duct tape. Fill the bag with white vinegar and cover the showerhead with it, making sure that the head is covered by the vinegar. Tape the bag to the showerhead arm with the duct tape, and let it soak overnight. When you take it off in the morning, you'll finally get the shower you've wanted. (Test the vinegar on your fixture first; it can discolor some brass and other finishes.) The same strategy applies to clogged faucets, too.

Bag your photos

Photos of the family are de rigueur at reunions, get-togethers with long-lost friends, and other meetings of family and friends. Keep your pictures pristine by placing two back to back in a clear plastic sandwich bag. You can then show them with pride without worrying about fingerprints—or worse!

Keep moisture out of outdoor padlocks in winter. Simply cover the locks with plastic sandwich bags.

Protect padlocks

Keep moisture out of outdoor locks in winter. It freezes and thaws over and over until it damages the lock. Simply cover the locks with plastic sandwich bags. The bags help keep rust off, too.

Decorate a cake

Writing good wishes on a cake has never been easier! Just fill a plastic sandwich bag with the frosting, squeeze out the extra air, and seal the top. Cut a corner of the bag on a diagonal—make a small cut at first, since you can always enlarge it later—and squeeze out the words you want to write.

Cushion your treasures

Whether you're storing a fragile doll in the attic for your daughter's future children or shipping your favorite vase to your new home, you can protect your belongings with small plastic bags. Wrap your items as you normally would in newspaper, bubble wrap, or tissue paper, then surround them in the box with several plastic bags that you've inflated (by breathing into them with a straw) and sealed. The bags will protect your valuables from shifting in the box.

Polish sandals without a mess

Polishing shoes can be a messy undertaking, particularly when you're polishing sandals. Take the mess out of the equation by covering the hand holding the sandal with a small plastic bag.

string

String does so much more than tie things together. It polishes, measures—even waters plants. How? See below.

Polish silver forks

Silver knives and spoons aren't difficult to polish, but forks can be a challenge. How on earth can you get the edges between the tines to shine?

Easy. Cut a piece of string about 6 inches long, and run it through silver polish. Now thread it between the fork tines. Mission accomplished!

Create the sound of silence

The constant sound of a leaky faucet—drip–drip–drip—might make you want to scream, but you can stay calm with a piece of string. Tie a piece of string to the spout so that it hangs from the end of the faucet down to the bottom of the basin. The water will ride down the string quietly. Now call the plumber!

Water your plants

Let your plants drink up while you take a short trip. All you need is a large container of water and a few pieces of string. Place the water next to your indoor potted plants, and run a piece of wet string from the bottom of the water to each pot, burying the string in a few inches of soil. The string will deliver moisture to the soil as it dries.

Measure your waist

Or anything else that a ruler can't measure, for that matter. Then place the piece of string against a ruler (or yardstick) to determine the dimensions of your object.

toothpicks

Toothpicks are generally known for testing if a cake is done or playing a major role in a child's craft project. But these small sticks can do so much more. Let these little helpers help you in big ways.

A little lemon drop

Slicing a lemon in half to get a few drops of lemon juice for a dish just doesn't make sense. Get only the little bit you need by piercing the lemon rind with a toothpick and squeezing out a few drops. Tape the hole and save for another day.

Nail bread to cake with toothpicks

Why, you ask? Because the part of the cake exposed to air—where it's been cut—can get stale quickly. If you attach a slice of bread to the exposed part with toothpicks, you'll protect the moist cake. The bread will get stale instead.

Tighten your glasses

The teeny tiny screwdrivers designed for glasses may be cute, but they're a waste of money. Tighten the screw that holds your frames together with a toothpick instead.

First aid for flowers

If your flower has a bent stem, tend to it using a toothpick as a splint. Stick the toothpick in the soil, then attach it to the stem with a loose circle of transparent tape.

The toothpick test

Pretend your garden bed is a cake. How do you know if your cake has finished cooking? Insert a toothpick—if it comes out clean, it's done baking and ready to come out of the oven. Stick a toothpick in the soil of your garden, too, to see if it needs to be watered. If it comes out clean, it's ready to be watered. If it comes out with soil attached, you can wait and test it again the next day.

towels

Gone are the days when you only used a towel to dry yourself—or your dishes. You can use towels for your plants, your pants, a wine bottle, and more. Check them all out!

Use a towel to iron your shirt

Metaphorically, anyway. If you have a wrinkled shirt but don't have access to an iron—but you do have access to a dryer—toss your shirt and a damp towel in the dryer. Run the dryer on air-dry for 10 or 15 minutes. Your shirt will be wrinkle-free and ready to wear.

Keep your plants wet

Don't use towels to dry your plants—use them to water your plants the next time you go on vacation. Place already-watered, saucer-less plants on a damp towel in your sink or bathtub. Let cold tap water drip—and only drip—onto the towel. As long as you leave the water slowly dripping and as long as the pot's drain holes touch the towel, you'll return home to healthy, well-watered plants.

Don't whine about the wine bottle

Don't get discouraged if you can't get a cork out of your wine bottle. Instead, get a towel, soak it in hot water, and wrap it around the neck of the bottle. The neck of the glass bottle will expand slightly, and you'll be able to pull out the cork.

Ship packages with towels

Skip packing peanuts, bubble wrap, tissue paper, and newspaper the next time you ship a package. Instead, send an additional gift—towels! Use them to protect your cargo and fill the box so that the contents don't shift. The recipient will be happy to receive a package in one piece, and delighted to have packing material that she can use!

Support your back

Driving doesn't have to hurt your back, and it won't if you use a lower back support. Make your own with a towel and old panty hose. Fold a medium-size bath towel in half lengthwise, then roll it from one long end to the other. Cut the leg off a pair of stockings, and slide the towel in. Trim the stocking so it fits neatly around the towel. Place the support between the car seat and your lower back and drive away in comfort!

Speed dry your clothes

Say you're in a rush to get to a party but you need to wash your party outfit first. Run it through the washer, then put it in the dryer—with a few clean towels of a similar color. The towels will help speed up the drying process by absorbing the moisture.

wax paper

What's up with wax paper? It seems like it's not terribly handy around the house—can you name three ways to use it?—but it can surprise you with its worth. Here are a few alternate ways it can earn its keep.

Start a fire

On its own, wax paper works well as fire kindling. Consider taking it along on camping trips for food purposes, and then tossing it into the fire for a second use.

Keep your fridge clean

Cut a piece of wax paper to fit the bottom of the fruit and vegetable drawers in your refrigerator. When the drawers get messy—and they will—just pull out the sheet of wax paper and replace it with another.

Give your chrome a shine

Make your chrome bathroom fixtures sparkle by rubbing them with wax paper after you've cleaned them. The wax paper will keep them spot- and smudge-free for longer than usual.

Protect your cookie sheets

You may be careful to use plastic spatulas on your nonstick cookie sheets, but do you protect them as well when you store them? Place a sheet of wax paper between each cookie sheet when you put them away, and you'll keep them from getting scratched.

Stop struggling with corks

Wrap your wine bottle's cork with wax paper the next time you have a drink, then put it back in the bottle. The wax paper will prevent chips of cork from getting in your wine, and will make opening the bottle for your next drink easier.

Repair your iron

If your iron is coated with a nonstick substance but still sticks to your clothes and even stains them, call in wax paper reinforcements. Crumple some wax paper into a ball and rub it over the warm soleplate. Your iron will stop sticking and staining.

WAX PAPER

Although wax paper may look like parchment paper, the two are quite different and not interchangeable—especially if you want to line cookie sheets. Wax paper is paper coated in wax. If you use it in a hot oven, the wax will melt. This will not add a desirable taste to your cookies. Parchment paper, on the other hand, is coated with silicone, is very heat resistant, and won't melt, stick, or add unwanted flavor. So don't get in a situation where you'll have to toss your cookies—keep wax paper out of the oven.

AISLE 5

HOUSEWARES

DOLLAR STORES ARE A PARADISE FOR shoppers seeking housewares. From basters and buckets to candles and coat hangers, this is the place to look for those everyday, utilitarian items we all need to run our homes. And part of the pleasure of shopping at a dollar store, once you've stocked up on certain staples, is that you never know what you'll find. A selection of variously shaped bottle openers, perhaps? Ice cube trays in cheery colors? Bathtub appliqués that look like circus animals? Whatever you find there, you'll be able to find a wealth of uses for it with these tips and suggestions.

aluminum foil

It has been many years since aluminum foil was tinfoil and actually made from tin. It has also been many years since we could do without this indispensable workhorse of the kitchen.

Keep your oven clean

Why do fruit pies always bubble over? By the time your dessert is done, there's a blackened mess on the bottom of the oven, and you'd better remember to clean it off before you turn on the oven again. Or, you could just line the oven with foil and discard the whole mess.

Make temporary hair curlers

You daughter wants her hair in curls for her school play tomorrow but it's been ages since you last saw your curlers. No problem! Tear off strips of foil, fold them over, roll a damp lock of hair around each, and fold them over. By the time her hair dries, she'll have perfect ringlets. Curl the whole head, or make pincurls to frame her face.

THE TWO SIDES OF ALUMINUM FOIL

The reason the two sides of your aluminum foil look different is a direct result of how the foil is made. During manufacturing, sheets of foil pass through giant polished rollers in layers; the side that contacts the rollers comes out shiny and the other side remains matte. The foil itself is made of aluminum—so why do so many people refer to it as "tinfoil"? It is a matter of habit: Household foil was made of tin until 1947. Some old habits are hard to break!!

Help soap last longer

Most of us let bars of soap melt away in water in the soap holder. Wrap a piece of foil around the bottom of the bar so when people swipe their wet hands against the top, the base won't end up in a puddle of water.

Cover stovetop drip pans

If you have removable drip pans beneath the heating elements on your stovetop, cover them in foil, shiny side up, to protect from drips. When they look dirty, discard and re-cover in clean foil. The shiny foil will also reflect heat when the elements are on.

Prepare a taco salad shell

Ball up a piece of foil on a baking sheet; the ball should be about 4 inches in diameter. Brush a large corn or flour tortilla lightly with olive oil and drape it over the ball. Bake at 350°F for about 10 minutes, until it's crisp. Cool and fill with your salad!

Make ironing more efficient

Lay a sheet of foil under your ironing board cover, shiny side up. It will reflect the heat back up, so you need fewer swipes to get your shirt smooth and wrinkle-free.

Wrap a gift

Use a sheet of foil, shiny side out, to wrap a present (ideally something in a box). Top with a sparkling metallic bow for a novel and arresting giftwrap.

Cut down on static cling

It's frustrating to find all your synthetic socks clinging for dear life to your pants and shirts when you remove them from the dryer. Reduce static in the dryer and avoiding peeling clothes apart by tossing a crumpled ball of foil in with the clothes.

> Make a spare dustpan by simply cutting an aluminum pie pan in half.

Wrap a doorknob

Foil makes a tight seal to keep paint off doorknobs while you're painting. Press down the foil right up to the edge of the doorknob and its fitting, then run a utility knife around to make a neat edge you can paint right up to.

aluminum pie pan

You meant to make a homemade crust for that apple pie, but somehow you just ran out of time. No worry. With a readymade freezer crust, you get pie *and* a hugely useful item to have around the house.

Catch paint drips

No matter how carefully you think you wiped the edge after pouring, it's almost impossible to keep paint from dripping down the sides of a paint can. But keep an aluminum pie pan handy and set the can back down in it. It will still drip—but only into the pan!

Scoop up garbage

Why is there never a dust pan around when you need it? Make a spare by simply cutting an aluminum pie pan in half. The thin plate makes for a much sharper edge that will sit flat on the floor, letting you sweep even the finest crumbs right into the pan instead of underneath it.

Stack pies for storage

At the holidays, counter space can quickly get scarce with all the desserts arriving with visitors. Create some more room by turning one clean and empty pie pan upside-down atop a full pie pan. Now you can stack a second pie on that, then turn another pie pan upside-down to cover the stack.

Stop grease from spitting

Some brands of bacon "spit" hot grease when cooking more than others, no matter how carefully you fry. Protect yourself and the top of your stove by poking a few holes in the bottom of a pie pan, then turn it upside down over the spitting food. Use tongs to lift it when you're ready to flip the bacon, and discard (or recycle) the clean pan when you're done.

Tote dinner to a neighbor

If you share food with neighbors or friends who might be elderly or unwell, keep empty pie pans to serve as portable, disposable plates. Dish up the food as if it was a dinner plate, then cover with foil. It can go straight in the oven to reheat.

baster

Suction in the roast's juices to squeeze over the top or suction off the fat and discard— basters seem to be highly specific in their uses. If you think so, you might just be surprised at what else you can do with one.

Water hanging plants

Are you tired of pouring water down your arm when you're trying to reach a decorative plant hung high? Suck up water in a baster that you save for just this purpose and push the tip right into the soil. Squeeze gently—no more drips.

Clean an air conditioner

You can use your fish-tank cleaning baster for this job: If your AC is blowing musty air into the room, chances are the drain hole is clogged. Take off the front of the unit and use the baster to suck out any standing water you may see, then blow through the drain hole with the baster to clear the blockage.

Lower the level of coffee water

Half asleep while making the morning coffee and you overfilled the reservoir? Use a baster to suck out the excess, and soon you'll be happily brewing.

Make perfectly even cupcakes

Spooning batter into cupcake papers can be a messy job. Drips dot the pan, and woe to you if you spill a bit between the paper liner and the cup. And it's hard to get them all evenly filled, meaning some are short while others burst out like mushrooms. Use a baster to suck up the exact amount of batter and squeeze it into the paper liner with accuracy.

A no-spill way to handle paint

Pouring paint from a large can into a small one for touch-ups can be a messy job. Keep a dedicated baster as part of your paint supplies, and suction up the amount of paint you need. This also works for transferring paint to a roller tray. When you're done, rinse with water and let dry. You'll be able to use the same baster time and again for this job.

bathtub appliqués

While they might seem like an item from the past, people still have bathtubs, and dollar stores still sell the appliqués that make the floor of the tub less slippery. What you may not know is that you can do a whole lot more with them as well.

Make your slippers nonslip

Nearly broke your neck in a new pair of slippers or sandals? There's no need to throw them away. Cut pads out of the bottom of nonstick bathtub appliqués and apply them to the soles of your shoes. This is great for the slippery bottoms of a pair of kiddie "footie" pajamas.

Keep a sippy cup in place

A sippy cup banged down on a food tray wet with food has a good chance of hitting the floor. Cut a circle of bathtub appliqué to fit the bottom and stick it on. You've got a much better chance of Junior's juice staying on top of the tray.

Keep a baby comfortably in his high chair

Little ones wriggle and slip around in high chairs, especially when they first start sitting in them, and you can find your tot sliding down even if she's not trying to get out! Put a couple of appliqués on the seat of a high chair to keep baby from slipping around.

Make wading pools safer

Before you put water in that plastic baby pool, stick down a handful of bathtub appliqués so that little feet can get a better grip while they toddle around in the water.

Anchor your computer

Replace your computer's missing feet or add ones that you wish were there, by cutting out little circles of bathtub appliqués and applying them to the base of your laptop or keyboard. They don't need to be large to get the job done.

bottles and jugs

Whether you save old bottles and jugs and wash them out or buy specific sizes new at the dollar store, you can bet there are heaps of uses for them all.

Save on every flush

Even if you don't have a newer toilet that's designed to use less water, you can still live a little greener. Fill a clean, label-free 1-liter bottle with water and put it in the tank. You'll save water, and money, on each flush.

Design a string dispenser

Cut the bottom half off a 2-liter soda bottle and mount it upside down on the wall near your desk or kitchen—wherever you wrap packages or roasts or anything else that requires twine. Put a ball of string in the top so the end hangs down through the top of the bottle (which is now the bottom of your dispenser). You can easily pull out what you need, tangle-free.

Stay prepared for winter ice

Keep two gallon-size milk bottles full of grit, sand, or kitty litter in your car during the snowy season. If your wheels are ever caught spinning on ice or slush, you can pour the sand or grit in front of the tires to free your vehicle.

Make your freezer more efficient

A half-empty freezer is a freezer that's costing you more. Keeping it full of frozen items actually uses less electricity. If your freezer is on the empty side, fill in the empty spaces with plastic gallon jugs full of water (leave a few inches empty for the water to expand as it freezes). The freezer will run more efficiently, and you can also put one of these frozen jugs in a cooler as you pack a picnic.

Create a paint storage system

With a disposable funnel made from a soda bottle, pour leftover water-based paints into clean plastic milk jugs. Add a few marbles to the jug before screwing on the cap. When you need the paint again, you can shake the jug and the marbles will help mix the paint. Write the manufacturer, color name, and date directly on the jug with a permanent marker.

Save a bundle!

bottle openers

A simple bottle opener might seem like an unimportant item, unless you can't find yours! It's the only tool for that particular job. Fortunately, it does several other jobs as well.

Make a dedicated grill scraper

Grill brushes can easily wear down by the end of the season, but you can make a super-efficient one that will last and last with a church-key bottle opener and a metal file. File a notch in the flat end, and use it to scrape along each bar of the grill rack.

Make creative party favors

Make original and memorable party favors by customizing bottle openers for every guest. Use a hot glue gun to attach rhinestones or sequins, or paint designs (or names of the recipients) on each opener with brightly colored nail polish. String beads on a wire and loop it through the hole in the handle for added color.

Hull strawberries

The pointed end of a church-key opener is exactly the right size to hull strawberries. When you've been out picking berries and find that you need to clean a couple quarts of them fast to make jam, use the church key to nip out the leafy top without trimming off extra berry.

buckets

A house can never have too many buckets. Big and small, dull metal or brightly colored plastic, they have endless uses—including some slightly more unusual ones.

Make a garden on your fire escape

No outdoor space in your apartment? Fill some brightly colored plastic buckets with some big stones, then pebbles, then potting soil and seeds or plants. You'll have enough of a drainage system from the rocks that you don't need to drill holes in the bottom.

Shower in the great outdoors

A large plastic bucket with holes punched in the bottom can serve as a shower when you're camping. Hang it from a sturdy branch, and fill with another bucket—ideally one you've left in the sun all day to warm up. Punching fewer holes means a slower drip but a longer shower!

Lock up your food

Bears are getting smarter and smarter at opening "bear-safe" food lockers at campsites. But there's still not a bear with the digital dexterity to open a sturdy 5-gallon plastic bucket with a tight-fitting lid, so it's a great way to store food on camping trips. The bucket also helps seal in the odors that summon bears to your campsite.

Store extension cords

However you wrap them, long extension cords are inclined to tangle. Coil them down into a bucket with a hole drilled in the side near the bottom to pull out the pronged end of the cord. The other end lifts out of the top, so you can pull out as much or as little as you need.

cans

You open a can of food, rinse out the can, and toss it into the recycling, right? Not so fast! Cans have so many special uses that you won't want to hurry to throw one away.

Stack it like a restaurant chef

If you remove the top and bottom of a clean tuna can, you're left with the same tool that high-end restaurant chefs use to "stack" food for beautiful presentations on the plate. Put the ring on a plate and make a mashed potato base topped by beef stew, for example, or put down washed mesclun mix and top with chicken or shrimp salad. Pull off the ring, and it's like you're dining in a fancy restaurant.

Poach eggs to perfection

That same tuna can ring can make perfectly round poached eggs. Bring a skillet of salted water to a boil and drop in three or four clean tuna "rings." Break an egg into each ring and your poached eggs will be beautifully even.

Plug a mouse hole

Old houses often have major holes in the floorboards or skirting that mice have gnawed over the decades. To really seal these up, you need metal, and a can lid is ideal. Carefully nail it over the hole (ideally from behind or underneath a carpet or rug) and your little visitors will be thoroughly foiled.

Lock table legs together

Remember back when you sat at the kiddie table at a family meal? More often than not, it was a couple of card tables stuck together. Make a kiddie table that's kiddie-proof by setting the adjacent legs of each table in empty cans. If those tables do move, they'll be in lockstep.

candles

It's always good to have a handful of candles on hand. Not only do they light the occasional pleasant meal, but they're good for emergencies when the lights go out. And with these tips, you can use them for other things, too.

Stop a saw from sticking

Here's a trick from professional carpenters' shops: When you're cutting wood, rub a candle over the saw blade. It will help it glide more easily through the wood. Reapply as often as needed.

Make sleds (and skis) slide faster

Rub the metal runners of the sled with a candle, and soon you'll be schussing down the hill at the head of the pack.

Fill a scratch

Got a hairline scratch in the surface of your dining room table or coffee table that resists all efforts to polish it out? Rub it with a white candle to fill the scratch, then buff to a shine with a soft, lint-free cloth.

Help a drawer slide smoothly

Kitchen drawer keeps sticking or squeaking? Remove the drawer and rub a candle all along the runners. The drawer will slide smoothly back into place.

cheesecloth

If you think a sheet of cheesecloth is little more than a flimsy dishtowel, you need to read these tips. You may soon find cheesecloth indispensable in your kitchen.

Create a fine-mesh strainer

Trying to clear a stock or drain yogurt to thicken it? Your regular colander won't do the job. Put a layer of cheesecloth in the bottom and you'll have a chef-worthy sieve.

Wrap bay leaves and herb sprigs

When a recipe calls for stewing a dish with several bay leaves or a sprig of fresh herbs such as rosemary or thyme or even whole cloves or allspice berries, you want to be able to fish out the stems or inedible bits with ease. Just wrap the herbs or spices in a small square of cheesecloth and tie with kitchen string. When you're done, remove and discard.

Avoid tiny items when vacuuming

A vacuum nozzle is a great way to clean up dust from the tops of bureaus or the edges of shelves, unless you sweep up earrings, marbles, or other tiny items. Fix a square of cheesecloth over the end of the nozzle with a strong rubber band and clean away! The cheesecloth filters out the items you don't want sucked up but lets the dust through.

Dry herbs for use all year

Drying herbs you grew yourself is such a romantic idea, until they're crumbling all over your kitchen. Wrap individual bouquets of the herbs you want to dry in cheesecloth and tie with kitchen string. Hang these upside down in a dry area such as the pantry. When you want to use some rosemary or thyme, untie the bag and take what you need.

coat hangers

Whether you get them free at the dry cleaner or buy them in bulk at the dollar store, coat hangers are endlessly useful for tasks other than just hanging coats.

Cultivate a window-box greenhouse

If you have a window box, you're halfway there. Bend several lengths of wire coat hanger into wide U shapes and insert each end on either side of the window box. Cover the wires with tough plastic, such as a storage bag you've cut for the purpose, and your seedlings will stay warm.

Make a bright mobile for a baby

Fit two white wire hangers together at 90-degree angles, twisting the hooks so they both point the same way, and secure them by wrapping ribbon around the hooks, overlapping it to cover the metal. Now you have the frame for a baby's mobile. Dangle pieces of brightly colored ribbon off the bottom and hang toys, such as tiny stuffed animals or shiny race cars, from the ribbon. Hang it well out of reach of the crib, where it can swing in a light breeze and enchant a little one.

Stopper a caulk tube

With a wire cutter, trim off a short piece of a metal hanger and twist it into a U-shape. When you're finished caulking a job, insert one end into the tip of the caulk tube. It will seal it completely, preventing leaks and preserving the rest of the tube unclogged for another job.

Unclog that drain

You know you dropped something down the sink or Junior tried to flush a toy or a washcloth got abruptly sucked down the bathtub drain. Don't panic. Untwist a wire hanger, keeping a small hook on one end, and probe the drain for the offending object. You might just loop it back up—and save yourself a fortune on a plumber!

coffee filters

The fine-textured, food-grade paper of the typical coffee filter makes it perfect for lots of things other than filtering coffee.

Make a disposable funnel

Need to pour something potentially messy, such as cooking oil, solvents, or motor oil? Avoid the cleanup by making a quick and effective funnel from a coffee filter. Snip off the bottom and fold it to fit the neck of the container you're pouring in. A filter has just enough stiffness to complete a speedy pouring job, and when you're done, no cleanup—just throw it away.

Keep the soil in the pot

Layers of rocks and pebbles let the water drip down in a potted plant, but over time, all that watering washes the soil down into the rocks, compacting it and washing it away out the drainage holes. Put that day off for a long time by putting down a layer of a couple of coffee filters before you pour in the potting soil. Water will filter through; dirt won't.

Apply shoe polish

Shoe polish can be a mess waiting to happen. Instead of risking stains when polish rags touch other items, simply apply the polish with a soft, basket-style filter (not a cone filter) and polish with a second, clean filter. Discard both after use.

Detail a car

The absorbent, lint-free paper of a soft pleated filter will get every last speck of dust and dirt off the dashboard and electronics in the interior.

Filter cooking oil

Those fritters were terrific at dinner, but now you've got a saucepan full of oil and floating bits of food. How to salvage it? Cool the oil and filter

Melitta
Coffee Filters

Amalie Auguste Melitta Bentz was living in Dresden, Germany, in the early 1900s. Thirty-five years old and busy raising children, she was displeased with the bitter grounds she tasted in her coffee each day. She was sure the metal and porcelain filters on the market could be improved—so she took a metal pot, punched holes in it, and lined it with paper taken from her son's notebook. Grounds-free coffee dripped out of the bottom. Bentz took her invention to the Imperial Patent Office in Berlin. In June 1908, she was granted legal protection for her "filter top device with filtration paper." More than 100 years later, the German-based company manufactures its popular Melitta Coffee Filters in Clearwater, Florida, and at other factories around the world.

it through a coffee filter and you'll get every last bit of grit out. Use a second filter as a funnel, and put the oil back in the bottle. Live to fry another day!

Diffuse light for a photo

Avoid the harsh look of a flashbulb when taking closeup interior shots, especially of people's faces. Hold or tape a single thickness of a coffee filter over the flash. When you take the shot, you'll find that the faces will look more like a professional, softly glowing studio portrait, and not a police mug shot.

colanders

A bowl that won't hold water sounds totally useless. But call it a colander and you can do all sorts of things with it besides drain pasta!

Make a slow-drip watering system

If you've just planted delicate seedlings and need to water them, do this: Line a colander with one layer of coffee filters, place the colander right next to the seedlings, and pour in water to the top. It will drip through slowly, and your seedlings will be happy.

Keep bath toys fresh

When you gather up damp bath toys after a child's bathtime, storing them in a bucket or other container can quickly lead to mold. Gather them in a bright plastic colander, and they'll drip dry, remaining fresh bath after bath. During baths the colander itself is a great toy. It's equally at home in the sandbox.

Store grapes perfectly

Tucked away in a plastic bag, grapes will sag and mold quickly. But rinsed in a colander and stored uncovered in the colander in the refrigerator, they'll stay fresh longer, and they're right at hand, ready to eat.

Prep the pasta platter

Here's a simple trick to serve up piping hot pasta every time. Put the serving dish in the sink and set the colander on top of it. When you drain the cooked pasta, the hot water pours right over the serving dish and heats it up. Pour off the water and wipe dry with a dishtowel before adding the pasta and sauce.

curtain rings

Metal curtain rings are especially useful when it comes to tasks other than hanging your shower curtain. Buy a pack and see for yourself.

Keep your keys nearby

Always fumbling in your bag for your keys? Loop a metal shower curtain ring through a fastener just inside your purse, such as the zipper on an inside pocket. When you put your keys away, open the shower curtain ring and slip on the keys. They'll be hanging just inside so you don't have to search around when you need them.

Improvise a baby lock

Special baby locks for cabinets can be expensive. Why spend all that money when your grandchild is only visiting for a few days? Keep little hands at bay temporarily with a metal shower curtain ring locked between the two handles of a lower cabinet. It might not keep a clever 2-year-old out forever, but it will give you time to get there first.

Organize your backpack

When camping or hiking, you can make extra space *outside* your backpack. Most metal shower curtain rings can hold just enough weight to make them useful for clipping a small flashlight or canteen to the outside of your pack. Hang items such as a pair of sneakers or leisure-time sandals on the outside and save valuable room inside.

dustpans

You've probably never given your dustpan a second thought. But if it wasn't there, you'd have problems! Keep it on hand for its basic job—and for all these other ones, too.

Make a scoop

A mini-dustpan, intended for quick cleanup jobs, can seem useless compared to the amount of kitchen floor you have to clean. But you're looking in the wrong place. A mini-dustpan is ideal for scooping cat litter or scattering salt on an icy sidewalk or spreading sawdust on a greasy garage floor.

Use to shovel sand

Headed out for a day by the waves? Pack a plastic dustpan for your little beachgoer. It's much more effective than those flimsy plastic shovels that usually come with beach sets.

flowerpots

A basic terra cotta flowerpot can do so much besides hold a plant. For many of these jobs, a decorative one will do the job very prettily.

Create a yarn dispenser

Some balls of yarn won't unspool smoothly when you're knitting, forcing you to stop every few rows and pull another length free. When you're faced with a stubborn ball of yarn, take out a clean flowerpot. Put the ball of yarn under the upturned pot and thread the end through the hole in the bottom. The weight of the pot holding it down lets the yarn pull free with ease.

Line one pot with another

Turn a medium-size pot upside-down inside one of those large decorative pots and you can decrease the amount of soil you need to fill it, and thus decrease the weight—very helpful if you need to move it around or if it sits on a balcony.

Store kindling

Baskets for kindling are nice-looking, but they let dirt and dust from the kindling sift down onto your hearth. Make an equally attractive container by putting a piece of duct tape over the hole in the bottom of a large clay flowerpot, and store your kindling there. Nothing will sift out onto the hearth, and kindling and sticks will be readily at hand. Put a second large one on the other side of the fireplace and store logs there.

Give it a lift

Want to elevate a potted plant to give a space some height? Invert a taller pot and place the plant on top of it. Instant pedestal!

Make a drainage system

Even broken, a clay flowerpot has its uses. Use the shards to line the bottom of other flowerpots instead of stones and pebbles. They're lighter weight than rocks and naturally drain well.

funnels

Big, small, metal, or plastic—there's a huge variety of funnel types and a huge amount of things you can do with them.

Separate eggs with ease

It can be tricky to separate the whites from the yolks, and that foolproof trick—breaking it into your hands—is a big mess. Try this: Break the egg into a funnel. The whites will trickle out the bottom and you can pour the yolk into a bowl or cup.

Make a funnel phone

Despite the wonders of modern technology, kids still love a string telephone. Run a length of string up the bottom of each of two funnels, and tie each end firmly to a large button to hold the string in place. Instant funnel phone! Remind kids that the trick to a string phone is to pull the string tight between the rooms before talking into the funnel.

Dispense string

A plastic funnel makes a terrific dispenser for kitchen string. Nail or screw it to the wall and drop the ball of string in it with the end hanging down through the funnel. String is at hand whenever you need it, for tying up roasts or packages—or making funnel phones.

ice cream scoops

While ice cream scoops might seem designed to do one job and one alone, in fact they're great for a wealth of tasks.

Scoop potting soil

Once you move a plant to its new pot home, it's hard to top it off with dirt without spilling all over. A plastic ice cream scoop that you keep dedicated to gardening is ideal for putting dollops of soil all around the roots before patting it smooth.

Make a seed planter

A mini-scoop is perfect for making holes when you're planting seeds in spring. You can make holes of an even depth, sprinkle in the seeds, and cover back up with the scoop of dirt in your hand.

Shape butter

Patting softened butter into molds seems like such a throwback to the days when ladies had nothing to do but lunch. Nonetheless, shaped butter really *is* cute on a holiday dinner table. Use mini-scoops or

melon ballers to make small rounds of butter to put on individual bread plates, or use a larger scoop to make an even round for a central butter dish.

Keep cookies round

Love those large, perfectly round chocolate chip cookies you get in bakeries? If you've always wondered how they get them so perfect, the answer is a full-size ice cream scoop. And you can do it too! Scoop up a level portion of dough and plop it down on your baking sheet, leaving several inches between each scoop so the cookies can spread.

Shape meatballs

Homemade meatballs are a treat but the task of rolling and browning can make you hesitate to start. Put meatballs back in your repertoire with the super-easy scoop method. Use a small scoop to put balls of the meat mixture right onto a baking sheet, and then brown them in a 350 degree oven for 15 minutes before adding them to your sauce. You skip rolling and the mess of pan-browning in several batches, which you may find is well worth the tradeoff of having a meatball that's flat on one side.

Make melon balls

There's no reason why melon balls (traditionally made with a melon baller, which is really just a miniature ice cream scoop) have to be tiny. A delightful way to enjoy watermelon is in balls, so use a standard ice cream scoop instead.

ice cube trays

All those neat and tidy little compartments in an ice cube tray must be good for something besides freezing water, right? Right. Read on for much, much more.

Freeze baby food

Any mom who has ever struggled to make homemade foods for her fussy little darling will

9 More Nontraditional Ways to Use ICE CUBE TRAYS

A DIFFERENT Solution!

1 Start Your Garden
Put some soil in each compartment of the tray, plant seeds, and get your season started early with indoor sprouting!

2 Treats for Tots
Ice cube trays make an excellent mold for Jell-O cubes. Make several trays, each a different flavor, and mix them together for a fun presentation of "finger foods" that kids will love.

3 Pair Up!
Searching for an earring is not the way to start your morning. Keep an ice cube tray (or two) in your top drawer and you have the perfect place to store earrings together. The trays can hold a dozen pairs and they stack nicely.

4 Egg Whites in a Hurry
Want to save time on your morning routine and still maintain your diet? On the weekend, crack some eggs and pour the whites into an ice cube tray. When frozen, pop them into a freezer-proof container. You can grab egg whites out of the freezer without having to crack a single egg—a great time-saver for your weekday morning rush!

5 Improve Canine Table Manners
If you have a toy breed of dog that eats so fast that indigestion is a problem, an ice cube tray can be a dog's best friend. Simply distribute your pet's normal portion of food between the empty cube holders. Your pooch will have to slow down to get at the food. It will take longer to finish the meal and this will aid in digestion.

6 Real Fruit Snacks
Try this for a delicious, healthy snack: Fill an ice cube tray with springwater and drop one seedless grape into each cube. Frozen grapes are low-fat and taste great. You can also freeze summer berries this way, and if you don't want to eat them individually, fill several trays and then store the berries in freezer bags. You can make a smoothie whenever you have the urge to snack.

7 Fresh Herbs all Year Long
Chop herbs coarsely and use a tablespoon to drop them into an ice cube tray. Top with a little water and freeze. When you want to add fresh parsley, sage, thyme or rosemary to a dish, they'll be right at your fingertips. Plus the freezer maintains their vibrant color.

8 More Delicious Edges
Do you have an old metal ice cube tray? Then you're in luck! Remove the metal divider from the tray and insert it into brownie dough before baking. You can bake with the divider in place, and when the brownies are done and cooled, pull it right out. You will have precut brownies, and each piece will have a delicious, crispy edge.

9 Now That's a Tomato
Why is it that recipes call for 1 or 2 tablespoons of tomato paste when you've just bought a whole can? Don't throw the extra away. Freeze it in an ice cube tray, then transfer to plastic bags and store it in your freezer for future use.

know the value of this tip: Once you have gently steamed and carefully pureed that butternut squash, portion it out into ice cube trays and freeze. After it's frozen, pop the cubes into a ziplock plastic bag for storage. Not only does it make all your hard work go further, but the trays make the ideal portion size for baby's dinner.

Make flavored ice cubes

Tired of your cold drink getting diluted by melting ice? Make a tray of ice cubes out of whatever you're drinking, be it coffee, tea, lemonade, or anything else that's not fizzy.

Freeze leftover wine for cooking

Leftover glass of wine in the bottom of the bottle? Freeze it to add to a stew or sauce in weeks to come. When the cubes of red or white wine are solid, pop them out and store them in a plastic bag.

Pretty Up a Special Drink

How lovely would floral ice cubes be in a glass full of your favorite beverage? Add a festive touch to your summer brunch or celebration drinks by placing an edible flower (pretty herbs or berries work well too) in the center of each cube. Start by filling the ice cube tray ¼ full with water then top with the flower, herb, or berry. Cover with water and freeze. Your guests will love the special touch!

jars

You can buy a huge range of different types of jars at the dollar store, from basic canning supplies to jars big and small for everything from storing flour to cutting cookies. You can do a lot more with them, too.

Bake big cookies

Want great big cookies like grandma used to make? Then you need her special cookie cutter.

So use the wide mouth of a clean empty jar to cut out those cookies from your childhood.

Make a homemade piggy bank

Charity starts at home, they say. Let it start with a piggy bank that you and your child or grandchild can make together. Put the jar lid on a work surface and hammer a flathead screwdriver tip against it to make a slit for coins. You can file the inside edges to make it safe and smooth. Then let your child decorate the jar with poster paints or permanent markers. Make it a regular thing to put coins and money inside—some for the child, some for your favorite charity. You can see through the glass when enough has been saved to take it back out!

Store flours and grains

The best way to keep flours and grains fresh as the day you bought them is to decant them from their store packaging into jars. Place them in the refrigerator to keep them for up to six months.

Make a mini-terrarium

In a large mason jar, place about half a cup of potting soil. Using a skewer, make holes in the soil and carefully drop in seeds. Water, place in a sunny spot, and voila!

Organize a workbench

Large glass jars, such as pickle jars, are ideal for organizing the bits and pieces that clutter a workbench. Screw the metal lids directly to the underside of a wooden shelf, then fill the jars with nails, screws, bolts, washers—whatever is making your mess—and then turn the jar right into its lid. It's out of your way and your items are plainly visible.

jar lids

Jars are so incredibly useful that even the lids are indispensable. With the spares that you're not using to top a jar, try some of these tricks around the house.

Keep counters clean

A large metal jar lid is an ideal spoon rest. As you occasionally stir that simmering spaghetti sauce all afternoon, set the red-coated spoon down into the upturned jar lid. You won't get hard-to-scrub dried stains all over the countertop, and you can toss the lid into the dishwasher with everything else.

Organize earrings and pins

If you tend to take off your jewelry and toss it on the dresser top, you need a handful of metal jar lids. Put earrings in one, rings in another, pins and brooches in a third. No more fumbling for your favorites in the morning.

Protect tabletops

Even the best-intentioned family member can't help putting that sweating glass of ice tea down on your wood surfaces now and then. Remind them that you prefer no white rings on the tabletops by leaving out a few coasters, ready to use. Glue rounds of felt to the inside and outside of an attractive large metal jar lid, and keep one or two of these in potential trouble spots.

Catch drips

Many condiments, such as honey and soy sauce, drip down the outside of the bottle after use, leaving sticky rings on your kitchen table and in your cupboards. Prevent the mess by storing the bottle in an upturned plastic or metal jar lid, both on the table and in the cabinet. The lid will catch and hold the stains, leaving the underside clean and un-sticky for storage.

Cover a glass or bottle

Kids left half a glass of milk on the table after lunch? Can't find the cap for the salad dressing bottle? A jar lid is just the thing. Cover the glass and put it in the fridge, so that milk can be drunk for dinner, or seal off that bottle—the cap will turn up one of these days!

paper bags

In addition to being an overall test of general ability ("He couldn't write/act/find his way out of a paper bag"), the paper bag has other, more practical uses.

Blackout your windows

Unless you want to spend big money for blackout curtains, the lower priced versions rarely do the job completely. But as any parent of a very young child will tell you, well-darkened windows can be the difference between a baby who wakes up at the first rays of dawn, and one who slumbers till 8 in the morning! Whether you're the tired parent of a toddler or a nightshift worker who needs some daytime shut-eye, darken your windows by taping up brown paper bags slit open.

Wrap a gift

Homemade wrapping paper can be as precious to a grandparent's eye as what's inside. Cut open a large paper bag to lie flat, and let your child decorate it with markers, stickers, ribbon, paint, whatever you like. Then wrap the gift as usual and watch the recipient's eyes shine.

Microwave popcorn

Why spend money on pricey popcorn packs? Put 1/4 cup of kernels in a lunch-sized paper bag and fold the top down. Pop on high for a few minutes (it may take a couple of trial efforts to get it right) until you have fresh bag of fat-free, low-price popcorn.

Separate linens

Can't find the pillowcases that go with that sheet set? Avoid tearing apart the linen cupboard by storing the whole sheet set together in a paper bag after washing. The paper lets your linens "breathe" so they won't have the musty smell they can get from plastic storage, and you can even slip

WHO KNEW? WHY PAPER BAGS HELP RIPEN FRUIT

Why does fruit ripen more quickly when stored in a loosely closed paper bag placed out of direct sunlight? The reason is simple: The bag helps contain ethylene, a gas fruit releases as it ripens. Ethylene triggers the creation of enzymes, which cause starches and acids in fruit to turn into sugar; they also break down cell walls, softening fruit. Paper trumps plastic, because plastic bags trap and condense too much moisture, causing spoilage. If you have unripe stone fruits and want to speed up the paper bag process just put an apple—which produces a lot of ethylene—in the bag along with your plums and peaches.

in a sachet or a dryer sheet so they smell sweet when you need them.

Clean up a wax spill

Tall tapers are lovely on the dinner table, but wax dripped on the tablecloth isn't quite so charming. Scrape off any excess, and then lay the wax-stained area over a heavy brown paper bag on the ironing board. Press the waxy area with a hot iron, melting the wax and transferring it to paper bag. Launder as usual to remove any remaining traces.

Contain a messy project

Cleaning a catch of crabs, peeling shrimp, or perhaps coring heaps of apples? Cut open a large paper bag and cover your work surface. When you're done, you can gather together the whole messy pile, paper and all, to discard (or toss on the compost pile).

Line drawers

Heavy-duty brown paper grocery bags make ideal drawer liners, both in the kitchen and the bedroom. Brown paper bags are sturdy, hard-wearing, inexpensive, and absorbent, keeping damp and odors from foodstuffs or fabric. Cut the bags to fit and lay flat in drawers. The heavyweight paper will lie flat, no adhesive needed.

Keep mushrooms fresh

As soon as you bring home mushrooms from the store, whip them out of their plastic or foam packaging and put them in a paper bag in the fridge. This way, you can keep them up to a week without the mushrooms browning or growing those large unappetizing "gills" on the underside.

Dry herbs

Trim the plants by the base and store them upside down in paper bags. Seal the tops and let them sit undisturbed in a cool place to dry. The bags let the herbs gently breathe, avoiding mold and mildew as they dry. Once they're completely dry, pick off the leaves and store in glass or plastic to keep them pungent.

Keep ice off windshields

Snow is easy enough to sweep away but ice on windshields is a hassle. Avoid the problem with a paper bag. Open a large paper bag and lay it over the windshield, holding it in place with the wipers. In the morning, just lift it off. You'll have clear windows and be ready to go.

paper plates

Every cupboard seems to have a pack of paper plates, way up in the back, kept for those pizza nights or when you just can't face the dishes. Now you can move that package closer to the front of the shelf and start using it for other jobs.

Microwave mess-free bacon

Microwaved bacon leaves a greasy mess on the plate, even when cooked between sheets of paper towels. Put a paper towel on a paper plate, then lay on bacon slices in one layer and top with a final paper towel. When you're done, eat the bacon and throw the mess away.

Catch paint drips

A paper plate under an open can of paint will save a world of tears in spills and drips. As the paint drips down the side, the can will end up sticking to the plate. When you pick up the can to move it or to pour more paint into a roller tray, the plate will stay intact to prevent more drips.

Make kids' crafts

Kids stuck at home on a snow day? Give them a stack of paper plates, scissors, glue, and markers, and let their creative sides go nuts! Staple three together and trim around the middle and top plates to make snowmen. Put a handful of beans on one plate and staple another one on top, sealing the sides, for a tambourine.

Create a safe Halloween mask

Many parents worry about close-fitting plastic masks. Kids can't see well from odd-shaped eyeholes and they can't draw a deep breath through tiny mouth holes. Cut large eyes and breathing holes in a paper plate and let your kids make their own masks, scary or funny. They can glue on ribbons and feathers or make additions from construction paper.

Cut large eyes and breathing holes in a paper plate and let your kids make their own Halloween masks.

> Toss a clean pillowcase into your luggage the next time you travel, and you can shift dirty clothes into it each day.

paper towels

You already knew that paper towels have a thousand uses in the kitchen every day, but here's a roll call of beyond-the-ordinary things to do with them.

Help thaw frozen bread

Before you freeze a loaf of bread, slide a paper towel between the loaf and the bag. When you thaw it, the ice crystals that have formed in the bag will melt and be absorbed by the paper towel, not the bread, leaving it dry and fresher-tasting, not soggy and freezer-burned.

Make crystal-clear stock

Even when you've poured off the solids from your homemade stock, you may find that it still has tiny bits of solids, not to mention a layer of fat. Clear your stock by pouring it into a fresh pot through a strainer lined with a paper towel. It will strain out any bits and a lot of the fat, too, for stock that's crystal clear.

De-grease a soup or stew

You're ready to eat but there's too much grease floating on top of your food. And it's too late to cool it down and wait for the fat to solidify. Remove excess grease by slowly dragging a paper towel over the surface. You want to soak up the grease, not the sauce. Discard the greasy towel and use another until the food is de-greased and ready to eat.

Clean a can opener

Have you ever noticed that strange gunk that collects on the cutting wheel of your can opener? You don't want that in your food. Clean your can opener by "opening" a paper towel. Close the wheel on the edge of a paper towel, close the handles, and turn the crank. The paper towel will clean off the gunk as the wheel cuts through it.

pillowcases

Yep, just a plain cotton pillowcase. It keeps your pillow clean and makes a smooth, soft surface for sleeping. And it does dozens of other things, too.

Dry lettuce

Making a big salad for a large picnic? Nobody has time to wash and dry six heads of lettuce in a salad spinner—unless you have a really big spinner.

Fill the sink with cold water, break up the lettuce heads, and wash all the leaves. Lift them into a clean cotton pillowcase, then take it out into the backyard and spin your arm like a propeller. The water will fly in a big circle, and the pillowcase will get wet, but the lettuce leaves will be dry as a bone. Seriously, don't do this indoors.

Line a wicker basket

Why pay for fancy fabric-lined baskets when you can make your own. A pillowcase is the perfect size to line a small wicker wastebasket, ideal for holding items such as skeins of yarn, socks, or anything you like.

Make a dress for a little girl

If you have a pillowcase with an embroidered edge, you can make a darling dress for a child. Cut off the seam on the short end, and slit the side seams just enough to make armholes. Fold over the tops and make a deep hem. Thread with two lengths of ribbon to tie over the shoulders. You'll have perfect summer dress!

Cover a changing pad

The covers on baby's changing pads need washing frequently, which isn't surprising considering the use they get. Instead of investing in lots of pricey covers, slip a pillowcase over the pad, or even lay it flat on top. You can change it quickly as needed, and wash and dry with ease.

Travel with a laundry bag

Toss a clean pillowcase into your luggage the next time you travel, and you can shift dirty clothes into it each day, rather than having to pack them next to your clean clothes. Take another one to hold shoes, if you like, so you don't have to stack shoes directly on top of your shirts.

plastic bags

If you're just using plastic bags to line your garbage cans, you're missing out on a huge range of other things you could be doing with these versatile, inexpensive items.

Make a temporary mattress cover

Grandkids sleeping over or perhaps a family member is recovering from surgery? You can make a protective mattress cover for a few days by sliding a large plastic garbage bag over the mattress.

Make a garment bag

Need to protect a suit or dress for the season? Make a small slit in the middle of the bottom seam of a large plastic garbage bag and slide it down over the item on a hanger, letting the hanger's hook poke out through the slit. Leave the bottom of the bag open so the item can breathe.

Protect an antique vase

Love that vase from the antique store but you're not sure it's watertight? Don't risk it. Line the interior with a heavy-duty plastic bag, such as a ziplock bag, and fill it with water. After you add the flowers, push the top of the bag down below the rim of the vase so it's invisible.

Make steel wool last

One use and your piece of steel wool is already rusting by the sink. Keep it to scrub pots again and again by instantly sealing it in a ziplock sandwich bag after use. Shake out the water, then pop it in a bag and press out the air as you seal. No air, no rust.

A DIFFERENT Solution

9 Nontraditional Ways to Use PLASTIC BAGS

1 The Cat's...Meow
Plastic bags make changing cat litter easier—dump the box into the bag and the bag into the trash.

2 Diaper Duty
Carry some bags when you're away from home with baby—they can contain soiled diapers.

3 Foot Protection
Considering shoes at a tag sale? They're not yours yet. Use plastic bags as a hygienic covering as you try on the footwear.

4 A Traveler's Tip
Use old plastic bags to stash your dirty clothes when you are traveling. This will keep your suitcase neater and smelling fresh. It also makes unpacking a breeze—carry your bags of dirty laundry straight to the washing machine.

5 You're Soaking in It!
Want a quickie mini-manicure? Coat your hands with a moisturizer and cover them with plastic bags for a quarter of an hour. The plastic will keep in your body's warmth, and your hands will emerge soft and smooth.

6 Bury Them!
If you have a large planter to fill, crumple plastic bags to fill the bottom of the container first (keep the drainage hole clear!). Then fill the rest of the planter with potting soil. The planter will be lighter and therefore easier to move.

7 It's a Wrap
Keep an eye out for colorful plastic bags. An unexpected way to wrap a gift is to triple or quadruple-bag a present—and then tie all the sets of plastic handles into a knot. Once everything is secured, cut the tops of the handle loops and fan the pieces out into a multicolored plume.

8 Ship 'Em Out!
Use the bags as packing material to ship fragile items. Stuff the box full to support the item enclosed, and your recipient will be grateful that you didn't use messy foam peanuts when she unwrap it with ease.

9 Keep a Paintbrush Wet
Time for lunch? Time to quit? Just because you're stopping a paint job for awhile doesn't mean you need to wash your brushes before the work is done. Wrap wet brushes tightly in a plastic bag and you can leave them overnight. If you want to stop for longer—say, several days or a week—stick the bag in the fridge.

Dispose of a holiday tree

There's nothing sadder after Christmas than dragging the dead holiday tree out the door, leaving a trail of sticky needles. Avoid the whole rigmarole by pulling a large plastic garbage bag over the tree from the top down. You'll have far fewer needles to vacuum.

Prepare crumbs easily

A ziplock bag is the ideal way to make crumbs neatly. Put cookies or graham crackers, cornflakes or dry bread, whatever you need, in a bag, seal it, and crush with your hands or a rolling pin. Store the extras in the same bag.

Tote an umbrella cover

Who wants to climb back in the car with a sopping umbrella dripping all over? Keep an appropriately sized plastic bag in the car and toss the umbrella in the bag as you climb in. You'll keep your seats and your floor mats dry and clean.

plastic containers

There's an endless variety of plastic containers available at the dollar store, from tiny containers that could hold salad dressing in a lunch box to huge containers ready to transport a fleet of cupcakes. And somewhere within that variety is just the size you need for a home task that lets you think outside the (plastic) box.

A wide plastic container is an ideal dog dish for both food and water when you're traveling.

Feed your dog on the road

A wide plastic container is an ideal dog dish for both food and water when you're traveling. They're lightweight and disposable. Take along a stack so you can toss one away or into the recycling bin when it gets dirty or worn.

Prevent ants on picnic tables

When you're having a picnic, ants are not invited to the party. Keep them from gate-crashing their way up the table legs by setting the picnic table legs into plastic containers. If you want to make doubly sure that no ants arrive, pour some water in the containers.

Give wasps the heave-ho

You can use a plastic container to make an extremely effective wasp trap that will keep your outdoor dining sting-free. Fill a small or medium plastic container with sugary water (3 parts water to 1 part sugar works well). Cut a hole in the lid and cover the container tightly. Wasps crawl in but can't crawl out.

Saran Wrap

In 1933, Ralph Wiley, a lab worker employed by Dow Chemical, came across a vial used in experiments for developing a dry-cleaning product. The vial was covered in a film and had an offensive odor. Try as he might, he couldn't scrub the container clean. He dubbed the stuff "eonite," after an indestructible material in the comic strip *Little Orphan Annie*. The invincible substance was soon made into a greasy, dark green film, and renamed "Saran." The first practical use was military: Saran was sprayed on fighter planes to guard against salty seawater. Eventually Dow improved Saran's appearance (and odor), and by 1953 Saran Wrap was being marketed nationwide as the first cling wrap designed for household use.

Serve beer to slugs

Slugs love beer but it doesn't love them! Keep slugs off your plants by digging a hole in the garden and setting in a plastic container so that the rim is level with the ground. Fill with stale beer. If you like, you can put slices of potato around the rim to attract them. In the morning, you'll see slugs who have attended their last party.

plastic tablecloths

If you're decorating the room for a kid's birthday party, a plastic tablecloth is quick and makes for easy cleanup. But these inexpensive items can do much more than cover a table.

Collect leaves

You can get special leaf cloths, but why pay for such a specialty item when you can use a plastic tablecloth? Lay it next to the pile, rake the leaves onto it, and gather the edges to transport the leaves.

Dress up the bathroom

Can't find a shower curtain pattern you like? Look at the selection of plastic tablecloths, where you can find a wide variety of colors and patterns. Use a hole puncher to make 12 holes evenly spaced along the hem, 1/2 inch down from the edge. Loop shower curtain rings through the holes or use ribbon to tie it to the rod.

Make a drop cloth

When you're done with using a plastic tablecloth for a meal, don't throw it away. Save it to serve as a painting drop cloth, or spread it under a toddler's high chair while she eats.

Upholster a vintage dining chair

Picked up a tag sale chair with a torn seat? Upholster it with a heavy-weight plastic tablecloth in a cool design. Remove the old seat, place it top

> Make a simple and effective protector for your keyboard out of a sheet of plastic wrap.

down on the tablecloth, cut out the replacement plus 5 inches all around, and fasten with furniture staples. Fun, nifty, and easy to clean!

Have a picnic!

The very best picnic blankets aren't the plaid wool ones that we remember from our childhoods. Plastic tablecloths are easy to wash, inexpensive, and there's no reason to get upset when you accidentally dump your relish all over it.

plastic wrap

Besides covering food, plastic wrap is useful for some very surprising jobs *outside* the kitchen.

Protect your keyboard

Computer keyboards are like dirt magnets. Every bit of fluff that drifts by seems to get trapped between the keys. Make a simple and effective protector out of a sheet of plastic wrap. Cut it larger than the keyboard and tape it down loosely at the sides. Don't stretch it taut or you won't be able to push the keys. Replace as needed. It might feel funny till you get used to it, but if you spill a cup of coffee over your laptop, you'll be glad you had a protector on there.

Heat up a sports cream

When you spread a heating sports cream over aching muscles, you get relief for a short time, but the effectiveness often seems to cease before the pain is gone. Enhance the effect of a liniment by wrapping a sheet of plastic wrap around the affected area after you apply the cream. It will increase the heating effect and treat the pain better. (This treatment is so effective that you may want to test it on a small patch of skin to make sure it doesn't burn you.)

Keep a cast or a bandage dry

Don't fumble with plastic bags when you need to keep a cast or large bandage dry. Wrap the limb or area with plastic wrap, circling high above and below the area to protect. You can pull the wrap tight to keep water out during a brief shower, then dry the skin on either side and remove the plastic wrap quickly.

Roll up a (plastic) rope

Need a length of sturdy twine for a household job? Trying to tie up a package or box? Don't look further than the kitchen. You can pull out a long piece of plastic wrap and twist it into an extremely strong and flexible rope.

Seal a drafty window

Are winter winds blowing in a small window in your basement? Lots of heat can be lost that way. Food wrap is thinner than industrial plastic window sealers, but in a pinch, you can use three or four layers of food-grade plastic wrap to seal a drafty window. Tape it firmly to the sides with duct tape.

Popsicle sticks

Tongue depressors, Popsicle sticks, craft sticks, little wooden thingies—whatever you want to call them, craft sticks are great for more than just doctors' offices and frozen treats.

Use for finger paints

Most kids adore the mess they get to make with finger paints, but more than a few actually don't like sticking their fingers in the cold wet stuff. There's no need for them to miss out on the fun. Give your picky young one a handful of Popsicle sticks and let him paint with them to his heart's content.

Label the garden

Seed packages on a stick look charming, but by the time the seedlings are coming up, the packages have faded and blown away. Avoid the confusion by writing the name of each plant in permanent marker on a craft stick and stick it in the ground at the end of the row.

Keep a record of your house paints

By the time you need to make a spot repair on the living room wall color, that paint color's name will have escaped you. When you finish a paint job, dip a craft stick into the color and when it dries, use a permanent marker to write the color name and the room where you used it. Keep these memory sticks in a safe place on your workbench.

Make a temporary splint

Got a broken finger? You'll need to go to the emergency room to be sure. But until you get there, hold the injured digit stable by laying it against a craft stick and wrapping it with gauze.

Steady a bookshelf

Is that bookshelf rocking a little unsteadily? No need to go to the hardware store for shims. Just use one of these!

Make skewers for kids

Got a picky toddler? Make food fun by skewering healthy bites on an easily grabbed craft stick. Pieces of chicken breast, chunks of fruit—with food on a stick, every meal becomes a game.

Pack an impromptu "spoon"

Sending along a container of yogurt or pudding in your kid's school lunch but you're out of plastic spoons? Grab a craft stick and toss it in the lunch box to serve as a handy utensil for eating creamy foods.

Give a kid his own "knife"

Little ones always want to do what the grownups are doing, but you're still not comfortable handing down a dinner knife. Instead, let kids spread their own jelly or peanut butter with a craft stick. It does the same job as a metal knife, and you can throw it away when they're done.

pots and pans

Dollar-store pans aren't always made to last forever. The metal can be thin or the nonstick finish may chip. But those lightweight metal pans can be ideal for some things.

Catch the drips from your grill

When you're grill-roasting a large piece of meat, you need to put a pan underneath to catch the dripping fat so it doesn't flame up. Instead of using and throwing away a disposable aluminum pan each time, keep a metal baking dish as your grill pan, and use it over and over.

Improvise a grill

Grills don't have to be huge, high-octane affairs with enough surface space to cook for a football team. Take a page from the Japanese, whose tiny hibachi grills are just big enough to cook supper for a small family. Build a charcoal fire in a large old pot and cook on a rack set over the top. When you're done, use the lid to smother the fire.

Make a big scoop

A small saucepan with a narrow rim and a single handle is an ideal scoop for scattering grass seed out of a big sack or sprinkling lime or fertilizer over your yard. If you've got a big dog, use one as a dog-food scoop.

Change your oil

A large pot is just the thing for draining your car's oil. Stick it under the drain plug, empty out the old, and put in the new. Use a funnel to pour the old oil into the empty containers for disposal.

Make a birdbath

Set a wide pan on top of an overturned flowerpot and partially fill it with water. Your feathered friends will hone in on it instantly for a quick bath on their way to visit your bird feeder.

saltshakers

Usually found next to the pepper, a saltshaker is such an ordinary household item that you may not have realized that you can do more with it than season food.

Apply colored sugar

Want to get an even layer of colored sugar on top of your cookies or cupcakes? Pour the sugar into a clean saltshaker. If you're making holiday cookies, fill as many shakers as you have colors.

Keep a dedicated cinnamon-sugar shaker

Some people actually buy shakers of premixed cinnamon and sugar at the store. Don't even consider it. Make your own blend, with as much or as little cinnamon as you like, and store it in a shaker near the toaster. Refill as needed.

Be creative and frugal!

Dust with flour

When you just need a little flour, such as a dusting on top of a pork chop you're about to sauté, a saltshaker makes a convenient and speedy distributor. Mark it clearly with a label so you don't accidentally dump flour in your clear soup, but keep it by the stove so you can add a few teaspoons to a sauce or dust a chicken breast.

Cut down on your sugar use

A little sugar in your coffee, a sprinkle on your cereal, a dab on top of sliced fruit—pretty soon all those little bits add up. If you're trying to cut down on sugar consumption, put the sugar in a saltshaker, not in a sugar bowl, and you'll automatically use less.

sandwich and freezer bags

Small plastic bags, whether ziplock-style or fold top, have a lot of uses besides keeping your sandwich fresh for lunchtime.

Pack cosmetics for travel

Even when you're not flying, it's useful to keep cosmetics in a small sealable bag. Toothpaste can squeeze out, shampoo bottles can leak. Put individual items in sandwich bags in your cosmetic kit or bag to prevent messy drips and leaks.

Waterproof a youngster's shoe

Does your little one want to walk in every mud puddle? Keep the wet out with a plastic sandwich bag. Pull one on over each sock, then put the bagged feet in the shoes. Her shoes may not be dry when she gets home but her feet will be.

Freeze a washcloth for a cold pack

It's hard to predict when someone in your household will next suffer a burn, teething pain, or another bump or scrape. Be ready. Freeze a wet washcloth in a sandwich or freezer bag. Pull it out of the freezer the next time someone needs some cold care.

Grease cake pans

Getting a pan thoroughly greased to stop a cake from sticking can be a messy job. Make it tidier by putting your hand in a sandwich bag and scooping up some shortening or butter. Grease away; your hand will stay clean.

Carry a damp washcloth

Carry a sealed ziplock bag with a clean wet washcloth in it. You can wipe a dirty face and hands before mealtime with no funny aftertaste.

Stash clean and dirty clothes

Heading out the door with a small child without a change of clothes is a mistake. Pack the fresh clothes in a ziplock bag, and, after whatever spill or accident, pack the damp or messy clothes in there for the trip home.

Use as a rubber glove

A sandwich bag or two makes a perfect hand covering in a pinch. Whether you're working on a messy project or you need to answer the phone while kneading bread dough, slip your hands into a pair of plastic bags and you can do the job with ease, then discard the bags.

shower curtains

A large sheet of lightweight but sturdy plastic might be just the thing to keep the water in the tub while you shower. Then again, it might be good for a whole lot more, too.

Make a picnic tablecloth

Going on a picnic? Don't forget to take a shower curtain. A clean shower curtain can either cover the tabletop or a bench at a public park, or it can serve as a waterproof blanket to keep you dry and comfortable when you eat on the grass.

Protect a tabletop

Worried about people putting hot or wet stuff down on your walnut dining tabletop? Sure that the grandkids will turn over their milk glasses? Sometimes a tablecloth just isn't enough. Lay a clean shower curtain on top of the table and then place your tablecloth over it. Nobody will ever know it's there, and you can dine in peace, no matter what gets knocked over.

Line kitchen cabinets

A new shower curtain makes a sturdy liner for kitchen shelves. It's waterproof and durable. Cut to fit, and glue or tack in place, folding the front edges under for a smooth finish.

Keep weeds out of a flowerbed

Put a piece of an old shower curtain, cut to fit, on your newly cultivated flowerbed. Cut large X-shaped slits through it to set in your bedding plants. Top with more dirt, and cover up with mulch to hide any hint of that shower curtain.

straws

Kids already know that ordinary drinking straws contain a world of fun. Besides blowing bubbles into chocolate milk, kids will always find more uses when they're playing with straws. Now you can put straws to other uses as well!

Arrange flowers

You weren't paying attention when you trimmed that bunch of flowers and now you don't have any taller ones for contrast. Push a few stems down into straws, and hide those plastic stems in the middle of the bunch.

Create a protective mat

Lay eight drinking straws side by side, and hold them at the top with a heavy book. Use yarn to weave in and out, over one straw and under the next, circling at the end and weaving back the other side. Use the resulting mat under planters, preventing water stains on furniture. The mat will eventually flatten out under the plant, but it's easily replaced by a new mat!

Make a dropper for liquids

If you need to add a little liquid to something, such as a drop of milk in icing to get the texture right, use a straw in the liquid and then put your thumb over the end to lift out a tiny bit.

> To use a straw as a dropper, put the straw in the liquid, then put your thumb over the end to lift out a tiny bit.

toothpicks

Some people treat a toothpick almost like a chewable mint when they leave a restaurant, keeping it in the corner of their mouth for hours. They know that it has a value beyond the one contained in its name. Update your supply of toothpicks at the dollar store, and you'll find more to do with them, too.

Clean in the cracks

Like auto detailers who clean around the radio dial with a cotton swap, a toothpick will let you "detail" areas in your house that are hard to clean. Dip the tip in a little rubbing alcohol and run it around the dials on your stove, the cracks in the phone, the lettering on your fridge—anywhere those fine lines accumulate dirt.

Light candles

A paper match always burns down before you can light more than one or two candles. Use a round wooden toothpick when you're lighting up a room with candles. It will burn long enough to light a lot of them.

Mark steaks or burgers

Why can't everyone just eat medium? Or rare? Or well-done? But people are different, and we all want our food the way we want it. So the next time you're on the grill doubling as a short-order cook, use toothpicks to mark which steak or burger is which. One toothpick means rare, two mean medium, three mean well-done. Everyone can pick up whatever they want.

Clean the gaskets on a gas stove

If your flame is running yellow, it means that your gaskets are probably stopped up. Turn off the gas, remove the grate, and clean each gasket by sticking a toothpick in it.

twist ties

When you don't want a twist tie, they're lying all over the countertops—off the bread, from the potato bag, off those apples. When you want a fresh one, don't go scrounging. Just lay in a fresh supply from the dollar store, and you'll have them for uses beyond the kitchen.

Rein in your electrical cords

The back of your desk looks like a spaghetti junction with all those cords and cables hanging down. Use twist ties to gather them together, tying off coils or bundling together long falls of cord. It will be tidier and far less dusty than a jungle-like tangle.

Find your house key

Does your ring full of similar keys get confusing when you need to open a door in a hurry? Use different colored twist ties through the holes to mark the keys you reach for most often: a green twist on the front door, a red one for the security lock. You can stop fumbling for the right key and go on inside.

Secure Christmas ornaments

If you don't want Fluffy the kitten to bat your precious ornaments all over the house, secure them to the branch with a twist tie.

vegetable peelers

Whether they're swivel peelers, or fixed, you can use your trusty kitchen companion for far more than just carrots.

Sharpen an eye or lip pencil

Can't find your makeup pencil sharpener? Don't put your eye and lip pencils into the kids' pencil sharpener lest you get a graphite pencil shaving on the tip of your cosmetics. Instead, use a clean vegetable peeler to shave off enough to turn on the color.

Make chocolate curls

Ever wonder how pastry chefs make those elegant, delicate curls of chocolate? The answer is in your drawer. Chill a chunk of chocolate in the refrigerator for 20 minutes, then run along the surface lightly with a vegetable peeler to make curls. Make them thin or thick; you'll get the hang of it quickly. Shave right over a cake or onto a plate, and arrange them on the cake as you like. Don't handle them too much or they'll melt.

Butter toast with cold butter

Your toast is hot but your butter is cold and hard. Never mind! Get out a vegetable peeler and shave off a few thin scrapes of butter right onto the hot toast. It will soften right up, and you can spread it with ease.

wax paper

Sandwich bags are handy, sure, but there's nothing like unwrapping a sandwich from a crisp and crinkly square of wax paper. While you eat, digest these other uses for this versatile wrapping.

Clean garden tools

Crumple up a sheet of waxed paper and rub it briskly over the work surfaces of your garden tools before storing them. You'll remove the dirt and add just enough lubrication to protect from rust.

Grease your shower rod

Not many of us pay attention to our shower curtain rod until it starts to get a bit rusty. If you have metal shower-curtain rings, they might start to squeal like failing brakes when you shoot back the curtain. And the plastic rings will stick

and bunch, perhaps causing you to nearly tear down the curtain as you pull. Keep your shower rod running smoothly by bunching up a handful of wax paper and rubbing it along the length of the rod. The rings will run smoothly along the slightly waxed surface.

Clean a can opener

Whether manual or electric, a can opener's gears will eventually get gunked up with all the bits of food that can leach out as you open cans. Keep your can opener operating smoothly by running a sheet of wax paper through it as if you were opening a can. The wax will clean away any grime and coat the wheels to keep the opener running smoothly.

Cover a cutting board

Experts recommend that you keep two cutting boards, one for meats, one for fruits and vegetables. But if you don't have a second, you can still keep meat juices and their potential bacteria out of the pores of your board by covering it with several sheets of wax paper every time you cut meat. When you're done, bundle up all the paper and scraps and throw it away. You should still wash your board before you use it for veggies again, but the risk of cross-contamination drops significantly.

Make a pastry bag

Don't have a special bag and tips for piping frosting onto cakes? You don't need one. Pull out a big sheet of waxed paper and fold it in half for strength. Roll it into a cone and spoon frosting into the open end. Twist shut, pushing the frosting down to the tip. Snip off the end, always starting with a small cut that you can enlarge as needed, and start piping.

NOTIONS

IF THE WORD "NOTIONS" CONJURES UP something your mother shopped for while you loitered, bored, in the aisles as a child, you obviously haven't visited the notions section in some time. In case you haven't hit a craft or sewing store in awhile, notions are those sorts of small, lightweight items that facilitate domestic comfort and harmony—needles, thread, ribbons, buttons. These days, however, notions can mean so much more, from a huge range of craft and scrapbooking materials to beads and rhinestones, fasteners, felt and fleece. The extent of how many notions a 99 cent store carries may vary, but you can always find something that will inspire you either to create something new—or use the item for something completely different from the manufacturer's intent!

adhesive fabric spray

Originally sold in the notions aisle as a fast way to secure a fallen hem until you could fix it with needle and thread, adhesive spray has terrific uses in virtually every room of the house.

Fix it quick!

Spray adhesive might be great for putting down appliqués on fabric, but it works just as well for making minor home repairs. Wallpaper curling in a corner of the dining room? Piece of linoleum peeling up in the kitchen? Border in the bathroom beginning to come unstuck? Spray the back of the paper or tile lightly with adhesive, then spray the wall or floor behind it. Let dry for a minute or two, then press down firmly, smoothing from the inside edge outward to remove any bubbles, and you've got a fix that may well be permanent.

Make storage boxes

For a fraction of what you'd pay for them in a specialty store, you can make stylish fabric-covered boxes good for storing anything from family photos to baby booties. Cut a square of fabric that's 1.5 inches larger than the box all the way around. Spray adhesive all over the base, and center the box on the fabric. Press to smooth and continue around the sides, spraying and smoothing on the fabric for a tight fit. Fold the ends as if gift-wrapping a present, then fold and spray-glue the top edges inside. Do the same with the lid, spray-gluing a piece of batting on top first, if you like, for a padded effect.

Design your own labels

If you've got spray adhesive and paper, there's no need to buy labels ever again. Whether you're identifying a storage box of summer clothes or putting your own logo on a jar of homemade jam, make up your labels on any kind of paper, whether you're printing straight off the computer or hand-tinting a piece of rag paper for a special gift of peach preserves, then cut the paper to size, spray lightly with adhesive, and apply.

baskets

Old-fashioned, lidded sewing baskets are perfect for holding more than just needle and thread. The trick is finding them! Once you do (and you may have to look in unusual places, like a tag sale or even your own attic), you're in for a multipurpose organizer that works everywhere.

Create a towel holder

Make it clear to guests that yes, indeed, those fresh towels really are meant for their use by placing a basketful of small folded towels right next to the sink when you're having a party or gathering. To underline the point, if you have enough guest towels, you can toss a used towel into a second basket farther away from the sink, which will invite others to do the same.

Make a small-stuff tool kit

A few small tools are needed over and over around the house—tape measures, screwdrivers, hammers, picture hangers and nails, duct tape. Rather than taking up kitchen space with a large and ungainly tool chest, make a tool basket of the little things you need repeatedly. Tuck drills and larger items away elsewhere while keeping a basket of the little stuff right on your pantry shelf.

Never lose your mittens

In wintertime, the whole family comes in the door and shucks off mittens, gloves, hats, earmuffs, and scarves. While boots and overcoats can go in their appropriate closet, the smaller items of cold-weather gear tend to pile up higgledy-piggledy.

Designate a particular basket to hold all those much-needed items, making it easier for everyone to find their own gear each morning and giving you a storage container ready to be put away when spring comes again.

Make a makeup kit

It's too hard to rummage through a messy makeup drawer in the bathroom or to unpack your whole makeup bag when you're looking for that tube of pink lipstick that must have fallen to the bottom. Keep makeup in a basket on the bathroom counter where you can readily find the items you need. Sort other toiletries into different baskets, as necessary, so your cotton balls and hair bands aren't jumbled cheek-by-jowl with your nail clippers and eyelash curlers.

Create a remote holder

A basket is a far, far better place than deep inside the sofa cushions to keep the endless jumble of remote controls that build up around the living room. Put them all in one place—a basket kept right on the coffee or side table, for example—and perhaps you can add that week's TV schedule.

Prep an after-school snack basket

Kids come home ravenous each day, and whether there's a cook in the kitchen or not, they love to rummage through the cabinets, sometimes leaving a trail of destruction in their wake. Head them off at the pass with a designated snack basket that puts everything in plain sight. Fill it with fruit and packages of granola bars or cookies, along with drink boxes, and perhaps a note reminding them that carrot sticks or kid-friendly yogurt and juices are just inside the door of the fridge.

Build a thank-you note station

Even in an Internet age, many of us still try to write thank-you notes by hand and send them via snail mail. Make it easy on yourself by keeping everything you need in one place. With note cards, envelopes, pens, and stamps, along with perhaps a few dried flowers or sequins to drop into the envelope just before sealing, you can dash off a thank-you (or a casual missive to brighten someone's day) the moment you think of it, rather than wishing, too many days later, that you had gotten that note in the mail.

Tote a table-setting caddy

It's hard enough to get food on the table every weeknight, much less remembering to set the table before dinner is ready. It's the same old task night after night, and whether you're doing it or asking the kids to do it, it's easier if you keep it all in one place. Put placemats, napkins, knives,

Wrap your hot water heater in batting, then surround it with heavy-duty foil, taping it down with duct tape.

forks, spoons, coasters, candles, or anything else that's a regular at your table in a basket that you keep in the kitchen or pantry just for the purpose of getting dinner on the table with ease.

batting and fiberfill

There are many more uses for this notions aisle standby then just providing cushioning on chairs and the like. All it takes is a little ingenuity!

Make a dog bed for a small pooch

Cut two equal circles of toweling or sturdy scrap fabric a little larger than the dog when it's curled up. Stitch a thick layer of batting between the circles. Sew a couple of layers of batting to the back of a soft towel or a contrasting piece of fabric.

WAY BACK WHEN...

What Was in Grandma's Quilt?

Long before quilters and sewers could just stroll out to their local five and dime or notions department to pick up a roll of batting, they stuffed their quilts with whatever was available: old rags, children's clothes that had been outgrown, even used oilcloth. Always looking for a way to use absolutely everything, country folk often cut apart flour sacks for use as quilting pieces. (The next time you find an antique quilt, look at it closely for the telltale signs: flour company logos!)

Roll this piece up into a soft border for the bed and hand stitch it around the round base to make a cozy, cuddly sleep spot for your favorite dog.

Quilt your windows to keep costs down

Tired of that winter draft blowing in through your windows? They need blankets! Use lengths of lightweight batting to line curtains. Making "window quilts" that keep in heat and keep out the cold will help cut fuel bills and make your house cozy in cold weather.

Wrap your water heater

A plushy roll of thick polyester batting can provide as much insulation as natural down, especially when combined with a reflector such as aluminum foil. Wrap your hot water heater in batting, then surround it with heavy-duty foil, taping it down with duct tape. It's a cheaper and safer alternative to fiberglass insulation.

Baby-proof your living room

Anxious parents and grandparents can spend hundreds of dollars buying specialized products to prevent little ones from falling against the sharp edges of coffee tables or railings around the home. But the need for this kind of protection only lasts a few short months. Instead, use heavyweight fiberfill to wrap the edges of sharp furniture while baby is learning to toddle.

Make a homemade oven mitt

Use batting and pieces of felt and toweling to make a custom set of oven mitts. Whether you need to replace your own worn-out mitts or create a great homemade gift, trim felt into squares and stitch on a thick layer of cotton batting. Cover with a smaller square of cotton terrycloth, and fold the felt over the edges of the terry, using a decorative zigzag stitch to finish.

beading

Doesn't matter if they're big or small: Dime-store beads are good for far more than embellishing fabric. Start right here to learn more!

Make a key saver

Tired of losing your keys all the time? Make a keychain that will help them really stand out. Tie two 8-inch lengths of twine or leather strips to your existing key ring, so that the four ends dangle loose. Then string on the chunkiest, funkiest beads you can find and tie knots at the ends. Your keys will never again disappear into the clutter on the hall table!

Count your calories

Make a bracelet that will remind you not to casually eat three cookies just before dinner and help you keep on track with your favorite diet plan. If you're trying to keep your daily calorie limit to 1,500 calories, for example, string 15 beads on a length of string or a leather strip. In the middle of the strip, tie a single knot that's just big enough for you to push a bead across it. Tie the two ends together to make the bracelet just tight enough to slide on and off your wrist. First thing each morning, put your bracelet on. As you eat approximately 100 calories (a slice of bread, an apple, etc.), push a bead across the knot. When all your beads have migrated to the other side, you're done eating for the day.

Build a bookmark

Tie a knot at one end of a narrow ribbon and wrap cellophane tape tightly around the opposite end. String on a handful of colorful beads, pushing them all the way to the opposite end, and tie a knot just above the beads to hold them in place. Then tie a knot 3 or 4 inches above the taped end, string on a matching or complementary pattern of beads. Remove the tape and tie off that end, and you have

THE MEANING OF BEADING

The history of beads dates back a whopping 40,000 years! The word "bead" comes from the Anglo words *bidden* (to pray) and *bede* (prayer). Traditionally, beads have been used through the ages for prayers, protection, worries, money, and adornment.

a bookmark with ribbon to lie between the pages and beads to show the place.

Decorate a box

Bring fresh life to an old jewelry box or knickknack by gluing beads in a meandering pattern all over the surface. You'll have a unique item that's as lovely and decorative as the jewelry inside.

Score your golf game

Can't keep track of how many strokes you hit on one hole? String together 10 small beads on as thick a cord as will pass through them, and knot the cord on both ends. Tie it onto your golf bag or attach it to your belt loop, and with every stroke, move one bead down. Tally your score at the end of each hole.

Buy it for this, use it for that!

bias tape and binding

Designed to be used on the raw edge of any material, bias tape and binding is very strong, hence its use on the most stressed part of a garment. Here are some other uses for this lifesaver!

Preserve a quilt top

Is the filling all bunched and lumpy in the quilt your grandmother made? Picking apart, relining and re-quilting is a huge job. Instead, save and preserve a favorite old quilt by using seam rippers to carefully detach the backing and batting. Then stitch a suitably colored binding or bias tape all the way around the outer edges and use the resulting lightweight blanket as a bedspread or coverlet. Your bed covering will be good as new, and only you will know the trick!

Replace a drawstring

Bias tape is cut at a 45-degree angle to the cross-grain of a fabric, providing the maximum possible strength and support. Thus double-fold bias tape, which is less likely to fray since the edges are folded inside, can take the place of string or straps in lots of places. Use brightly colored cotton bias tape to bring new life to a frayed drawstring bag or backpack.

Play baby blanket bingo

Looking for something special and practical to give to a new mother or a mom-to-be? Buy a bright colored blanket (pink or blue!) and cut it into four or six squares. Bind the edges with a wide satin binding in a matching or contrasting color, as you prefer, and the new mom will have a blooming garden of baby blankets to keep in the car, under the stroller, in the diaper bag, near the rocker—anywhere she likes.

Get hung up

Bias tape's strength and range of finishes can make it better than ribbon for some decorative uses. Strong and narrow, it's ideal for hanging Christmas ornaments or serving as a hanging loop on a potholder or dishtowel. Sturdy (and inexpensive to replace), it's also great for looping through the handles of kitchen tools so you can hang that stirring spoon or spatula right by the stove.

buttons

Whatever shape or size—big, little, round, square—buttons are a basic notions department find and can run the gamut from plain to gorgeous. But don't keep them hidden—use them all over your house!

Keep a pot from scorching

If you've ever let a steamer or double-boiler dry and burn, you'll never want to let it happen again. A few metal buttons in the bottom of a pot of boiling water will start to rattle and clank loudly as the water gets low, serving as an alarm to remind you it's time to refill the water.

Stitch on sock puppet eyes

When you're trying to get some work done, give your favorite preschooler a couple of old wool or tube socks, a very large plastic needlepoint needle threaded with a length of yarn, and a selection of coat buttons. Little fingers can be surprisingly adept at stitching on the big buttons to make sock puppets—and the challenge of sewing like a grown-up keeps small hands occupied for a long time!

Replace a game piece

Lost a few checkers or backgammon pieces? The fun doesn't have to end. Replace with large plastic buttons and the game goes on. With the huge range of colors available, you can likely find a button the same color as your missing piece.

Metal buttons in the bottom of a double boiler can serve as an alarm to remind you it's time to refill the water.

Decorate a frame

Eye-catching buttons such as those with glittering or pearly finishes make a striking decoration when glued around an inexpensive picture frame. The only limitation is your imagination, so have fun.

Perk up a planter

Glue plastic buttons in a swirling pattern all over the exterior of a clay plant pot to make a hard-wearing surface that will brighten a patio or porch. Blooming flowers in the pot will be icing on the cake!

Make a curtain

If you come across a large cache of mixed buttons, you're in luck. String them on heavyweight thread or dental floss—or single-fold bias tape, if the buttons' openings are large enough—to make a gleaming garland that will fascinate children and adults alike. Drape it around a Christmas tree or over a doorway. If you have enough buttons, make several ropes and tack or tie them to a wooden dowel. Affix it the top of a doorway or in the kitchen window for a shimmering curtain of buttons that both catches the light and discourages flies and other insects from entering a room!

Dress up a vintage jacket

Have an old jacket that you just love but find, well, a little bit drab? Replace the buttons with some pretty ones, and everyone will stop you and say, "Nice buttons!"

clips, d-rings, and fasteners

Used to secure fabric in clothing, bedding, and more, these handy dandy items have a host of other uses throughout the home.

Tie back curtains

Attach two D-rings to one end of a fabric tube or a ribbon, then tack it to the edge of a window frame to make a distinctive curtain tieback that you can open and close with ease each day.

Close a backpack or messenger bag

If Junior has broken the buckle on his backpack, you can repair it by attaching a strip of webbing or ribbon to the backpack—one side to the flap, another to the bag. Then put a pair of D-rings on the piece attached to the bag and thread the other end through—no homework will get lost on the way to school this way!

Fashion a belt from scarves or ties

Any distinctive piece of fabric can become a stylish belt with the addition of a pair of D-rings. Vintage men's ties that you pick up at a consignment shop make a belt that the hippest college student would be proud to wear. Attach two D-rings at the narrow end of the tie and thread the whole tie through your pants loops. If the wide end of the tie is too big to thread through the D-rings to fasten it shut, you may need to trim the sides and stitch that end down a bit narrower.

Grip a nail with a clothespin. This way you can hammer the nail and not your finger.

Seal a special book

Glue one end of a wide ribbon to the inside back cover, then stitch on two D-rings just where the ribbon leaves the book. Then loop the ribbon around the back and over the front cover and catch the opposite end in the D-rings on the back.

Close a gaping tote bag

Tired of losing things out of that open-top beach tote? Use four pieces of ribbon—two on either side—and D-rings or any dollar-store clips to seal the top in a decidedly stylish manner.

Put a new strap on a purse

Stitch one D-ring on either side of a purse with frayed handles, and attach a length of chain, a fabric tube, or a strip of leather to either end to breathe fresh life into your old handbag.

clothespins

Invented to hang up damp laundry on a clothesline, these babies were designed by the Shakers and date back to the early part of the 18th century. Their uses are widespread around the home, even in the playroom!

Get your shoe closet in shape

If your method of storing shoes is to open closet, throw in shoe, you need clothespins. You can still use your favorite technique, but before you toss that shoe, clip it to its mate with a clothespin. It will speed up the search each morning.

Build a better bib

So many baby bibs are tiny little half circles, when what kids learning to eat really need is a drop sheet. Make a broader bib for your little food thrower by wrapping a dish towel around your child and clipping it at the back of the neck with a clothespin.

Fill in the (bulb) blanks

When a bulb in your carefully planted bed doesn't bloom in spring, press a wood clothespin into the dirt above the spot. When it's time to plant new bulbs in fall, you'll know exactly where to replace one.

Save your thumb

Trying to fit a nail into a hard-to-reach place or at a funny angle? Grip the nail with a clothespin, and that way you can hammer the nail and not your finger.

Seal a snack bag

You don't need specialty clips or sealers to close your chip bag. Pop on a clothespin or two when you fold down the top to keep snacks fresh.

12 More Nontraditional Ways to Use
CLOTHESPINS

A DIFFERENT Solution

1 Make a Coupon Holder
Glue a magnet to a clothespin and hang it on the fridge door. As you clip coupons, stick them in the clothespin, and you'll always have them in one place.

2 Fasten a Dryer Sheet
Before turning the machine on, fasten a dryer sheet to a piece of clothing. When you remove the clothes, the dryer sheet is easily found and reused for another load.

3 Clip Your Keys to Your Purse
Run a clothespin through the O-ring and clip to the inside of your purse to keep from misplacing your keys.

4 Clip Your Book Where You Left Off
Use a clothespin instead of a bookmark.

5 Keep Your Skirt on Its Hanger
Clip the corners and that skirt will never slip off again.

6 Clip Outgoing Mail to Your Purse
Never forget to mail a letter when you head out the door.

7 Clip a Tarp
Help keep tarps in place on outdoor furniture by anchoring them with clothespins.

8 Clip Those Mittens
Attach mittens to your kids' coats so they don't go missing.

9 Close a Bag of Dog Food
Got a big bag of pet food in the pantry? Keep it fresh by clothes pinning it shut.

10 Keep a Cookbook Open
Clip open the page, and the book won't shut while you're cooking.

11 Stand-in Barrette
If your hair is long and you're out of barrettes, just clip with a clothespin and keep hair out of your face.

12 Make a Car Seat Protector
Before you put Fido in the backseat, clip an old sheet in place, attaching it to side-hung seat belts.

Pin up Christmas lights

Deck that holly bush with lights, but don't wind them around the stems to keep them in place. Clothespins are tough enough to survive the winds of winter. You can clip them to gutters, trees, anywhere you like, and they'll keep your lights in place all holiday season.

dyes

They started out life as a way to turn old clothes into "new" ones, especially during the Depression. But today, dyes can be used in a myriad of ways. Here are just a few!

Paint unfinished furniture

Get a highly distinctive look on a piece of unfinished wooden furniture by carefully painting on fabric dye with a foam brush. (It's best to wear gloves to protect your fingers from the dye.) Paint the whole item, a section at a time, always moving the brush in the direction of the wood grain, then use a soft rag to rub off any wet patches before beginning a new section. After the item dries, cover it with a few coats of a clear water-based finish.

Freshen up a slipcover

A small slipcover, such as for a chair or a loveseat, can be dyed in your washer if the slipcover is 100 percent cotton. Put the item in the washer, fill with hot water, and push the cover down until it's fully submerged. Follow package instructions to dissolve the appropriate amount of dye in the water, and then add it directly to the washer. Close the lid and allow it to agitate for a few moments before opening the lid and allowing it to sit for one hour. Allow the cycle to finish, and dry the item in the dryer.

Make custom tablecloths

Use a resist medium such as wax to paint figures or a design on a tablecloth border, then dye the

fabric any shade you like to cast your masterpiece into beautiful relief. You can also mix a concentrated portion of dye and use a paintbrush to paint designs on placemats or a table runner. (Wear gloves and work on a well-protected surface with a thick covering of newsprint.)

elastic cord and tape

Elastic can be used to do everything from letting out trousers that have gotten a bit snug to attaching to the bottom of pants to keep them in place on a bike ride. What are some more uses?

Dress up a T-shirt

Cut off the hemmed neckline and sleeve edges of a dull, store-bought T and make it look like high couture by stitching fold-over elastic tape around the hems. Use a zigzag or straight stitch, whatever you prefer. Stitch the neckline flat, but you can gather the sleeves for an instant puffed sleeve.

Shape a bouquet

If your flowers—real or silk—keep falling over in the vase, use a length of elastic cord to shape and support them. Tie the bunch just under the rim of the vase where it will remain invisible to the eye as it keeps the flowers standing beautifully at attention.

Make a yoga band

A 24-inch strip of wide elastic tape serves perfectly as a yoga band for keeping your upper arms toned and stretched—and it costs a tiny fraction of what a yoga band found at a store.

Bead a stretchy bracelet

Narrow elastic cord is perfect for letting kids make jewelry. Give them a handful of beads and several lengths of elastic, and they can make bracelets that easily slide on and off their wrists. It's also a fun project for a birthday party to let kids string round candy or mints with a hole in the center to make colorful edible bracelets.

embroidery hoops

Not so long ago, ladies would spend bucolic afternoons embroidering fabric that was held in place by a round, adjustable frame, which would stretch the fabric taut like a canvas. Well, you can still get those hoops, only now there's a lot more you can do with them!

Use them as frames

Use colorful plastic embroidery hoops just like you would a picture frame. You can showcase the piece of needlework you've just completed by trimming off the excess fabric and tying on a ribbon at the top for hanging, or you can fit the hoop over a picture your child has created on a piece of fabric with markers or fabric paint. Embroidery hoops can also frame paper, including wedding invitations and birth announcements. Fold and curve the paper's edges over the bottom loop of the hoop, then stretch it smooth with the enclosing top hoop and hang.

Create a Christmas ornament

Use the smallest size embroidery hoops to make personalized holiday ornaments. Hang them on your Christmas tree or make a garland of five small hoops over a doorway. Use your imagination to create a holiday series unique to your home. Use the hoops to showcase a series of patterned holiday-themed fabrics, such as a hoop with fabric showing bells, one with Christmas trees, and one with candy canes, for example, or you can create a holiday series of individual cross-stitch vignettes—perhaps a wreath, a candle, a reindeer, a gingerbread man, and a snowman.

Personalize a wall hanging

Put swatches of bright, eye-catching graphic fabric into a series of different sizes of embroidery hoops, from large to small, and hang them on the wall in a varied group. This is an excellent way to brighten a dark wall or decorate a nursery and also to highlight an exciting remnant of fabric that you couldn't resist buying. Craft hounds have a name for these beautiful groupings of embroidery hoop frames enclosing fabric with bold patterns: swatch portraits.

Make a door hanging

Stretch a piece of plain, light-colored fabric across a hoop and trim it close so no overhang shows in the front. Use fabric pens or glue to write and illustrate a message on it such as, "Welcome Home!" or "Let It Snow!" Decorate as you like by gluing on beads or buttons. Glue a length of lace trimming all around the front rim of the embroidery hoop and glue on a bow at the top, covering up the metal clasp. Use a pushpin to hang it on an interior door.

Hang up a kitchen towel

Paint an embroidery hoop a bright color. Tie a small piece of wire to the top of it and twist the ends, creating a loop. Hang the loop from a nail and a kitchen towel from the hoop.

fabric

They might be inexpensive remnants from a tag sale or on-sale bolts from the notions aisle. Either way, bits of fabric are perfect for many other uses, including these.

Make cloth napkins

Found a fabric remnant that you love, but it's too bright or the pattern is too busy for a dress or shirt? Cut it into 18-inch squares and hem them on all four sides, either with a machine or iron-on hemming tape, to make a stack of cloth napkins. They're good-looking, absorbent, and much greener to use than continually throwing away paper napkins. In some European countries, each family member ties his or her cloth dinner napkin in a distinctive knot and uses it for several days running.

Replace paper towels with clean rags

One way to go green in the kitchen with ease is to quit buying, using, and discarding paper towels. Cut up absorbent cotton, such as a T-shirt knit, into small squares and use them, unhemmed, for quick kitchen cleanups like spilled juice. Then throw these used kitchen rags into the wash. Save the paper towels only for the greasiest cleanups, such as draining cooked bacon.

Use cotton squares for mopping cloths

Those household mops and sweepers with disposable wipes fitted to the mop head seem like a great idea until you realize you have to buy replacement cloths over and over and over—they get expensive very quickly. Instead, cut absorbent cotton scraps into a suitable size replacement and use real fabric instead of those pricey store-bought replacements. To make a dry duster, spray the cloth with a bit of furniture polish. For wet mops, use a rectangular strip of terrycloth or toweling.

FELT IS EVERYWHERE

Felt dates back to 6500 BC and is used everywhere from the automotive industry to children's storytelling (a felt board is a great way to tell a visual tale). It's also used on musical instruments. It wraps the bass drum and timpani mallets, and on drum cymbals, it protects the cymbals from cracking and ensures a clean sound. And those hammers on your piano? They're covered with felt!

Clean your spectacles

Over time, tissues and paper towels can scratch the surface of your lenses when used to clean eyeglasses. Instead, cut 4-inch squares of soft, 100 percent cotton cloth. Store one in your eyeglasses case, one on your desk or by the bed—anywhere you might need to give your specs a rub. Gently polishing with these unhemmed squares, which can be easily replaced when soiled, will give your glasses longer life and give you a clearer field of vision!

Carry a coin purse

Tired of collecting change in big jars on the dresser? Start spending coins as you go instead of lugging them to the bank or rolling them. Make a small coin purse and seal it shut across the top with Velcro or snaps, then pull it out every time you make a purchase. No cashier minds waiting an extra second while you count out the change—and you'll likely find that the paper money goes a bit further when you eke it out with the coins.

felt

The oldest known fabric in the world, felt is created by matting, condensing, and pressing fibers together for a thick, dense result. It's used everywhere, from making children's toys to billiard tables. Here are a handful more uses!

Turn felt into a toy

Like paper dolls, but with felt! Turn felt scraps and a shoebox into a toy that kids will play with for hours. Use a pale color of felt such as light blue or beige to cover the lid of a heavy-duty plastic shoebox (a square-ish shoebox, such as those from a pair of boots, is ideal), tucking the ends under the inside of the box lid. Use different colored felt scraps to cut out shapes and figures that kids can stick to the felt board. Try a theme, such as "The Little Old Woman Who Lived in a Shoe," and cut out the old woman, a big brown shoe, and as many kids as you like, along with their pets and even mix-and-match clothes for each figure. Use markers for detail, or let kids decorate their felt figures themselves.

Stop wood floor scuffs forever

Use heavy-duty felt to cut out circles to fit under the feet of every piece of furniture you own that sits directly on a wooden floor. These protective pads, will prevent those inadvertent scratches and scrapes on wood that result from over-enthusiastic rising from an armchair.

Make an insole

Those new loafers were a terrific bargain, but they're a little loose around the heel. Pull out the insole and use it as a pattern to cut a layer of mid-weight felt the exact same size. Slide it into your shoe and return the insole over it. You may need one or two more layers to get comfortable. Real cotton felt won't make your feet sweat like synthetic liners, and your shoes will fit like a glove!

Top a table

Do you worry when guests set their hot cups on top of your grandmother's dining room table? A regular tablecloth can't protect the surface from the bangs of flatware and heat from dishes. Buy lightweight felt by the yard and use it to cover your tabletop completely. Then lay your tablecloth directly over the felt layer, for a smoothly padded, plushy surface that mimics the dining experience at the world's most expensive restaurants—and keeps your tabletop safe for generations to come!

Weather-strip windows and doors

Casement windows rattling in the wind? Wind whistling around an old wooden door? Cut strips of lightweight felt and use adhesive spray, double-sided tape, or glue to attach the felt to the jamb of the door or window. Use a neutral color such as beige, white, or gray—whatever matches your window or door frames most closely—or an appropriate contrast, such as dark-green strip against a mahogany door. When you pull the rattling parts shut, you'll get a snug, secure fit that keeps the heat in and the winter weather out.

> Use heavy-duty felt to cut out circles to fit under the feet of every piece of furniture you own that sits directly on a wooden floor.

Polarfleece

Polarfleece, the synthetic fabric that changed the way we dress for cold weather, was invented at Malden Mills in Lawrence, Massachusetts, in the late 1970s. The market was ripe for cold-weather clothing that was warmer, easier to care for, and less allergy-inducing than wool. Synthetic Polarfleece wicked moisture away from the body, it was warm, and it dried quickly—though it did pill after a few uses. Still, it was almost perfect. At about the same time, a company in Ventura, California, called Patagonia, was developing clothing for people who were serious about their outdoor sports. Malden Mills worked with Patagonia and improved its fabric to reduce pilling. Patagonia used the fabric in its clothing, and sales were fantastic. Today there are many makers of fleece, but the original fabric is now marketed in various forms under the name Polartec, the company which acquired Malden Mills.

Cut a bouquet that won't fade

Trim felt into a vibrant bouquet of flowers that will brighten your home year-round. Cut a simple flower shape, then trim two or three smaller ones and stitch them together, with the largest flower on the back. Finish them off with a bright button center, and attach them to a bamboo skewer for a stem.

fleece

Pound for pound, there is no other fabric as resilient or warm as manmade fleece (which is patterned after sheep's wool, which dates back thousands of years). The uses for fleece are endless and include the following.

Add absorbency

If you use cloth diapers for the baby in your life, putting one or two layers of fleece inside will add a lot of extra absorbency for nighttime or when you're going out. Cut the fleece into narrow rectangles to fit without adding a lot of extra bulk. Wash along with the diapers for repeated uses.

Make a comfy throw

With nothing but fleece, a few pins, and a pair of scissors, you can make a double-layer fleece blanket at lightning speed for a lovely handmade gift or to warm your own tootsies on a winter night. Cut two pieces of fleece to the same size—it's nice to use a solid color on one side and a complementary pattern on the other—and pin them together in several places to keep them from slipping while you work. Clip a fringe about 4 inches deep at 1-inch intervals all the way around the blanket. Tie the fringe together all the way around, remove the pins, and you're ready to snuggle.

Wrap up in a no-sew scarf

Cut a strip of fleece 12 inches wide and 3 to 4 feet long. Use scissors to trim each end into a fringe

3 inches long at 1/2-inch intervals. That's it—
wrap it around your neck and hit the slopes!

Tempt Fifi with a fleecy toy

Your kitten or puppy will go nuts for a fleecy ball.
Fleece is frequently sold in 60-inch widths. Cut
four strips 1 inch wide and 60 inches long (if your
fleece is 36 inches wide, cut seven or eight strips).
Hold one hand flat and wrap the fleece strips very
loosely around your palm. Slide the ball of strips off
your hand and tie it tightly around the center with
a piece of string. Use scissors to cut through all the
fleece loops on either side of the string and fluff
them up into a big, soft round ball. Here, kitty!

Throw on a no-sew poncho

Perfect to keep a little girl toasty in cool weather,
you can make a fleece poncho in less than an
hour. Cut a 30-inch square of fleece, then fold it
in half and cut a 5-inch slit from the very center
for a neck hole. Open it and trim the edges all
around into a fringe, as long or as short as you
like. If you have time, you can string a bead on
each strip of a narrow fringe and tie a knot in
the bottom to hold the bead on. Voila! A stylish
poncho in minutes.

liquid fray preventer

**We've all had it happen: The edge of a
favorite garment begins to fray and that shirt
is history. But a little dab of fray preventer
will help keep things where they're supposed
to be. Even better? There are lots of uses for
this miracle liquid. Here are just a few.**

Stiffen a bow

Did you ever spend time tying a beautiful bow
for a gift-wrapped package or holiday wreath

only to watch the ribbon sag like an old balloon?
A little fray preventer along the outer edge, once
you've tied your bow to perfection, dries stiff and
colorless and keeps it looking perfect throughout
the holiday or until your gift is opened!

Repair a stuffed animal

If Junior's most beloved teddy starts to show
wear at the seams, extend its life by stitching up
any visible holes with a needle and thread, then
anoint the joint with a few drops of fray preventer
to toughen up the area. You might make the bear
last long enough to get your little one to stop
sucking that thumb!

Prevent button loss

Buttons always seem more likely to pop off a
brand new shirt than an old one—the old ones
have stood the test of time, while new ones are
more likely to have been loosely stitched at the
factory. Whether you've just finished a button
repair or you're about to don a brand new shirt or
cardigan, put one or two drops of fray preventer
at the threads on the underside of each button to
keep them locked firmly in place.

Appliqué any print

You can make your own appliqués by cutting out the picture from any type of printed fabric and stitching it directly onto the front of a pillow or the side of a backpack or bag without hemming the cut edges. Apply a thin band of liquid fray preventer all around the outside edge of the cutout picture and you're done.

glue sticks

These familiar items started out life as a sewer's helper; place a little bit on a hem to use as a guide or to keep a hem taut, and then start sewing. Over time, they've found their way into school desks, but their uses go much further than that!

Wrap a gift

You've just squared the paper perfectly on the corner of a box you're gift-wrapping—but then you need two hands free to rip off a piece of tape. Instead, use a glue stick to secure the paper, and you have one hand to hold the paper down and one to apply the glue.

Fold up an envelope

The handmade invitations for your spouse's birthday party are ready to go out, but it seems a shame to stick them in a white business envelope. Use colored paper and a glue stick to make your own envelopes—the glue stick holds immediately and doesn't need to dry like liquid glue, and it won't seep through and stick to the front of your invite.

"Pin" a seam

Use a swipe of a washable, water-soluble glue stick to hold together a simple seam instead of pinning it. Whether you're making a pillowcase or repairing the ripped edge of a shirt, it's far faster and easier to glue the edges together and stitch them up than to laboriously pin them first.

Make a wreath

Glue twists of brightly colored craft paper to a wreath shape to make seasonal decorations, whether you're using yellows, reds, and golds for autumn or pastels for spring. Push a pencil eraser down in the center of a square of paper and wrap the paper up tightly around the pencil, then use the pencil to press each twist of paper down as you glue it to a foam wreath or a flat wreath shape that you have cut out of a cardboard box. The base of each twist should be glued together closely, letting the ends of the twist bloom and curl around the wreath.

Secure a vase

Where there are animals and breakables, there is breakage. Rub the glue stick on the bottom of a vase and place it where you want it on display. If the table gets bumped, the vase will stay in place.

no-sew/iron-on hem tape

Ever step on your own pants leg and tear out a hem? This great product is designed to let you iron on a bit of special tape, with no muss or fuss. More uses? Absolutely.

Replace paper napkins

You bought that beautiful linen remnant with the idea of making some classy hem-stitched napkins, but the fabric sits and sits because you can never find the time to commit to that project. Don't drive yourself crazy—use iron-on hem tape instead to make napkins in a hurry. When making a set of napkins isn't such a laborious process, you can pick up other appealing fabric remnants and make a grab-bag of pretty napkins so your table is always set with something nice. (And it's greener than throwing away paper after every meal.)

Hem curtains

While iron-on hem tape is perfect for quick jobs like shortening a pair of pants you want to wear the next day, it's also acceptable for long-term jobs such as a hemming a set of curtains. Cut the curtains to length and iron in the self-stick hemming tape, using the hottest setting acceptable for the fabric. While hem tape isn't meant to last forever, well, neither are curtains—and your hem will likely last for years, no matter what the tape's label says.

Relax with a heating pad

Make a flexible and renewable heating pad by using hem tape to stitch up two sides of a rectangle of cotton fabric to make a pouch. Fill the pouch about half full with rice or dried beans,

then fold over the flap and use hem tape to seal it (the filling can fall to the bottom while you iron the top). When your neck or shoulder aches, heat the bag in the microwave for 1 to 2 minutes, until the filling is warm to the touch, and drape it over your aching part, reheating as needed. A few cloves added to the mix will provide a soothing scent for many moons.

Make café curtains

A simple, durable pair of café curtains for a kitchen window can be yours in moments with hem tape. Find a cute pair of tea towels and use hem tape to iron on a 1-inch hem at the top of each. Thread a curtain rod through the hem and string 'em up! Since café curtains are intended to hang on the bottom half of a window, you won't need to hem the other side.

interfacing

This is the stuff that is sewn between a garment's lining and surface material. It helps protect both surfaces and provides warmth. But it also has more uses....

Prevent a pocket from wearing through

Men tend to keep their wallets, loose change, and keys in the same pocket of their pants, whatever pants they're wearing. And a heavy wallet, jingling coins, or a set of metal keys can wear through a lightweight pants pocket in no time flat. Turn the pants inside out and cut lightweight fusible interfacing to fit exactly around the pocket. Sew it up on three sides to make an interfacing pocket, then stitch it directly to the interior seam where the pocket attaches to the pants. Lightly iron to fuse the interfacing to the pocket.

Add life to upholstery jobs

If you're going to make the effort to recover a piece of furniture yourself, you want the job to last as long as possible. Before recovering a stool or chair seat with padding and fabric, wrap a layer of thick, heavy-grade interfacing around the surface of the wood or metal frame to be covered. That additional layer of strong, hard-wearing interfacing prevents hard edges from rubbing through the surface.

Trace a pattern

Bought a multisize paper pattern you love but your family wears different sizes? Use interfacing to fit all concerned. Trace the pieces from each size on the pattern onto lightweight non-fusible interfacing and cut them out. Use the interfacing "pattern" you've now made to cut out the pieces in each size. You can also use this trick to extend the life of a pattern. The interfacing will last much longer than the delicate paper, letting you make that perfect pair of pants or dress several times without needing to buy the pattern again.

knitting needles

They are exactly what they say they are: needles for knitting. Here are a few additional uses that will save you time and money!

Put up your hair

Wooden or colorful plastic needles make a stylish coiffure when you use them to hold a bun or chignon in place. Twist your hair up behind your head and push in two matching or contrasting needles like hairpins to hold the bun in place.

Stuff a doll or pillow

Use the blunt end of a knitting needle to push fiberfill or batting into the far corners of an item you're stuffing. A knitting needle will let you reach and plump out those difficult edges, as well as the main body.

Turn a tube

Use a large-gauge needle to turn projects that have been stitched together inside out. A large needle helps you turn corners and narrow strips, such as the arm on a stuffed doll or the stitched tube of a purse handle.

Make kebabs

String chunks of cut fruit on colored metal knitting needles and serve them with a dip of melted chocolate or plain thick yogurt flavored with vanilla and a little powdered sugar. Children love the novelty, and it makes a lovely presentation for a party.

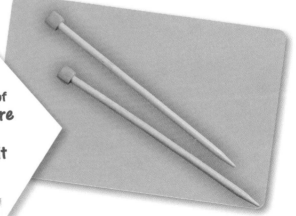

Press a knitting needle into the center of baked goods, and you'll know they're ready if the needle comes out with a few crumbs clinging to it in place of raw batter.

marking pens

Marking pens are a necessity in every sewing kit. But their uses outside of sewing are multitudinous.

Sign your work

Use a fabric marking pen to sign your name to the back or bottom of any handmade item such as a quilt or purse. Other artists sign their work—why shouldn't you record your authorship for posterity?

Decorate a T-shirt

A clutch of permanent fabric-marking pens in different colors can be used to make much more intricate designs than fabric paint. For a terrific birthday party activity, let children run riot with a white cotton T-shirt and a handful of colorful permanent fabric pens. Or you can do something a little more sophisticated, such as sketch a curling vine and a few blooming flowers around the sleeve or neckline of your favorite white V-neck.

Hide a repair

Does your pale thread show up on a seam you've repaired on a dark garment? Use a permanent marking pen that's a similar color to the fabric and "color" any visible threads to hide your stitches.

Create a needlework template

Use fabric marking pens to make your own designs for cross-stitching or embroidery. There's no need to buy preprinted kits when you can design your own, for a much more personal and distinctive piece of needlework.

Blow up (or shrink down) a design

Want to transfer an existing photo or design to your piece of fabric for needlework and make

Enjoy the savings!

your finished work either bigger or smaller than the original? Mark or overlay the picture with a 1-inch grid, then mark a 2- or 3-inch grid on your fabric (to enlarge) or a 1/4- or 1/2-inch grid on your fabric (to shrink). Then you can easily sketch what's in each box in the original into the corresponding box on your ready-marked fabric.

Cover a bleach spot

Accidentally splashed a dot of bleach on your favorite T-shirt? Color it in with a matching fabric pen. It may not totally disappear, but it will become far less noticeable. After you wash the shirt, color it in again.

oilcloth

Oilcloth was originally invented as a way to keep roofing and walls dry during construction. Today, it shows up everywhere from home porches to picnics. Where would you use this great material?

Weatherize porch furniture

That cushion on your wicker chair was supposed to be "weather resistant" but after a month of rain, it's got dark spots that won't wipe clean. Make your outdoor sofa and chair cushions weatherproof, not merely resistant, by re-covering them with covers made of PVC-coated oilcloth. The same bright lengths that make such ideal washable tablecloths can be sewn easily into envelope-style, wipe-able cushion covers that will keep the rain out, extending the life of your outdoor furniture.

Make a place mat

Why waste money on place mats for the kitchen table, especially if you have young kids who spill food all over them anyway? Cut rectangles of a brightly patterned vinyl cloth and use them for place mats instead. To keep the edges from rolling, use scissors or pinking shears to cut a 1-inch fringe all around the edges. When the place mats get worn or dirty, cut fresh mats!

Line a drawer

Decorative kitchen paper for lining drawers and shelves can be pricey, but you can save yourself money and prevent wear and tear on your cabinetry by lining your kitchen storage with vinyl instead. Cut lengths to fit, and either tack down with thumbtacks or use a light spritz of spray adhesive under the corners.

Protect a baby's bottom

Many parents hesitate before setting their child into a shopping cart at the grocery store or before using a grubby high chair or booster seat at a restaurant, especially in winter, when colds and flu are rife. Plonk that little bottom down with impunity when you carry along a square of fabric-backed oilcloth. Just unfold and place it over the seat before putting down your precious cargo. You can also use your vinyl square as an impromptu changing pad when using public changing tables. When it starts to look at all worn or dirty, throw it away and cut a fresh square!

Cover a book

Just bought that new hardcover everyone is talking about? If you're getting ready to take a plane trip or a long car journey, chances are you're going to rip or scuff the paper dust jacket. Instead, cut a rectangle of vinyl that's 3 inches taller than the height of the book and 6 inches wider than the open book lying flat. Fold the long sides of the rectangle (the top and bottom) by 1 inch, gluing these folds flat with glue or spray adhesive, then fold in the edges to make a 2-inch wide flap on either side, gluing these just at the very top and bottom edges. Remove the dust jacket and insert the hardcover flaps in the edge flaps of your brand new, waterproof, wipe-able, reusable "travel jacket."

pipe cleaners

Traditionally, they're used for exactly what they sound like they're used for: as a way to clean a pipe. But there are so many more ways to use these familiar items.

Scrub in a tight space

True to their original use, pipe cleaners fit well into narrow spaces. But you don't need to limit their cleaning abilities to pipes. Use one to dust

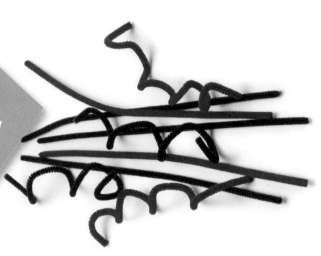

Use a pipe cleaner to dust off your sewing machine's tight corners, clear a pressure cooker safety valve, or clean other tight spaces.

off your sewing machine's tight corners, clear a pressure cooker safety valve, or clean the dust from around the trackball of the computer mouse. You can also use one to clean the little vents on your gas stove top to keep the ring burning clear.

Keep your shoe on

Just busted a shoelace but you're on your way out the door? Grab a pipe cleaner and thread it through the top of your shoe just like a lace. It will keep your shoe on until you get to the store for a replacement. It's tougher than a twist tie—but a pipe cleaner can replace one of those, too!

Twist up a set of holiday napkin rings

Give the kids or grandkids a task while you finish preparing the meal. Have them twist together pipe cleaners of seasonal colors—use yellow, orange, red, and brown for Thanksgiving, for example—and tie up the napkins for dinner.

Keep kids busy on the road

Parents panic about what to take along to keep little ones entertained on long road trips or flights. Don't overlook pipe cleaners. Take along a colorful heap of them for kids to twist together into animal shapes or make necklaces and bracelets.

ribbons

Ribbons are among the very first materials used to adorn garments and date back beyond the Middle Ages. Even Geoffrey Chaucer mentioned "ribbands" in *The Canterbury Tales*. Overlooked and often forgotten, they are divine used in many other circumstances.

Hang a picture

For an old-fashioned look in your picture hanging, use a length of heavy, wide ribbon and tie the ends through the two metal D hooks on the back of a picture frame. Loop the top over a decorative hook (or even a nail) on the wall several inches above the frame, or use a longer length of ribbon for a more dramatic presentation and drape it high above off a picture rail.

Update a necklace

This season's fashion-forward style in jewelry includes necklaces that tie with ribbon rather than clipping with metal fasteners. Hang a favorite pendant off a narrow length of dark grosgrain ribbon and tie it to any length you like. For a more exciting and contemporary look, press grommets into one end each of two lengths of a wider ribbon, and suspend a length of an old

necklace between them. Use a twist of chain, a collection of funky beads, or a length of river pearls—any old necklace that needs a new look.

Personalize a photo, card, or note

Use a hole puncher to make holes in a photo mat, birthday card, or piece of notepaper. Use long and short lengths of ribbon either to tie bows between two holes or to weave back and forth through a series of holes for a fun, funky personalized look to any heavy piece of paper.

trimming

Trimming is used to add a bit of pizzazz to fabric on a garment, upholstery, curtains—everywhere. Buy it in bits and pieces to give a little zip to anything and everything around you.

Decorate a gift

Pre-tied bows and curling paper ribbons on a gift-wrapped present are so dull. Make your wrapped gifts highly distinctive by tying a length of decorative trimming around the box. From a run of tatted lace to a dangling golden fringe to colorful cotton bobbles, your package will shine on a table of ordinary gifts. With a colorful and cheerful length of trimming, you can even skip the paper. And the lucky recipient can put the trimming to his or her own use after opening!

Perk up a lamp shade

With very little effort, you can bring a whole new look to a living room or lounge by adding some striking trimming to the base of the lamp shades. Go for an elegant gold braid all the way around the top and bottom, or put a long fringe around the base of the shade on a tall standing lamp, or get a hip mod look by hanging bobbly fringe all over a little shade. Brightening up the lamp shades in a room is like dressing the room in new clothes. Your room will be ready to party!

Have a Victorian Christmas

Get an old-fashioned look by draping your holiday tree with yards and yards of wide lace trimming instead of tinsel or sparkling ropes. Make small paper fans out of folded craft paper and clip them to the branches. Finish the look with white lights and a few gauzy bows tied here and there. You'll hear a chorus of approval singing as you work!

Update a photo frame

Glue braid, bobbles, a strip of lace, or a short fringe all around an ordinary photo frame and make the picture inside spring to life!

Give a dress a swing

Make up your own flapper dress that's reminiscent of the 1920s by stitching row after row of long fringe all the way around a simple sheath dress. Whether you're wearing it for a Halloween party with a feather in your hair or simply to kick up your heels for a night on the town, you'll be the belle of the ball.

Velcro

Where would we be without Velcro? But who knew that it had so very many uses!

Replace duvet cover fasteners

It's hard enough to slip a full-size quilt or duvet cover back on after washing it, but worse is when you get to the bottom and realize you've buttoned the quilt cover on crooked and have to start all over. Replace your buttons or snaps with Velcro, and not only will quilt covers go back on with ease, but the ends won't poke out if you lose a button.

Keep a pen where you need it

Does your refrigerator pen always disappear the moment that you need to write something on your grocery list? Put a strip of Velcro directly on the door of the fridge and glue the other side along your favorite pen or pencil. Now you'll never forget to add peanut butter to the list while you rummage in a drawer for a pen.

Hang a smoke detector

To make it easier to take smoke detectors down twice a year to change the batteries, as recommended for fire safety, stick them to the ceiling with a wide strip of Velcro. You won't have to perch on a stepstool trying to jigger the detector down from its screws when you can just tear it away.

Secure a first-aid kit in your car

It seems like a good idea to keep a small first-aid kit in the car. It's there when you need it at soccer practice or when you have a flat and need a bandage after wrestling with the jack! But the plastic boxes slip and slide and end up all over the floor and eventually back in the house. Keep it firmly in place by putting a Velcro strip down in the back window ledge and putting the other side on the bottom of the kit. That bandage will be there when you need it.

Hold the car mat under the driver's feet

The floor mat that came with your car is usually carefully fitted so that it will lie flat under the driver's seat. But what if you get a replacement? Don't risk the dangers of a mat that slides under your feet or potentially bunches up under the brake pedal. When you put down a replacement mat from the auto store, be sure it's well secured on the left and right with Velcro. That way it will stay in place without question when you drive—and rip right up when it's time to clean.

> **Put a strip of Velcro directly on the door of the fridge and glue the other side along your favorite pen or pencil.**

Make a sink skirt

Put the zing back in a lifeless bathroom with a colorful sink skirt. Wrap the base of a plain porcelain wall sink with a wide strip of cheerful fabric that's long enough to reach the floor. Stick a strip of Velcro all the way around the base of the sink and stick on the skirt with the opposite side of Velcro. This way, you can whip it off in a hurry if you need to launder the skirt or dry it after a vigorous washing! Best of all, you can swap in a different skirt with ease if this one gets soiled or boring.

Replace buttons

Buttons on clothing can be very difficult as fingers get older and stiffer. Make dressing simpler for your older loved one by replacing tiny buttons or tricky snaps with small pieces of Velcro. For clothing, use the type that can be stitched on, not stuck on with double-sided tape, and be sure to use a small patch of Velcro to replace each closure, not a long wide strip. Too much Velcro can cling hard and make it just as hard to get clothes off as a stiff button.

webbing

Designed for use as belts, suspenders, sandals, and even back braces, polyester webbing has a plethora of other uses. Here are just a few!

Substitute for a bungee cord

Can't lay hands on your bungee cord when you need to strap luggage to your car's roof? Prefer to ensure that those bikes won't come off their travel rack on the back of your camper? Polyester webbing is strong and tough and can hold a knot well. Keep a roll of webbing in the back of your car and you'll have a strong, lightweight cord for any packing eventuality.

Weave a mat

Use natural jute webbing to weave a distinctive and hard-wearing floor mat or area rug. Weave over and under just like making the lattice top on a pastry, tacking down one end of each strip to your work surface so you can pull against it for a tighter weave. Use scissors to even off the edges

Put a zipper in the upper half of the front of a homemade Christmas stocking. When the presents are bulging out, you can pull down the zipper a little so they'll all fit!

of the finished mat and seal it all the way around with binding tape.

Make a tool belt

If you're a workman who needs a heavy-duty tool belt—well, chances are you've already got one. But if you're a weekend DIY warrior who just needs a hammer and screwdriver at hand while doing a few light home repairs, you can make a stripped down, lightweight belt that frees your hands while keeping indispensable tools nearby. Cut a long length of jute or polyester webbing that fits around your waist with an extra 2 feet to spare. Use a sewing machine to sew two loops into the webbing, about 5 inches each, just big enough to slip a hammer through and let it hang. When you need to do a few repairs, tie on your tool belt and get cracking.

zippers

Invented a good 12 years before the Civil War, the zipper was invented to, well, hold things together. They're everywhere now, but we've found even more uses for them than the obvious.

Pad a pajama pillow

Set a zipper up the front of a satiny pillowcase that's several inches larger than the pillow form that you have to stuff it. Then fit the oversize case over the pillow, leaving room inside for a folded pair of pajamas to recline on your bed all day.

Make a friendship bracelet

Perfect for the preteen set and an ideal activity for a girl's birthday party, make snazzy friendship bracelets by putting snaps or Velcro on the ends of 7-inch zippers. Kids can decorate the bracelets themselves with beads, sequins, buttons, and fabric markers.

Decorate a doll

Bring new life to an old rag doll by adding zippers. Put a zipper in an old dress to make it easier for little fingers to manage. And put a short zipper in place of the mouth on a rag doll's face and give new meaning to the phrase "zip your lips"!

Turn teddy into a secret safe

Use a seam ripper to open a discreet side or bottom seam on a stuffed animal such as a teddy bear. Remove a handful of stuffing—enough to make some space inside but not so much as to make the bear collapse. Stitch a zipper into the seam, and your secret home safe is ready for use. Put your jewelry into a soft bag and stuff it inside, or protect any cash you may have lying around. It's an easy way to hide anything you want in plain sight.

Zip up your (Christmas) stockings

For a charming and highly personal approach to holiday stockings, put a zipper in the upper half of the front of a homemade Christmas stocking. When Santa brings so many presents that they're bulging out, he can pull down the zipper a little so they'll all fit!

Be creative and frugal!

SCHOOL AND PARTY SUPPLIES

THANK GOODNESS FOR DOLLAR STORES!
They stock essential supplies for you and your
house—soap, shampoo, rubber gloves, laundry
detergent, paper towels, and so on—that you're
likely to use on a regular basis. But don't forget
that dollar stores can be fun to visit, too! Two
aisles in particular provide items that are a blast
to browse: school supplies and party supplies.
Whether you're looking for snazzy notebooks
for your child's first day of school or brilliant
bows and ribbons to adorn your best friend's
birthday present, you'll likely find a stunning
array of products that you need and want. And
don't forget that many of these items have uses
well beyond what their manufacturers intended.
Use your imagination—and the tips that
follow—to get the most use out of your new
school and party supplies.

adhesive tape

One of the most versatile school supplies available, adhesive tape can be used on everything from your face to your shoes and from your car to your cake. Forget about using it to stick two pieces of paper together. It's way too busy doing other more important jobs around the house!

Help flowers stand straight

If your cut flowers are a few days old and have started to droop, use transparent tape to bring them back to attention. Remove the flowers and fill the vase with fresh water. Place several pieces of tape across the top of the vase, leaving small gaps for the stems. Put the flowers back in the vase and enjoy several more days of your bouquet.

Remove a splinter

As long as the splinter is sticking out of your skin, you may be able to remove it without tweezers or a needle. Lay a piece of adhesive tape over the affected area, and rub your finger gently over the tape until it makes contact with the splinter. Pull the tape up, and the splinter may come with it. This method works particularly well if you find many small splinters near the surface of your skin. It also works if you need to remove small cactus prickles from your fingers.

Get rid of a furrow

If you're a deep thinker or a big worrier, you may have a deep furrow in your brow. And if you don't want it, you can get rid of it with tape. Just rub your regular moisturizer into the furrow at night before you go to bed, then pull the skin taut, and put a piece of tape across the smoothed-out wrinkle. Make sure the tape sticks onto dry skin, rather than on the moisturized skin, or it may not last through the night. Do this every night for a month, and you'll see results you like.

Protect your library card

And your bus pass, your lunch ticket, your car registration, and any other small piece of paper that you use repeatedly or need to protect in your wallet. Cover them with transparent tape. (Clear shipping tape works well, too.) Tape both sides of the card, then cut the excess tape at the sides of the card. You'll keep the card in good shape, and scanners will be able to read it well.

Think like a shoelace

Wrap the ends of string or ribbon tightly with transparent tape to make it look like a shoelace. Stringing beads, macaroni, or anything else you want will be much easier.

Nix the adhesive

Ignore the adhesive on the permit sticker that you need to attach to the inside of your car's windshield—it makes removing the permit messy and difficult. Instead, simply tape the permit where it belongs. You'll have no trouble removing the sticker when its time has come.

Keep your sweets safe

Protect your cakes, cookies, and other sweet treats from ants by surrounding the goodies with a circle of adhesive tape. Place the tape sticky side up and you—rather than the ants—will have a yummy dessert.

Clean your comb

Even if your hair is always as clean as a whistle, your comb will still need to be cleaned occasionally. Pick up loose hair and accumulated dirt between the teeth by pressing adhesive tape on one side of the comb and then removing it. To fully clean your comb, soak it in a bowl of warm water and shampoo or a bowl of white vinegar. Scrub it with a toothbrush, rinse it, and let it dry.

Find the beginning of plastic wrap

Anyone who has ever used plastic wrap has undoubtedly had trouble finding the beginning of it on the roll. Here's an easy way to avoid that trap: Wrap tape around your finger with the sticky side out. Tap your finger on the plastic wrap until you discover the edge, then use another piece of tape to lift the edge off the roll.

Help chains travel well

Cover your necklace chains with tape before you take them on the road. The tape will prevent them from tangling.

X marks the spot

Make an X out of tape on your wall the next time you hang a picture or drive a nail into the wall for any reason. The tape will keep the wallboard from cracking or the plaster from chipping. It will also keep the paint from peeling off if you need to remove the nail.

Protect your wood floor

Don't let your grandmother's rocking chair ruin the finish on your wood floor. Just place a piece of adhesive tape along the bottom of each rocker, and your floor will be safe.

balloons

Balloons may be colorful, whimsical, delightful decorations, but they're otherwise useless, right? Pop that thought right now, and consider all these jobs balloons can do.

Put your bouquet in a balloon

You won't have to wait until the last minute to buy a bouquet for your hostess if you know how to keep the flowers fresh as you travel. Here's the trick: Fill a balloon with 1/2 cup of water, and pull the mouth of the balloon over the ends of your flowers. Prevent the balloon from falling off by wrapping a rubber band around the top.

Run off rabbits

Cut deflated, used metallic birthday balloons into vertical strips and use them to scare rabbits, squirrels, and birds away from your garden. Hang them from poles near your plants to keep them safe.

Travel with a balloon

Toss an uninflated balloon in your suitcase on your next trip in case you need a cold or hot pack for a twisted ankle or sore muscles. If you need an

Toss an uninflated balloon in your suitcase on your next trip in case you need a cold or hot pack for a twisted ankle or sore muscles.

ice pack or a heat pack at your destination, just fill the balloon with very cold water or very hot water and place it on the problem area.

Keep your bandage dry

Helping a cut heal means keeping it clean and protected and dry. Getting through the day without getting a cut on a finger wet is almost impossible—unless you get help from a balloon. Slip a balloon over your affected finger when you need to get your hands wet (in the shower or doing dishes, for example) and you'll keep your cut dry.

Chase cats off the couch

Tie some small inflated balloons to your couch or chair if you want to keep your cat off the furniture. The loud noise of popping will scare off your cat and keep him at a safe distance.

Scare off skunks

Tie bunches of blown-up latex birthday balloons (or congratulations balloons, or any other kind) around your house to ward off skunks. Be sure to place them wherever you suspect the skunks might lurk—on your patio, around the perimeter of your house, or near your trash. The rustling balloons will frighten them into leaving. A bonus: Raccoons are scared of balloons, too.

binder

Dollar stores sell plastic three-ring binders in a rainbow of colors. Designed to help students keep loose-leaf paper organized, they can be used for more than loose-leaf paper and for more than students. Check out the tips below.

Organize your garden

Devote an entire binder to keeping your garden organized. Make notes on what is planted where; when you planted seeds, bulbs, and seedlings; and the names of what you've planted. Make sure your binder has pockets for plant tags and receipts—even seed packets, as long as you won't forget you've stored them here.

Keep contacts under control

Make lists of contact information—phone numbers (including cell phones), addresses, e-mail addresses—of police and fire departments, gas and electric companies, doctors and dentists, and so on, and keep them handy in a binder. Organize the binder by type of contact: medical, home repair, financial, family, and more, and keep the binder where everyone in the family can find it.

Use regular old binder clips to seal bags of potato chips or cookies. The snacks will stay fresh longer.

Create a custom cookbook

It doesn't matter if you clip recipes or you write your own; insert plastic page protectors into the binder, organize by type of food or dish, and pop the recipes into the protectors. When you're cooking, just remove the whole page, which is now protected from splattering.

binder clips

Bigger and better than ordinary paper clips, binder clips also have bigger ambitions. They don't just hold pieces of paper together; they hold entire *pads* of paper together. And they can do so much more! Here are some big ideas for these big clips.

Mount a photo exhibit

String a piece of wire or rope from one wall to another nearby, and nail both ends into the walls. Put your photos in 8 1/2-by-11-inch clear document sleeves. Attach the photo holders to the line with binder clips, stand back, and admire your display.

Seal snacks for freshness

Forget about buying "chip clips" or using clothespins to keep bags of potato chips, tortilla chips, or cookies shut. Specially designed clips can be a waste of money, and clothespins may not keep the all the air out of the bags. Instead, use regular old binder clips to seal them. The snacks will stay fresh longer.

Clip open a cookbook

Reading a recipe takes time, and your cookbook isn't giving you the time you need if it can't stay open to the page you want. Hold the pages open with two binder clips—one for each side of the book—and you can finally relax while you read and cook.

BINDER CLIPS

Louis E. Baltzley invented the binder clip in 1911 as a way to help his father, a writer, join his manuscript pages more easily. Prior to this springy clip, his dad held pages together by punching holes and using thread. Invention ran in Baltzley's family: He was a grandson of Elias Howe, the first American to hold a sewing machine patent.

Keep travel documents handy

You need your itinerary, your airplane ticket, your boarding pass, your photo ID, your passport (perhaps), your list of important phone numbers, and more when you travel by plane these days. Rather than scrounging around each time you need to produce a document, keep them together with a binder clip. Staying so organized will (hopefully!) get you through security and check-in much faster.

Organize your money

Keep your bills handy by making a money clip out of a binder clip. Place your paper money in a neat stack, fold the stack in half, and attach a binder clip. Your money will be right at hand the next time you need it.

boxes

Dollar stores generally carry a wide selection of decorative boxes, and they display them in the party supply aisle. They are the perfect solution for gift-givers who don't like to wrap gifts, and they can serve other purposes, too. Check them out below.

Use a box for a gift

Not an original idea? It is if you put the wrapped gift in a decorative box, then put that box in a larger box, then place that box in a larger box still. You can leave the boxes unwrapped—they're decorative, after all—or you can have even more fun with the recipient by wrapping each box individually.

Think interior design

Stack three or four decorative boxes of descending size near a chair and place a small plant on top. The plant will cascade down the tiered boxes, creating a lovely focal point in the room.

Corral remotes

Stop losing your remote control—or several remotes, since so many electronics require so many remotes—by keeping them together in a decorative box. You'll clear up clutter, get organized, and add a touch of color to your TV stand.

Wrap it up

Store Christmas ribbons and bows, small pieces of wrapping paper, and scissors and tape in three different Christmas-themed boxes, and stack them in your living room. The holiday theme will enliven the room, and you'll have everything you need to wrap up another perfect Christmas.

Be creative and frugal!

Keep your appliances clean

Use an upside-down decorative box (without its top) to cover small kitchen appliances like mini food processors, blenders, and coffeemakers. It's a great way to keep them free of dust and dirt.

bubble wrap

Popping the bubbles in bubble wrap is entertaining, but not really the best use of the product. What's its best use? Most people use it to cushion items in packages they send. But they're not thinking of the glorious versatility of bubble wrap. Consider all the possibilities described here.

Take it shopping

Grocery shopping, that is. Particularly in summer, keep some bubble wrap in the trunk of your car so you can wrap up frozen foods to keep them from thawing out on the trip home. Even ice cream stays firm with an insulating layer of bubbles around it.

Protect your pants

Keep unwanted creases from imprinting themselves on the slacks you hang in your closet by wrapping the hangers in bubble wrap. Roll a layer of bubble wrap around the hanger bar, making sure that the smooth side of the wrap faces the pants and the bubbles face the bar. Keep the wrap in place with duct tape.

Plan a party on bubble wrap

Young kids like nothing better than to move and shake and make lots of noise. Fulfill all their wishes by holding a dance party on bubble wrap. Tape several sheets of bubble wrap together until you form a large square or rectangle, and make sure that the bubbles face up (so that the dancers will pop them as they boogie). You may want to duct tape the dance floor to your floor so that it doesn't move with the dancers. Freeze dancing is particularly fun on bubble wrap.

Shape up your shoes

Place a small piece of rolled-up bubble wrap in each of your shoes to help them maintain their shape. Roll up longer pieces to keep the calves of your boots standing upright—and to keep their shape.

Ride in comfort

Your car seat may be comfortable for short trips, but what about long ones? Make it dreamy by covering the seat and the back in a double layer of bubble wrap (with the bubbles facing out). The bubble wrap will support your body and provide a comfy ride over the long haul.

Sleep comfortably outside

Take a six-foot piece of bubble wrap with you the next time you go camping. Place it under your sleeping bag before you retire for the night. The bubble wrap will provide a cushion for your body and act as a tarp to keep your sleeping bag dry.

Protect tree trunks

Whether you mow your lawn or your lawn service mows for you, you'll want to protect small, fragile trees and tree seedlings. How? Wrap bubble wrap around their thin trunks. Keep the bubble wrap in place with masking tape. You can easily remove the bubble wrap when the lawn is done.

Insulate a doghouse

Bubble wrap is a safe, non-toxic option for insulating a doghouse to keep your pooch toasty in winter. And, unlike with fiberglass, if your pet gnaws at it, he'll merely get a surprise if a bubble pops!

Keep cold items cold

Heading out for a picnic? Wrap items you want to stay cold—cans of soft drinks, egg salad sandwiches, popsicles, and so on—in bubble wrap. Your picnic will be much more appetizing when you arrive at your destination.

Baby your tools

Protect your tools from each other and from the toolbox by lining the toolbox with bubble wrap. Hold the wrap in place with duct tape. The cushioning will help your tools last longer.

Make a perfect pillow

Pillows and camping don't mix, unless you make a pillow out of bubble wrap. Simply fold the bubble wrap a few times and place it inside a pillowcase. The bubble wrap won't get dirty and will provide a gentle cushion for your head.

Heading out for a picnic? Wrap items you want to stay cold in bubble wrap.

candy tins

Whether or not candy is part of the deal, candy tins are a good buy. They make nice decorative pieces and can also be used for assorted jobs around the house. Put them to work with the ideas below (and hope that they come with candy inside!).

Organize your workbench

Keep clutter to a minimum on your workbench by using several candy tins to hold small quantities of picture hangers, washers, nuts, and other pieces that don't have a logical home.

Corral quarters for your car

Keep a collection of quarters in a candy tin in your glove compartment. You'll be surprised how often you'll open the box—for parking, tolls, or even to buy a quick snack.

Create a mini-sewing kit

Store a few needles, thread, a thimble, straight pins, safety pins, and a button or two in a candy tin, and keep it in your suitcase as an emergency sewing kit. You'll have plenty of supplies to make quick repairs when you're on the road.

Round up a broken necklace

Don't let a broken necklace break your heart. Find as many pieces as you can, and store them in a candy tin. Take the tin with you the next time you visit the jewelry repair shop.

cap erasers

Pencils have a number of alternate uses, and surprisingly enough, pencil erasers do, too. Dollar stores sell pencil cap erasers in addition to pencils, and they work just as well as pencil erasers in their alternate universe.

Replace the back of your earring

The backs of pierced earrings seem to have a magical—and disturbing—way of disappearing, often at crucial times. As long as you have a pencil cap eraser (or even the eraser on a pencil) nearby, you can fix the situation pronto. Cut a small part off the eraser with a knife or scissors, and position it on the back of your ear. Place the earring in your ear as you normally would, and stick the eraser onto the earring shaft to keep it in place.

Erase marks on leather

Though scuff marks usually end up on a vinyl floor, they can show up on a leather couch or chair, too. Get rid of them by rubbing them with a pencil cap eraser. A regular pencil eraser will also work.

Get rid of grout grime

Cleaning bathroom tile grout can be difficult, especially in the corners of a tub and other tight places. Use a new pencil cap eraser (or a new eraser at the end of a pencil) to clean those hard-to-reach areas of grout grime.

WAY BACK WHEN...

Schrafft's Candy Tins

Back in the day, companies like Schrafft's, near Boston, sold its sweets in fancy tins. These containers had panache, and you can still find them in antique shops and online. A typical tin was round with a tapered top. Schrafft's candy company was founded in the late 19th century and has the distinction of sponsoring the first annual telecast of *The Wizard of Oz*.

chalk

Chalk isn't just for kids anymore. In fact, it can be used for very grown-up chores: filling holes, preventing rust, and even keeping ants out of your house. It has other uses, too (and you can always use it to draw on the driveway!).

Fill a hole

When you're filling a small hole with plaster, it's hard to keep the patch from sinking into the hole, however small. Break a few pieces of chalk and stuff them into the hole, wedging them against the sides, and then plaster over. The chalk both fills the hole and provides something for the fresh plaster to grab.

Set your screwdriver straight

Just as chalking a pool cue stops slippage when the cue hits the ball, chalking a screwdriver can stop slippage when the tool tightens a screw. Simply rub chalk on the tip of the screwdriver's blade before your next project for best results.

Keep a file functioning

Metal files tend to get their teeth filled up with debris from whatever you're filing. Run a piece of chalk back and forth over the file to leave a layer of chalk on it before starting work and the waste won't clog the file.

Draw a line in the sand

Actually, draw a line of chalk around windowsills and doorways to prevent ants from entering your house. Use the same tactic for protecting your outdoor plants from ants and slugs—scatter powdered chalk around the base of the plants.

Solve a sticking door mystery

If your door sticks but you don't know exactly where you should sand it, use chalk in your detective work. Open the door, and mark the sides of the door that touch the door frame with chalk. Shut the door, open it again, and take note of where the chalk is missing. Those are the areas that need to be sanded.

Prevent rust

Keep rust out of your toolbox—and stop your tools from pitting and rusting—by placing a few pieces of chalk in your toolbox. The chalk will absorb any moisture and keep your tools (and your toolbox) rust-free.

Place a few pieces of chalk in your toolbox to help keep rust out of it.

Liquid Paper

Bette Nesmith Graham was interested in art but had a child to support so she took a secretarial job. Meticulous, she developed a paint to match her office stationery; it hid typos better than erasing. Fellow typists wanted "Mistake Out," so Graham trademarked it as Liquid Paper. The Gillette Corporation bought her successful company in 1979 for $47.5 million plus royalties.

clipboard

Clipboards have such a singular purpose that it's hard to believe they can be used for anything other than holding a sheet of paper steady. But clipboards are surprisingly versatile, doing everything from hanging pants to holding maps while you drive. Here are some tips on how to use them differently.

Create a frame

Not all clipboards are dull and dark with a utilitarian metal clip on top. The latest generation of clipboards comes in a variety of materials, from plastic in neon colors to space-age aluminum. Hang one of these stylish clipboards on your wall and clip a photo to it. You can easily swap in a new photo whenever you like.

Corral school papers

Keep a clipboard designated for permission slips, school activity reminders, and tests that need to be signed in an agreed-on spot in your house. Your kids will know where to put important papers that you need to see, and you'll know where to look for them.

Keep your pants crease-free

If you don't have a hanger designed for pants and don't want to fold them over an ordinary hanger, use a clipboard to keep your pants looking sharp. Hang a clipboard from a hook on the inside of your bedroom door or your closet, and snap your cuffs to the clipboard. Your crease-free pants will be ready whenever you want them.

Organize your sandpaper

Most of the time, sandpaper is still good after the first or second time you use it. The trick is to find that used sandpaper again, often after several month. Hang a clipboard on a hook on your workshop pegboard. Just clip still-usable sandpaper to the board when you are done, and it will be handy the next time you need it.

Make a blackboard with a clip

Paint the clipboard with blackboard paint. Attach a piece of chalk to the hole at the top of the clip. Hang the clipboard by the phone or near the door. You can clip notes or bills to the top while scribbling messages on the board.

correction fluid

You'll find a lot of power in one little bottle of correction fluid. You can use it to fix tubs, cars, and decorative china—and that's not all! Make sure you keep a bottle of it on hand, because you'll find many unusual uses for it around the house.

Touch up your paint job

White moldings make any room look a little more elegant, but small marks and scrapes take away from that beauty. Return your room to its former glory by painting liquid correction fluid over any faults you find. To re-create the moldings' glossy look, cover the correction fluid with clear nail polish. (And don't forget that correction fluid works beautifully on small stains on walls and ceilings, too.)

Cover up a car's scratch

Don't despair if your nice white car gets a scratch; just get some correction fluid and paint it right on the mark. The scratch will be gone before the correction fluid even dries.

Fix a marred tub

Enamel bathtubs and other enamel surfaces can get scratched, no matter how carefully you care for them. The good news is that repairing a scratched tub is even easier than scratching it! Clean the affected area with a cotton ball

moistened with rubbing alcohol, and let it dry. Simply brush on the correction fluid for a quick and easy fix.

Welcome winter on your windows

Paint white snowflakes on your windows with correction fluid to usher in the winter season. When the snow outside has melted and thoughts have turned to spring, remove the snowflakes using glass cleaner, vinegar and water, or nail polish remover. If the correction fluid is particularly stubborn, you can get rid of it with a painter's tool: a single razor blade in a holder (used for scraping paint off of glass).

Repair decorative china

Use correction fluid to cover small nicks and dark lines or stains in white decorative china. Do not use correction fluid on anything that is intended for eating and drinking.

Cover a stain on fabric

Your white blouse is perfect except for a dot of ink on the cuff, and you can't get that drip of red wine out of the tablecloth. Use a tiny dab of correction fluid to cover the stains.

Instant savings!

crayons

Ah, to be young again—young enough to use crayons. But wait! You don't have to be under a certain age to use them, or even to use them for their original purpose. Check out the alternate ways you can use crayons, and use them to your (young) heart's content.

Fix furniture scratches

Whether your cat scratched your sofa's legs senseless or your young child scratched your coffee table with his scissors, you'll want to cover up the damage. How? Use a crayon. Find the crayon that matches the wood finish, and soften it with a hair dryer. Color in the scratches with the softened crayon, and then buff the repaired area with a clean rag.

Make a fire starter

A fire starter makes it easy to get a fire crackling in a fireplace. With crayons, making a chemical-free fire starter is easy. Melt crayons in a tin can set into a saucepan half-filled with water over medium heat. Wrap a pinecone loosely with string and roll it in the melted crayon, pulling out a tail of string to serve as a wick. Let the crayon soak into the pinecone, then let it cool and harden on waxed paper. To use, arrange twigs over the starter, add logs, and light.

Seal envelopes

Melt old crayons with a lighter over a cup lined with tin foil. Drip the wax from the cup over an envelope into pretty patterns before the wax hardens, or form a single spot and use a metal stamp to imprint a shape or initial you like.

Create colored candles

You don't have to be an experienced home candlemaker to get lovely results. Start with plain white candles. Melt a handful of crayons all the same color in tin can set in a pan half-filled with water over low heat. When the crayons melt, lift out the can onto a heatproof surface and dip the candles to coat them in a colorful way.

Decorate Easter eggs

Fancy Easter egg dye kits usually include a stick of wax for marking the egg before dipping it into the dye—the wax repels the dye and keeps the surface its original color. Forget about the stick of wax. Just use a crayon for a similar effect.

Color in the scratches on your wooden furniture with a softened crayon.

double-stick tape

Double-stick or double-sided tape can keep you organized, safe, and free from embarrassment. Who knew such a simple invention had so many important functions? You will, after you read this!

Repair a sagging hem

Staples and safety pins are good tools to use on a torn hem, but double-stick tape is even better because it won't show. Lay the pants or skirt on a table, counter, or desk, and cut a length of double-stick tape the width and length of the tear. Place the tape onto the hem, and then firmly press the two pieces of fabric together. Return to the world with confidence!

Secure throw rugs

Both people and pets can slip on a throw rug if it lacks a backing that keeps it in place. Don't put yourself, your family, and your dog or cat at risk of falling—just attach the rug to the floor with some double-sided tape.

Take a seat

Sliding off a chair during a dinner party would be considered very bad manners, so don't subject your guests to such a terrible faux pas. Stick the seat cushion to the chair with double-stick tape, and your guests will stay in one place.

Keep screws in place

Lay a few lines of double-stick tape on your workbench before you start a project. Stick nuts and bolts and screws to the tape as you work. You won't lose the pieces, and you'll know exactly where to find them.

envelopes

Envelopes have come a long way from just holding notes sent through the mail. No longer only plain white and a certain shape, envelopes come in all colors and sizes and have many more uses, too. Here are some of the best.

Feed the shredder faster

Whether you're disposing of ATM receipts, credit card receipts, or any other receipts that contain financial or personal information, you should shred them rather than toss them in the trash. And the fastest way to get rid of them is to put them in an envelope and shred the envelope, rather than individual receipts.

Get ready for the grocery store

Use an envelope as a shopping list—record what you need on the non-flap side—and keep coupons for items you plan to buy inside. When you go to the grocery store you'll have everything you need in one neat package.

Make a funnel

Refilling the salt and pepper shakers can be a messy job, unless you have a funnel. And don't despair if you don't have a funnel—you can make one quickly and easily out of a plain old envelope. Just seal it, cut it in half diagonally (suddenly you have two funnels), and cut a small corner off of each one. Now you have one funnel for salt and one for pepper!

Create family files

Need a place to hold gift cards after the holidays? Give each family member an envelope, and have them keep all gift cards in their designated envelope. You can keep all the envelopes or they can keep their own. Either way, the gift cards won't go to the wrong person. Use this system to keep other small family property divided, too.

The Pink Pearl Eraser

When the F. W. Woolworth Co. arranged to have a pencil named "Pearl" sold exclusively in its stores, the company had no idea it was helping to birth an icon. The A. W. Faber Pencil Co. took a revolutionary step: They attached erasers directly to their products, and the Pearl got a pink one. Erasers (when sold separately) were named after the pencils they first adorned. The Pink Pearl eraser is recognized as classic, and is a staple on back-to-school lists.

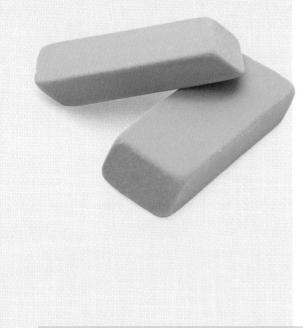

Secure teacher notes

Binders and backpacks are notorious black holes, particularly when it comes to notes sent home from teachers. Help your child keep those notes safe by punching three holes in one side of a manila envelope and placing it in the binder. Make sure notes are put in the envelope, and you'll never have to search for them again.

eraser

The main job of an eraser is to...erase. And erasers are generally used to remove pencil marks from paper. Here are a few completely different kinds of marks to remove, as well as jobs for an eraser that have nothing to do with erasing.

Rub away residue

Nothing destroys the joy of a new item more than the sticky residue left by the price tag. You scrub and you rub and you can't get rid of the gummy mess—unless you use a pencil eraser! Rub the goo with an eraser and get back to enjoying your purchase.

Clean a computer keyboard

When you've been pounding away on your computer keys for a while, you may notice dark grime building up on the curved face of the keys. It's risky to use water or cleaning products there, but you can rub the dirt gently away with an eraser, blowing to clear any eraser dust.

Clean spots off suede

Rub gently with an eraser not only to remove minor stains and marks from suede shoes and bags, but also to fluff up the suede fibers.

Erase the stain

If you find unidentifiable small smudges and spots on your walls, get rid of them with an art gum eraser. Rub the wall gently, and watch the stain disappear. You can also use an art gum eraser to rub fingerprints off wallpaper.

Make a pin cushion

Stop storing your straight pins in a box. They're too easy to spill and too hard to pick up, one at a time. Instead, stick them in a pencil eraser. You'll get exactly one when you want exactly one.

gift ribbon

When you tie ribbon around a gift, the ribbon serves only a decorative purpose—it's not really holding the package together. Why not give ribbon a real job to do? You can find one in the tips below.

Make stake ties

Use gift-wrapping ribbon to tie tall flowers like snapdragons and viny vegetables like tomatoes to their stakes. The ribbon is soft and flexible, so it won't hurt the plants.

Replace your lace

Shoelaces have a tendency to break at the worst possible time—usually as you tie them on your way out the door. If you don't have an extra on hand and have places to go and things to do, just replace your shoelace with a ribbon until you can buy another one.

Identify your luggage

Ever notice at baggage pickup how everyone on your flight has exactly the same suitcase you do? Set yours apart by tying a bright ribbon around the handle. You'll know it's yours, and if the ribbon is bright enough, you might even see it first!

grocery bags

Big paper bags—the kind your groceries are packed in—have multiple uses around the house. But the lunch-size paper bags you find at the dollar store have several uses, too, many of which having nothing to do with lunch. Here are big uses for these small bags.

Wrap small presents

Lunch bags are the perfect size to wrap CDs, DVDs, and small to medium-sized boxes. Cut the bag open, lay it flat, place the gift to be wrapped in the center, and wrap it as usual. Either tie a colorful ribbon around the plain brown wrap or decorate the paper with colored pencils, markers, or paint.

Gently rub suede shoes and bags with an eraser *to remove* minor stains and marks.

Keep your kitchen counter clean

Cut open a paper bag or two and place them on the kitchen counter the next time you peel carrots or potatoes or core an apple or pineapple. Use the bags to catch the mess. When you're done with your task, just roll up the bags and toss them into the garbage.

Make bread last longer

Transfer your bread from a plastic bag to a paper bag if you live in an area with high humidity. The bread will stay fresher longer—the crust will remain crisp and the center will stay soft.

Absorb cooking oils

Keep a couple of lunch bags on hand next Halloween when you prepare pumpkin seeds for eating. After you bake the seeds, put them on the lunch bags. The bags will absorb the oil or butter used in baking, and your seeds will be ready to eat.

Fill gift bags

Clean your paper shredder, then run a few lunch bags through it. Use the ribbons of brown paper as decorative filler in a gift bag. If you want to spice up the mix, shred a few pieces of construction paper and add those ribbons to the bag as well.

gum

Along with candy, dollar stores almost always stock chewing gum in or near the party and school supplies aisle, in addition to the checkout aisle. Gum makes a great addition to a goody bag that guests take away at the end of a party, but you might want to consider keeping some in the house—it fixes more than you might think. Chew on these additional ways to use gum.

Stop the wasps

If wasps have found a hole in your house and have decided to make a nest in the hole—and in your walls—bar them from entry by placing a wad of chewing gum over the hole. Plug the hole at night after you (or better yet, a professional) have killed the wasps. Wasps are least active between dusk and dawn, and you don't want to take the chance that any have survived.

Lunch bags are the perfect size to wrap CDs, DVDs, and small- to medium-sized boxes.

Fix clay pots

Don't toss a clay flowerpot or dog dish just because it sports a crack. Enjoy chewing a piece of gum, then use it to fill the crack. You'll save the pot and the bowl and a trip to the store.

Bid heartburn good-bye

Chew a stick of spearmint gum to relieve heartburn. The spearmint helps with digestion, and the act of chewing gum produces saliva, which in turn neutralizes stomach acid.

index cards

They're stronger than ordinary paper and a handier size. And they even have a life beyond recipes. Check out the other jobs index cards can do.

Shop strategically

Make several shopping lists on several different index cards depending on where you're shopping. Use one for the grocery store, one for the wholesale club, one for the dollar store, and so on. Using different colored cards for each store keeps you even more organized.

Make a handy reminder

Family members may claim they can't do the laundry because they don't know how. Tell them how, and then write simplified instructions on an index card, cover it with clear plastic (or transparent tape, if that's easier), and post it near the washing machine. No excuses now!

Toss your recipe book

Transfer your beloved ratty recipes to individual cards, slip them into index card protectors, and breathe life into them.

Count your pennies!

Level a table

Dinner table a bit wobbly? Fold an index card in half (or in thirds depending on how wobbly the table is) and slip it under the table leg. No more wobbles.

Make a bookmark

Why bother buying a bookmark when you can use an index card? Better still, you can write down favorite pages and passages, making it ideal for remembering the books that mean the most to you.

index card box

Chances are you fill an index card box with index cards. And chances are those index cards sport recipes. Consider taking a chance on using the index card box for something completely different!

File away your garden

Divide an index card box into sections, one for each part of your garden and yard: flowers, vegetables, shrubs, even your lawn. Make index cards for plant varieties you've tried and liked—and note how you've cared for them—and others for varieties you want to try in the future. You can even keep seed packets in the appropriate sections.

Ditch the address book

Using an index card box instead of an address book will keep you organized and on top of the paper tiger. Record the address, phone number, cell phone number, e-mail address, and any other pertinent contact information below the addressee's name on an index card. You can also add birth dates, anniversaries, spouse and children's names, and anything else you want to remember about that person.

Make a bookworm box

Big-time readers often have a tough time remembering what they've read. If you occasionally forget which books you've consumed, start a book file in an index box. Divide the cards by type of book—mysteries, novels, history, and so on—or by author.

Keep track of Christmas presents

Can't remember from one year to the next what you gave your loved ones? No problem. Assign each family member a card, write down their sizes and favorite colors, and each year write down what gift you gave them.

Buy it for this, use it for that!

magnets

You learned about the poles of magnets in school and why they repel each other. (Do you remember why?) But you never learned how to use magnets in unusual and creative ways. Here is what you missed.

Decorate your refrigerator

Picture frames can display only a limited number of the photographs you've taken. Enjoy more photos by cutting around the subject(s), gluing a small magnet on the back, and posting them on the fridge. You'll see your friends and family every time you have a meal!

Keep office supplies in order

Place a small magnet in your desk drawer to corral paper clips. They'll be easier to find and a snap to use.

Mount small metal helpers

Attach a series of small magnets or one magnet strip on the wall in the bathroom to hold the metal tools you use there: nail scissors, tweezers, a nail file, and so on. Just be sure to keep them out of reach of children.

Keeps nails in jars

Even if you're not a klutz, you may knock over jars of nails or screws or washers when you're busy at your workbench. Add small round magnets to these jars. Why? So that the nails and screws and washers won't scatter all over your workbench if you happen to tip over the jars. The magnets will keep them contained.

Clean up a metal mess

Suppose you spilled a container of nails and nuts and other small metal objects, but didn't have a magnet inside the jar to stop from making a mess. Use a magnet now. Turn a ziplock bag inside out,

9 More Nontraditional Ways to Use MAGNETS

1 Find a Stud

A handsome man may be your goal but another stud (the metal kind) can be found by running a magnet along a wall. Before picking up your hammer, grab a magnet—and save yourself some fruitless pounding.

2 Child's Play

You can make a wall in a child's bedroom more fun by coating a wall with magnetized paint. Magnets—the flexible sheet kind—will stick to the painted area, allowing children to create a "magnetic" focal wall.

3 Seal a Vent

Reduce heating and air conditioning costs by preventing hot or cold air from entering unused rooms. Just cut some flexible sheet magnet to cover your metal registers. Your home will be more energy efficient and comfortable.

4 Book Marked

Advertising magnets can take over your fridge. If you are tired of looking at pizza and dry-cleaning mottos, cover one side of a magnet with colorful packing tape. Then trim the edges so they are flush and cut the magnet in half. Hinge the two pieces back together with another piece of tape. You can use the result as a bookmark.

5 True North

If you have a straight pin, a piece of cork, a bowl of water, and a strong magnet, you can amaze your kids. Rub the pin across the magnet 50 times (in the same direction). Then push the pin through the cork and put it in the water. The pin will point north, no matter how you twist the bowl. Check it against a compass if your children don't believe you!

6 Magic Paper Clip

Drop a paper clip into a glass of water, and ask your friends if they can remove it without putting anything in the glass or dumping the water. Conceal a strong magnet between your fingers and touch the glass. After the paper clip attaches to the magnet, slowly move your hand up the glass. Your friends will be amazed at your "magic touch."

7 Ear, Ear

What do you do with a single earring? If it's pretty and you don't want to let it go, glue it to a magnet and use it to stick photos on your refrigerator.

8 Organize the Medicine Chest

Keep track of small metal items such as tweezers, in the bathroom by hanging them on magnets inside a cabinet. If your cabinet does not have a metal surface, attach the magnets with hot glue.

9 Keep Your Broom Handy

Use a screw to attach a magnet halfway down the broom handle. Then store the broom attached to the side of your refrigerator between the fridge and the wall. It will remain hidden until you are ready to use it.

and put a bar magnet inside. Pick up the nails with the bag—they'll stick to it—then turn it right side out to hold the metal pieces you've recovered.

Wear a brooch without a pin

Grandma's brooch may be beautiful, but do you really want to put holes in your favorite silk blouse to show it off? No you don't, and you don't have to. Take off the shaft of the brooch and superglue a magnet to the back. Once it dries completely, hold it where you want it on your blouse, and put the opposing magnet on the inside of the blouse. The magnets will hold the brooch just like a pin—but without the damage to your wardrobe.

Stop frozen locks

Cover your car door locks with magnets overnight in the dead of winter. They'll prevent the locks from freezing—and your hands from freezing as you try to defrost the locks!

Pick up pins and needles

Sewing hardly seems like a dangerous pastime, but it can be fraught with danger if you spill pins and needles on the floor. Before someone steps on them, use a magnet to pick them up. You'll spare your hands and their feet!

marbles

Marbles show up a lot as a standard party favor in 99 cent stores. They're inexpensive, fun to play with, and pretty. They can be more than window dressing, though. Here are several ways to put them to work. (Be sure to keep them out of the reach of small children because they are a choking hazard.)

Fix a fingertip

If you have a glove with a frayed fingertip, let a marble come to your rescue. Place it into the fingertip so that the fabric is stretched out and smooth—the way you want it when you sew.

Make a marble party game

Here's a way to occupy party guests at the beginning of a party while others arrive. Fill a jar with marbles—be sure to count them first—and set it out for everyone to see. Have each guest write down the number of marbles they think are in the jar. At the end of the party, give a prize for the closest guess—you can even give them the decorative jar of marbles to take home!

Prettify a vase

Clear glass vases are attractive, and they can be made even more so with the help of colorful marbles. Set a number of pretty marbles at the bottom of the vase, then fill the vase with water and flowers. You'll be amazed by the transformation.

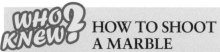 **HOW TO SHOOT A MARBLE**

The tried and true method to keep your marbles is to shoot with skill. Here's how:

1 With your dominant hand, fold your thumb into your palm and make a fist, keeping your thumb knuckle level with your index finger.

2 Stick out your index finger—the tip of your thumb will be held in place by your middle finger. Put your marble in the middle of your thumb knuckle, wrap your index finger around it tightly.

3 Kick out your thumb to shoot the marble from your hand!

masking tape

Masking tape is another item that can be found in several aisles; it's main purpose is to mask off areas that shouldn't be covered with paint during a paint job. But it also has other roles when rooms are painted, and even more roles outside those rooms. Here are the many things masking tape can do.

Speed cleanup

Before you start your next paint job, cover the bottom of the brush bristles and the top of the brush handle with about two inches of masking tape. (Make sure that 1/2 inch of that tape covers the bristles.) When you're done, take the tape off the brush and throw it away. The bottoms of the bristles will be cleaner than usual, since you've prevented the paint from seeping into them. Cleanup will be a breeze!

Pick up spilled beads

Dropping a box of beads—or watching a beaded necklace break and spill onto the floor—can be upsetting and potentially dangerous. Get rid of the annoyance and the danger by picking up the beads quickly and easily. How? With masking tape. Simply wrap the tape around your hand, sticky side out, until most of your hand is covered. Now pat your hand on your floor repeatedly, until you've picked up lots of beads. Brush the beads off into a container, and continue to pat the floor until you've rescued all the beads.

Label cans with tape

Paint cans can get messy—and the labels on the cans unreadable—after you've painted a room or two. Since you need to know which paint can contains which color, label the can with a piece of masking tape and a permanent marker. Note the date you painted the room, which room(s) you painted, and the name and number of the color.

Tape diapers shut

It doesn't matter if the sticky tabs have failed on a disposable diaper because your child has learned how to undo them or because you pulled them off one time too many trying to get them just right—what matters is that you need a new way to attach them. Masking tape will hold them shut just fine.

Control pet hair, hands down

Wrap both your hands in masking tape—with the sticky side facing out—and run your hands over your hairy couch or chair. Use both sides of your hands for best results. This works on pet-hair-covered clothing, too.

Use masking tape to tape disposable diapers shut.

Avoid overeeding fish

If your fish food container has too many big holes or is one big hole—which may result in overfeeding—cover half of the container's mouth or half of the holes with masking tape. You'll have better control over the amount you feed your fish.

Repair an umbrella

Fix a broken umbrella rib with masking tape and a coat hanger. Cut a length of wire from the coat hanger and attach it to the damaged rib with masking tape. You'll be ready for the next rainstorm.

Tape your locks shut

Prevent water from entering the locks on your car doors by taping over them with masking tape before you enter a car wash in winter. Why? So that the water doesn't turn to ice inside the locks and prevent you from locking or unlocking the doors. Take the tape off the door after you leave the car wash.

Keep a pen handy

You know how you can never find a pen when you need one in your car? Now you can—just tape a pen to the dashboard so you'll have it handy the next time you need to sign a receipt, jot down directions, or make a note of what you need on your next trip to the grocery store.

paper clips

Irons, eyeglasses, buttons, and CDs—what do they all have in common? Paper clips in general, and paper clips to the rescue in particular. Here are several alternate uses for the heroic little paper clip.

Repair your eyeglasses

When that delicate little screw disappears from the hinge of your glasses, it's easy to assume all is lost. But you can make a serviceable repair by using a small paper clip. Open one side and push it through the hinge. Gently fold the clip back down, and the glasses will hold very securely until you can get them fixed.

Attach a button

Don't hide in your office if you lose a button at work. You can fix it easily. Using the holes made by the original thread, push a straightened-out paper clip up through the garment, through one of the holes in the button, down through another hole, and back through the second original hole in the clothing. Twist the ends of the paper clip together, and bend them until the metal lies flat against your garment. Now get back to work!

Pick a lock

Not in a criminal way! Many of us have lost the tiny keys to diaries, jewelry boxes, or suitcases and despaired of ever getting the lock open again. Straighten out a paper clip and jiggle gently through the keyhole at the mechanism. It will likely spring open.

Rescue CDs and DVDs

CD and DVD players have been known to eat their discs. If your player refuses to return your disc, you'll have to rescue it without the help of the machine. Turn a paper clip into a hook, and place the hook over or under the tray. Jimmy the tray out enough that you can grasp it, then pull it out so you can take out your disc.

Lengthen a pull chain

Stop stretching or using a step stool to reach the chain on an overhead light or ceiling fan. Instead, attach a chain of paper clips to the end of the pull chain...and pull!

Mark the end of tape

If you've ever tried to find the beginning of a roll of transparent tape, you know that finding it is only half the battle—the other half is lifting the tape in one piece. Solve both problems by placing a paper clip under the end of the tape every time you use it. You'll never have either problem again.

Make a key chain

You always seem to have several key chains when you don't need them, and none when you do. If you need a key chain but don't have any on hand, thread several paper clips together into a chain and slip the key through the paper clip on the end. Instant key chain!

Remember your page

Beautiful paper bookmarks do an adequate job of keeping your place in a book, but an ordinary paper clip outperforms its paper competitor. A paper clip won't fall out and lose your spot if your book takes a tumble or gets upended in your book bag.

Unclog your iron

Minerals may be clogging the steam ports on the bottom of your iron if your iron doesn't emit steam the way it should. Unplug your iron, let it cool, and then try cleaning out the ports with the end of a straightened paper clip.

party straws

What is a party drink without brightly colored straws? And what is a garden without multiple straws? You may know the answer to the first question but not the second one. Find the second answer—and many more straw tips—here.

Thaw with a straw

Ice can wreak havoc on cars—particularly on locks, which can freeze in the winter. If you can't insert your key into a frozen lock, try placing a straw on the lock and blowing into it. The warmth from your breath should melt the ice, and you should be able to then insert the key.

Help your flowers stand straight

Place a straw next to a bent or drooping flower stem in your garden, and attach the stem to the straw loosely with transparent tape. The straw will act as a splint.

Extend a caulk gun

Whether you need to seal a crack in an awkward space in the basement or caulk the top of the tiles in the shower, you may need to extend your caulk gun. Let an ordinary plastic straw help! Attach it to the nozzle of the caulk gun with duct tape, and use the tool as you normally would—with better results.

Prevent knots in chains

Use a straw as a jewelry chain protector. Just run your necklace through a straw, then close the clasp. The straw will keep the chain from getting knotted and tangled. Your necklaces will always be ready to go!

WAY BACK WHEN...

Straws

We welcome paper straws today as an alternative to plastic, but they're not new. The patent was issued in 1888 to Marvin Stone (a manufacturer of cigarette holders). The Stone Straw Corporation made paper straws by hand-winding them until 1906 when the process was mechanized.

pencil

"Pencil pusher" is a derogatory term, but anyone who knows anything about pencils and all the jobs they can do would be thrilled to be called a pencil pusher. Here are a bunch of ways you can push pencils to your advantage.

A pencil marks the spot

A squirrel may be at the root of your missing bulb problem, and you can be sure a squirrel isn't going to fix it—but you can. Mark the spot where your flower didn't bloom with a pencil—push it firmly into the soil—so that come fall, you'll know where you need to replant the bulb.

Water plants the write way

Test the soil of your houseplant with a pencil to determine if it needs water. Push a pencil firmly into the soil and let it sit for half an hour. Pull it out and inspect the tip: If it's dry, you need to thoroughly water your plant. If the pencil comes up with dirt on the tip, the soil is moist enough.

Forget about a foot ache

Are your new shoes a little too tight? Did you walk a little too far? Did you stand in line a little too long? Ward off a foot ache—or stop one in its tracks—by doing a simple foot exercise. Place a few pencils on the floor, and pick them up one by one with your toes. You'll stretch your feet and feel relief.

Silence squeaky stairs

Don't let a noisy step keep you awake at night. Scrape some pencil lead into the seam where the flat part of the step and the riser—the back of the step—meet. The squeak will disappear. The pencil lead will eventually seep out of the joint, so be sure to reapply it when necessary.

Make a school picture frame

What could be more appropriate as a school picture frame than four pencils? Glue two sharpened pencils to the long sides of a frame and two shorter pencils (sharpen them down to size) to the shorter sides of the frame. The pencils and the picture will provide fond memories.

Lubricate your locks

Use pencil lead to "grease" your locks, rather than an oil-based lubricant, which may draw in dust and grime. Scrape the lead (which is usually a mix of graphite with a clay binder) of a No. 1 or No. 2 pencil onto a piece of wax paper with a knife, then rub the lead onto a key. Use the key to turn the lock a few times, and you're done. If you're pressed for time, just rub the point of the pencil against the key, then insert the key into the lock. Do this once or twice a year to keep your locks in tip-top shape.

Repair your zipper's teeth

If your zipper gets stuck moving up and down, lubricate the teeth by rubbing them on both sides with a lead pencil.

Tighten a loose screw

Eyeglass frames are dependent on those tiny screws that don't seem to stay in place very long. Don't let a loose screw get the best of you—just turn a pencil upside down, press the eraser against the screw so that it engages the screw, and turn the pencil. You'll fix the frame and create a handy new tool at the same time!

Remove a cactus

If you want to replant a small cactus, let the soil dry out a bit first. Then put the eraser end of a pencil into the drainage hole through the bottom of the pot, and slowly push the cactus out through the top. The root ball should come out in one piece.

Accessorize your hair

Stick two pencils into your bun so that they form an *X*. The pencils will help keep your bun in place.

pencil case

Why is a pencil case called a pencil case when, in fact, it holds so many other items? Pens, erasers, mini staplers—those are just a few of the logical items pencil cases carry. If you think outside the box—or the pencil case— you'll find several other items you should keep in your pencil case. Here are a few.

Carry cosmetics

Pencil cases make excellent cosmetic cases— particularly if they're made of waterproof plastic—and they're an awful lot cheaper than their cosmetic case counterparts.

Make a first aid kit

There's no need to buy a premade first aid kit when you have an inexpensive pencil case. Just add adhesive bandages, antibiotic ointment, aspirin, an instant cold compress, and any other items you feel are necessary. Keep it in your house or your car or anywhere you might need it.

Protect your stockings

Don't let your suitcase or its contents make runs in your stockings. Roll them up and stash them in a pencil case when you travel. They'll remain safe and run-free.

rubber bands

They're good for shooting at friends and enemies and making into bouncy balls. But rubber bands have a number of more practical and uncommon uses. Once you see the uses, you'll wonder why they're not more common!

Prevent carpal tunnel syndrome

Computers can help you get organized, save time, and provide endless entertainment, but they can also cause trouble. Avoid the effects of repetitive hand motion—like carpal tunnel syndrome—by stretching your hands every couple of hours. Touch your fingertips to the tip of your thumb, then surround your hand with a rubber band just below your fingernails. Slowly open your hand, spreading your fingers, then close them. Do this 10 times for each hand.

Wrap a rubber band around a container to help indicate how much remains.

Mark liquid content

Ever wonder how much liquid—like paint thinner, drain cleaner, or metal polish—is left in opaque containers? You can't tell by looking at the container—unless you wrap a rubber band around it to indicate how much remains. You'll never have to guess about the contents again.

Attach your tools to your stepladder

Making trips up and down your stepladder to get tools is a waste of time and potentially dangerous. Strap your tools onto your stepladder with large rubber bands. Stretch two rubbers bands around the folding tool shelf—or on the top step of the ladder, which you're not supposed to use anyway—and slip your tools under the rubber bands. They'll be at your fingertips the next time you need them.

Keep your cutting board in place

Stop your cutting board from sliding around the kitchen counter by wrapping a rubber band around each end. You'll have a much easier time cutting and chopping.

Protect your paint can

Want to keep the grooves in the top of your paint can from filling with paint every time you wipe your paintbrush on the side of the can? Place a rubber band around the can so that it stretches across the top of the can (and across the top of the paint). Wipe your brush on the rubber band rather than on the can to get rid of excess paint. You'll keep the grooves paint-free.

Organize your car

Get organized by wrapping two rubber bands around each sun visor in your car. You can use this newfound storage space for your garage door opener, maps, and directions.

Childproof your cabinets

Forget about buying expensive (and complicated) locks for cabinets that swing open. Simply secure them by tying rubber bands around the knobs.

Keep dresses on hangers

Dresses with spaghetti straps tend to fall off hangers. Keep your dresses where they belong by wrapping a rubber band around each end of a hanger. The dresses won't fall off.

rubber cement

People below a certain age don't even know what rubber cement is, but they should. It's a surprisingly versatile substance, even though it flies under the radar. Here are a few ways to use it that should put it back on the map.

Position a screw in a tight spot

If you can't reach the place where you need to insert a screw, you won't be able to hold the screw to start the job. How can you solve this problem? With a little rubber cement. Place a small amount of rubber cement on the slot of the screw, and put the tip of the screwdriver into the slot. Let the cement dry, then start work.

Cancel crayon marks

If your pint-sized Picasso got carried away and colored the (washable) wallpaper with crayon, don't worry that he's created a permanent masterpiece. Cover the offending marks with rubber cement, wait until it dries completely, then roll off the rubbery glue—and your budding young artist's work.

Fix a carpet burn

Don't despair if you find a hole burned in your carpet. Just cut the burned fibers out with scissors, then put rubber cement into the hole with a toothpick. Cover the ends of matching

> **Place a small amount of rubber cement on the slot of the screw, to help position the tip of the screwdriver.**

carpet fibers (that you've cut from a remnant or a hidden area of carpet) with rubber cement, and put them in the hole. Draw the tufts upright with a pin, then, when the patch is dry, blend the tufts into the carpet using the pin.

staples

You probably don't think of your clothing when you think of staples and staplers, but your life would be easier if you did. Check out how you can use staples on your clothes.

Hitch up your hem

Don't let a dragging hem get you down. If you don't have access to a sewing kit—or even a needle and thread—you can still repair your pants or skirt easily. Just staple the hem back where it belongs. You can even staple the hem from the inside of the garment so that very little of the staple will be seen on the outside. Best of all, the staples will come out easily when you have time to repair your garment properly.

Staple your pants shut

Splitting the seam of your pants is embarrassing in any circumstances and is particularly

mortifying if you're at work and can't change them immediately. Save face by ducking into a restroom with a stapler. After you've removed your pants, line the seam up as it was previously sewn, making sure about half an inch of material remains on either side of the seam—and staple the seam shut.

Tame your cords

Your computer and stereo cords, that is. Glue or tape a piece of thick cardboard to the back of your desk or stereo cabinet, and then staple the cords into place. No more tangled mess!

tissue paper

Tissue paper is a lot tougher than it looks. It may appear fragile, but it knows how to protect cookies; whip clothes, hats, and purses into shape; and even keep tabs on your dryer. Here's how.

Keep cookies crisp

Soggy cookies take all the fun out of having cookies in the first place, so help your cookies stay crunchy with tissue paper. Crumple some up and keep it in the bottom of your cookie container. It will draw moisture away from the cookies and keep them fresh longer.

Shape your hat

Stuff the crown of your favorite hat with tissue paper—more than you think is necessary—so that the brim doesn't touch the shelf when you place the hat on it. By resting the hat on the tissue paper, you'll keep the brim in shape, along with the rest of the hat.

Check your dryer door

If you suspect the seal on your dryer leaks, try this experiment. Close the door and turn on the machine. Move a piece of tissue paper around the edge of the door. Is the paper drawn toward the door? If so, the seal of the door needs to be replaced.

Aim for a soft collar

Starched collars often look harsh. Give your blouse or shirt collar a softer look by placing a twisted piece of tissue paper underneath it.

Prevent creases

Garments made of very thin fabric are often very beautiful, but they are also very susceptible to creasing. Place a sheet or two of tissue paper in

your favorite thin piece of clothing before folding it, and you'll minimize creases.

Keep your bags in shape

Stuff leather purses and briefcases with tissue paper to help maintain their shape when they're out of circulation. Plastic bags work well, too.

wrapping paper

Wrap up birthday and holiday celebrations in an environmentally friendly way by finding uses for all the wrapping paper you bought at the dollar store. Here are some ideas for that wrapping paper, whether new or used.

Protect your ornaments

Christmas is one of the biggest wrapping paper days of the year—and one of the biggest days of waste. Don't toss used wrapping paper just because it's ripped. Use it again to protect your ornaments when you store them for next year.

Pack your wrapping paper

Make your own packing material the next time you ship a package. Shred leftover wrapping paper and use it to protect whatever you're shipping.

Cover your book

Whether you have a title you want to keep to yourself or a textbook you want to protect, wrap the cover in wrapping paper. You'll end up with both privacy and a pretty cover.

Make pet bedding

Shred wrapping paper from birthday and holiday gifts and use it to create bedding for animals at a shelter or veterinarian's office. Be sure to ask if the shelter or the office needs bedding material before you drop it off.

Save a bundle!

9 More Nontraditional Ways to Use
WRAPPING PAPER

A DIFFERENT Solution!

1 Match a Matchbox

If you are giving a candle as a gift, a fun way to add to your present is to wrap a box of matches (the size you'd get at the supermarket) with wrapping paper that matches either the candle or the paper you've wrapped the candle in. This extra touch will delight the recipient.

2 Scrap to Keepsake

What can you do with wrapping paper left over from presents? If you have a pair of scissors and a wire coat hanger you can make a keepsake that can be reused each time the same occasion arises. Bend the hanger into a circle. Roll up a flattened piece of wrapping paper and cut it into 8-by-1-inch strips. Twist each strip around the coat hanger. Do this until your "wreath" is full and festive. If you have a leftover bow, pop it on!

3 Outside the Box

Do your kids have a lot of little toy figurines? Are you stepping on them because they're scattered all over? Box them up in a pretty way. Wrap an empty tissue box with paper that coordinates with your child's room. Now all of those toys that are outside the box have a home.

4 (Scrap) Book It

Some paper is just too pretty to throw away after you've opened a gift. Why not use some of it to decorate a scrapbook? You can create a page to commemorate the occasion the gift was received with the paper that it was wrapped in.

5 Holiday Theme

Take the mats from your framed pictures and wrap them in holiday-themed wrapping paper. This little decorating touch is inexpensive, but it will make a big impression on your guests. (This tip can work for birthday decorating, too!)

6 Cover a Corkboard

A corkboard is very useful but not particularly lovely to look at. If you want your corkboard to have some pizzazz, cover it with wrapping paper that matches your décor.

7 Book Wrap

Have you noticed how often high-end decorating magazines show monochromatic items on shelves? You can do this, too, by covering books of different sizes with solid-colored wrapping paper and then stacking them artfully.

8 Lovely Linens

Line the shelves of your linen closet with wrapping paper that makes you smile. Keeping sheets and towels washed and folded may not be your idea of fun, but seeing them all set on pretty paper can make finishing the chore more satisfying.

9 Framed

Beautiful paper can make very eye-catching (and inexpensive) art. Find a standard-sized frame and fill it with your favorite wrapping paper. This is also a good strategy if you are showing your home and want to "depersonalize" it without taking down all your framed photos.

TOOLS

THERE ARE PLENTY OF USEFUL, PRACTICAL, and everyday tools available very cheaply at your local dollar store—more than you might think, when you peruse the tool aisle—and also a lot of things you can do with them beyond their obvious purposes. The tool aisle encompasses a huge variety of utilitarian items way beyond hammers, screwdrivers, and alligator clips. This is the place where you'll also find such items as bungee cords and duct tape, hacksaws and car wax, paint scrapers and screening, weather stripping and wire. When you add up all the fantastic uses beyond the basic, you'll find the tool aisle an utterly invaluable part of inexpensive domestic bliss.

alligator clips

Like their namesake reptile, these spring-loaded clips have powerful jaws that close with a vicious snap. Whether you're using them for their purpose of making temporary electrical connections or for something else, keep your fingers off their serrated edges!

Hang cards and photos

Christmas cards mount up quickly in December. Put them on display by stringing up some ribbon or twine between two tacks on a wall, and then use alligator clips to hang cards up by one corner. You'll get to enjoy each card and keep surfaces empty.

Mount photos

Use alligator clips in coordinating colors to clip photographs to a piece of mounting board, matting, or stiff poster board. The board should be trimmed only slightly larger than the picture. The clips have a clean, post-industrial look that makes a modern and attractive picture frame out of any color board you like.

Create jewelry

For earrings, use the smallest alligator clips you can find and thread the loops from a discarded pair of earrings through the hole in the base of the clip. Use the serrated teeth to grab anything you want to display, from dyed feathers to squares of sassy satin to braided leather strips. For bracelets or necklaces, thread a strip of wire or leather through the hole, string on beads or charms or tie on ribbons or feathers, and use the clip to grab the other end and hold the jewelry on.

Make hair bows for little girls

Use a glue gun to attach ribbon bows, rosettes, or streamers to a clip. The alligator clip holds tight to a lock of hair, so little girls won't lose these once they go out.

Decorate a Christmas tree

Out of wire hangers for your holiday tree, or can't find a way to string up decorations such as paper snowflakes or cranberry garlands? Alligator clips are secure and easy. Either clip the item directly to a branch, or string fishing line or thread through the hole in the base and attach it to the ornament so it can dangle off a branch.

Count your pennies!

box cutters

These ubiquitous cutting tools come in different shapes and styles. Some hold a traditional razor blade in place with screws, others have disposable blades that snap off to reveal a new sharp blade. Some have angled cutting edges, others are flat. Whatever type you buy, you can use them for more than cutting open a box.

Cut out a pattern

Trimming a paper pattern into pieces before you pin it to the fabric can be a tedious job using scissors. Speed the process by laying the paper over a safe cutting surface (either a work table or, better, a cardboard box opened and lying flat) and zip through it with a box cutter.

Trim pastry

When you're making a fancy pastry, such as strips for a lattice top or little decorations rolled from the scraps for the top of a double-crust pastry, a box cutter with an angled edge is just the tool for cutting out leaf or heart designs. Brush with beaten egg before baking and your pies will look beautifully professional.

Unstick painted-shut windows

A sharp box cutter is the best way to slice open windows that are stuck tight with paint. Run it firmly around the edges of the window, angling the blade to push it into the crack and past the paint that's gumming up the works. Don't forget to cut top and bottom. It may take several tries to get it open.

Clean gum off a floor

A piece of chewing gum can get really embedded in a floor with a slightly porous surface such as brick or cement. Use the edge of a box cutter to work the offending article off the floor, scraping gently to remove the gum and being careful not to mark the surface. If you run a piece of ice over the gum first to chill it, the blade may be able to pick the gum up in one piece.

Scrape paint off a window

Use an angled box cutter to remove paint from the glass when you've accidentally touched the pane while brushing. The sharp tip is good for trimming off excess paint right alongside the mullions or glazing bars, to give a clean line to the finished paint job.

bungee cords

Bungee cords are springy elastics covered with nylon and with a hook at either end. They come in different lengths and widths, and they're commonly used in shipping and hauling (not to mention extreme sports). But they can do a lot more than their industrial origins suggest.

Make a travel clothesline

Carry a length of bungee cord in your suitcase while traveling and you won't have to drape your freshly rinsed undies over the radiator in a hotel room. Just stretch it across a corner of your hotel room and drip dry.

Seal a suitcase

After you overstuff your suitcase with souvenirs and goodies, you can close it with bungee cords for extra support. If you've ever experienced the airlines bursting open your suitcase in transit and returning it to you in a taped-up plastic bag, you'll find this trick a no-brainer.

Use it as a yoga strap

Why spend money on pricey specialty yoga straps for stretching and exercising? There's nothing you can do with those flat lengths of rubber that you can't also do with a cloth-covered bungee cord.

Hold up your pants

A narrow length of bungee cord is discreet and extremely effective. Buy the lengths of bungee cord by the foot so you can get the size you need and attach the hook ends yourself.

Train branches on a tree

If you're trying to train a young tree to grow in a certain direction or into a certain shape, a bungee cord is a great tool for gardening. Use bungee cords to hold up the branches or tie them down until your tree looks just the way you want.

Turtle Wax

What would you do if you noticed a man shining one fender of your car? Benjamin Hirsch, a former magician and the inventor of Plastone, hoped you'd buy his homemade wax and finish the job! In 1953, while visiting Turtle Creek, Wisconsin, Hirsch had an epiphany. The word "turtle" represented his product exactly: a hard shell of protection. Plastone was renamed Super Hard Shell, and his company became Turtle Wax. Soon, the main office in Chicago sported a gigantic turtle on the roof. It told the time and temperature—and held a can of wax. Hirsch knew how to catch people's attention!

car wax

Liquid waxes for your car might give you a terrific shine, if all you want to do is shine your car. But to do more with your car wax than, well, wax your car, be sure to buy paste wax and try the tricks below.

Take a ring off a polished surface

It happens: Someone puts a glass down on your wooden coffee table and next thing you know there's a white ring from the condensation. Put a little paste wax on your finger and trace the ring. Let it dry, then buff with a soft cloth.

Keep fingerprints off appliances

Keep your stainless steel appliances shining. Put a thin layer of car wax on appliances such as refrigerator doors, and then buff vigorously with a soft, lint-free cloth. The next time the kids put their fingers all over the door, they won't leave any fingerprints behind to mar the surface.

Fight mildew in the bathroom

If you're tired of cleaning mildew off the bathroom tiles, give yourself a break by waxing the walls. First, clean any mildew and soap scum off the tile walls of the shower. Wipe the walls dry, then apply car wax (only to the vertical tiles, not the bathtub itself, or it will be dangerously slippery). Allow to dry, then buff to a shine with a lint-free cloth. Your tiles will stay clean and shiny for many months.

Clear snow with less effort

Rub a thick coating of car wax on the surface of your snow shovel, and the snow will slip off more easily. The extra effort you save each time you toss off a shovel-full will make the whole job easier. You can also wax the chute of a snow blower to stop it from clogging.

Help drawers and windows move smoothly

Don't let a sticking drawer or a stiff window slow you down. You can use car wax instead of brute strength. With a soft cloth, smooth a little car wax all the way along the tracks of the windows or drawers, polishing away any excess. You'll find that the moving parts slide along much more readily, with a lot less effort on your part.

caulk

Acrylic caulk is water-soluble and thus makes for easier cleanup for home projects. Silicone caulk is waterproof, so it's very messy to work with but once it dries, it's completely impermeable to moisture. Decide which type is best for these unconventional uses.

Repair aged grout

Regrouting tile is a big job. Instead, make a temporary but long-term repair with waterproof silicone caulk. Squeeze a little caulk over the surface of the cracking grout to keep it from falling out of vertical joints due to expansion and contraction in the shower.

Fill nail holes

Use opaque acrylic caulk to fill nail holes. Press a little caulk into the hole, then push it in with your finger and smooth the surface with a putty knife. Allow to dry completely before painting.

Keep out ants

Even in the cleanest kitchens, food has to be out on the countertops now and then, and it's like a siren call to any nearby ants, particularly in the warm months. When you've tried every trick in the book to no avail, try caulk. Put out something sweet, and when the ants come in, trace them back to their point of entry. Whatever it is, seal it with caulk—along the edge of the skirting boards, around the electrical outlets, anywhere ants might enter.

Seal cracks in plaster

Make a repair job that might well last for years by spreading a little opaque white caulk across hairline cracks in plaster. Press it in with your finger and then smooth with a putty knife. Let dry completely before painting.

Use as an adhesive

Most caulk is white, but you can also get clear caulk, which makes a good industrial type adhesive for home repair projects. You can use it to stick together wood, Plexiglas, ceramics, glass, and more.

Repair inflatable toys

Clear silicone caulk is a terrific adhesive and sealant for inflatable items such as a kid's pool toy or even a small inflatable kiddie pool. Locate the source of the leak as you deflate the toy, then cover it with clear caulk and seal it with a patch such as another piece of plastic or rubber. Let dry completely and reinflate—your patch will hold the rest of the summer!

Use it this way!

charcoal briquettes

The dusty black chunks of charcoal that seem so messy to handle are in fact a great weapon in keeping all sorts of domestic places and items dry and clean. Be sure to buy plain charcoal briquettes, not the easy-lighting type that contain lighter or starter fluid.

Keep stored clothes dry

When you seal up seasonal clothes in plastic containers, any dampness inside (perhaps you put the clothes away on a humid day) can create an environment where mildew might grow. Keep clothes as dry as possible by wrapping charcoal briquettes in paper towels and storing a few of these moisture-sucking bundles in each container or sealed bag of clothes.

Remove mothball odors from an RV

Many people close up their RVs for the season with mothballs inside to protect against vermin. But when traveling time starts again, that mothball scent can be pervasive and lingering. Leave several bowls of charcoal briquettes (the plain type without lighter fluid) in the interior before you hit the road, and the odor will disappear.

Keep a cooler fresh

Before storing a cooler all winter, wrap a few briquettes in paper towels and put them inside. That way, even with the lid on, the cooler will still be dry and fresh inside when you open it for your first picnic the following summer.

Make a path

After burning charcoal in your grill, don't dump it in a garbage pile. Sprinkle the cooled ash along a garden path. Footsteps on the path will tamp it down into a lightweight, durable groundcover.

Keep flower water fresh

You've tried it all: bleach, aspirin, sugar. But the water in your flower vases still gets murky and foul-smelling in a day or two. Try a piece of charcoal and the water will stay fresher for days longer. Just don't use a clear glass vase and nobody will ever know!

clamps

C-clamps, so-called because of their shape, come in all sizes. Larger ones are generally used to hold two items tightly together while gluing. The smaller ones can have a host of other uses.

Crack nuts

Can't lay hands on your nutcracker, and a friend just dropped off an inviting bag of pecans in the shell? Use a C-clamp to crack them open.

Keep a cookbook open

Use a small C-clamp screwed onto each side so you can keep your place. That way, you won't swap from Irish stew to beef chili with the flick of a page mid-recipe.

Close a pet food bag

The thick, lined paper of some large, heavy-duty pet food bags can be difficult to keep closed. Use a couple of small C-clamps to hold the top rolled shut, and you can just slide them off each side when it's time to feed your pooch.

Hang holiday lights

The tiny C-clamps that look almost like toys are ideal for hanging a row of holiday lights in tricky places. You can attach them to the top edges of bookshelves or anywhere you can safely screw the clamp against an architectural feature, allowing the wire of the lights to hang off the "C," without needing tape or nails.

contractor trash bag

Contractor bags are super heavy-duty bags that can hold building waste without breaking. The plastic is strong and sturdy and won't tear under the weight of broken wall-board or tiles. That kind of strength makes it useful for other tasks as well.

Fashion a Halloween costume

Make a very convincing and inexpensive black robe for your little trick-or-treater with a contractor bag. Cut a large semicircle from the bottom center of the bag for a neck hole, then two circles from the side for armholes. Cut a strip off the top edge (now the bottom of the robe) to make it the right length, then cut that circle in half to make a belt. You can snip a fringe around the bottom and even slice it open up the middle to make an open robe—add a witch hat and a candy bag and you're done!

Go sledding

Thick snow falling and you can't find the sled at the back of the downstairs closet? Don't let your child miss out on the fun. Hand over a bag and let your kid "bum" down the hill with his bottom firmly planted on a tough plastic bag.

Store clothes

Contractor bags are sturdy enough to hold sweaters, heavy jeans, and winter coats for storage. Don't forget to add a charcoal briquette or two, wrapped in a paper towel or paper bag, to prevent humidity when you seal the bag.

Make a rain poncho

Need a hasty rain poncho to protect you in a downpour? Cut a neck hole and armholes in a contractor bag (they're big!) and keep your clothes totally dry.

cup hooks

These small metal hooks, usually with a screw tip at one end, are intended to fit under cabinets or shelves so you can hang a row of cups off them. Of course, they're also useful for lots of other things.

Hang keys

Never lose your keys again! Screw a row of cup hooks where you need it most––by the door. Whether you typically come in the front or backdoor, get in the habit of slinging your keys on the ring. When you're ready to go, there they are.

Hang toothbrushes

Take a lesson from nursery school and store your family's toothbrushes hanging upside down from a row of cup hooks mounted on the bathroom wall. When you hang toothbrushes upside down like this, they don't touch, preventing the spread of germs, and they dry quickly and efficiently after each use.

Create a necklace rack

If you're crafty, you can turn a strip of wood, a row of cup hooks, and some paint and glitter into a stylish and sophisticated necklace rack. Paint the wood in any design you like, then screw in the hooks at alternate levels across the strip. Mount on the wall and prevent your necklaces from ever again getting tangled up in a jewelry box.

Put up a hand towel

Got a work sink near the back door or in the basement? Make a handy towel rack by screwing in a cup hook nearby. Sling a hand towel over it and you'll have it ready to grab when your hands are wet.

drop cloths

Inexpensive, lightweight drop cloths are great for painting projects. They're disposable, so when you're done with the messy job, you can gather the whole thing up and throw it away. Cleanup doesn't get much easier. But there's plenty more to do with a drop cloth.

Cover furniture

Drop cloths are so inexpensive that you can buy several to protect your furniture during painting or renovation work. They're lightweight, so you can throw them on and off the sofa or chairs as needed.

Make a craft apron/paint poncho

Got a messy job? Protect yourself. Cut a neck hole in the center of a plastic drop cloth and pull it over you. It will fall in folds like a poncho, allowing you either to pull your arms out from underneath or cut slits to reach through. Either way, your clothing will emerge unscathed from dirty work.

Protect a tabletop

Whether you're trying to keep finger paints from getting out of hand, or you've invited your friends over for a shrimp boil, spread a lightweight drop cloth over the tabletop to catch all the drips. When you're done, gather it up and throw it away.

duct tape

Nowadays, more resilient space-age materials have replaced duct tape in the heating and air conditioning business—which frees up your roll of this silver miracle for other uses.

Prevent lockouts

Never get locked out of your car again! Tape a spare car key securely to the underside of your car with a couple strips of duct tape.

Line leaking gutters

The gutter might be mostly intact, but a few small cracks or holes here and there can leave leaks running down the side of the house. And replacing the gutters isn't in the cards right now. So let duct tape come to your rescue. Next time you're cleaning out the gutters in good weather, finish the job with a layer of duct tape stuck down the inside bottom of the gutter.

Remove lint and "pills" from clothes

Pat, don't rub, against the surface of coats and sweaters to remove lint and pet hair as well as those little "pills" of wool that tend to collect around the underarms and elbows.

Hem a pair of jeans

Sewing through thick denim is difficult—and it's frustrating when a child shoots up several inches the moment you finish the job! But you can make a sturdy, long-lasting hem with duct tape. It will last through several washes, and it will come off to reveal a few more inches of denim when that kid has another growth spurt.

Cover a blister

Breaking in a pair of shoes? A heel blister makes walking miserable, and most heel bandages rub as you go, worsening the pain. Put a gauze square over the actual sore, then cover your heel with a wide strip of duct tape and you'll be back on the road.

Hold a broken window together

If you have a lot of kids playing ball in your neighborhood, chances are you may have to replace a window sometime. Tape crisscrossing strips of duct tape over the broken glass before you lift it out of the window to prevent any (more) glass from falling.

6 More Nontraditional Ways to Use
DROP CLOTHS

1 Play Zone

Create a place where young children will play for hours. Cut a drop cloth to match the circumference of your dining (or kitchen) table. Include half an inch seam allowance. Then cut a piece equal to the height of your table and long enough to wrap all the way around it (add a one inch seam allowance on the top and bottom.) Sew the two pieces together and finish the edges. Leave an opening for a door! Let your kids paint on the details: windows, a doorbell.

2 Everyday Napkins

A green alternative to paper napkins can be made from a light-weave drop cloth. They're not fancy, so you'll use them every day, not just on holidays! Create a pattern out of stiff paper, making it 1/2 inch larger on each side than the final desired size. Trace the pattern on a washed piece of drop cloth and cut out your napkin. Turn the fabric under 1/4 inch and press with an iron. Turn under another 1/4 inch and sew the hem all the way around.

3 Guard Pillows

The pillows on garden furniture will eventually get rained on, but that doesn't mean mildew will set in, if cases are made from drop cloth with plastic backing. The backing keeps stuffing from getting wet and dries quickly. This type of drop cloth is sometimes called a "plastic laminated cotton dust sheet" and is easy to sew.

4 Sleep Longer

Drop cloths make fantastic blackout liners. Cut a heavy-weave drop cloth to the precise size of your expensive (but too sheer) drapes. Then hang the drop cloth behind the curtains (using clip-on hooks with rings—no sewing necessary!). You can darken any room you desire and sleep, sleep, sleep!

5 Dress Your Windows

If you have very tall windows, the thought of what curtains cost may fill you with dread. Not to fear: Drop cloths are here! They are cotton, a neutral color, and inexpensive. No sewing necessary if you use clip-on rings to attach them to curtain rods. The clean lines and raw fabric will look very modern.

6 Stop Food Splatter

Who said drop cloths were only for paint? Babies in high chairs are mess-making machines! Put a canvas drop cloth underneath the chair and save your floor. The cloth can be tossed in the wash and reused.

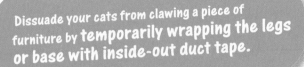

Dissuade your cats from clawing a piece of furniture by **temporarily wrapping the legs or base with inside-out duct tape.**

Discourage a cat from clawing

Cats can be very determined when set on clawing a piece of furniture. Persuade them otherwise by temporarily wrapping the legs or base with inside-out duct tape. (As you spiral up the leg, the stickiness holds the next layer.) Cats will back off quickly!

Fix a plastic trash can

For something that simply sits behind the house, trash cans take a lot of wear and tear. If the plastic cracks down the side, you can make a long-term repair by sealing it with duct tape inside and out.

Mend a metal screen

No time to take the door down and stretch a new screen? Make a repair that will last all summer by stretching some silver duct tape over the hole in the screen.

Seal your waterproof boots

Got a rip in your Wellingtons? There's no need to throw them away. Wrap them around and around with duct tape, overlapping the tape across the tear. You'll get the rest of the season out of them, at least.

THE TRUTH ABOUT DUCT TAPE

If it walks like a duck, talks like a duck... Johnson & Johnson manufactured the first duct tape to keep moisture out of ammunition cases during World War II. Army green in color, it was modeled after medical tape, made from cotton duck (woven cotton), and waterproof. Accordingly, people often called it "duck tape." However, during the post-war housing boom, it became indispensable for joining household ducts. The color was changed to silver (to blend in better) and the tape became known as "duct tape."

face masks

Disposable face masks are handy for low-grade filtration, when you're sawing wood or spray-painting or perhaps cleaning out a dusty closet. But they have more uses than that.

Make a comforting inhaler

Camphor and mentholated rubs are great when you're congested, but some people find that the rubs burn when applied directly to the skin.

Smear some on the inside of a disposable face mask and inhale in peace.

Cut onions

Add this to the folklore surrounding the ways to cut onions without tears. If you cover your nose and mouth with a face mask to avoid inhaling the fumes, the tears may never come. If it works for you, there's nothing to lose.

Create a cat toy

Drive your cat wild with this fabulous cat toy: Remove the elastic straps and put catnip in a mask. Top it with a second mask to make a hollow, rounded shape. Staple securely closed and toss it enticingly toward your kitty—it's more fun than a rubber mouse!

hacksaws

The narrow blades of a hacksaw have a jagged row of long teeth that are highly effective for sawing through tough substances. They are thin and flexible, which also means they wear out fast and are inexpensive to replace. Take one out of your workshop and into the house for tasks like these.

Cut up bones for stock

Using a kitchen knife on bone is the fastest way to ruin a quality knife. Use a small hacksaw kept in your kitchen just for the purpose and trim bones for stock and soup.

Prune branches off a Christmas tree

Once your tree is in the door and in place in the living room, it's too late to start doing any major hatchet work on the branches. But if a few of them are ruining the look, use a small hacksaw to reach back and remove branches without a lot of mess.

Construct a camping knife

If you've got survivalist instincts, you'll appreciate this canny use of a very inexpensive item: Use tin snips to cut a fine-toothed hacksaw blade in half and rough it out into a knife blade shape, with a dent in the "handle" for a fingertip to rest on. Use the hacksaw's teeth as the "spine" of the knife, and use a file or belt sander to sharpen the opposite side.

hammers

Dollar store hammers and rubber mallets are likely to be moderately lightweight, which may not be so great if you're driving nails, but is in fact terrific if you want to attend to different domestic tasks.

Pound meat

A meat mallet is nothing more than a hammer with a large head. Lay a sheet of plastic wrap under the steak or chicken breast you want to beat out, then a second sheet on top. Beat away with a small hammer or mallet until it's thin and tender.

Crush ice

Put the ice in a ziplock bag, lay it on the floor or countertop, and pound away. The more ice in the bag, the better, because it won't skip and skitter away with each stroke.

Crack nuts

Can't lay hands on your nutcracker? Use a hammer. Put the nuts on a thick layer of newspaper, then aim to crack each nut open with one stroke.

ladders

You won't find the sort of ladder that you can use to paint the outside of your house at a dollar store, but you may well find the sort of small, lightweight mini-stepladders that will let you reach the top of a cabinet with ease. But ladders can help you do more than climb heights.

Put light where you need it

A mini stepladder is ideal for moving a lamp to the task at hand. Whether you're cleaning in a dark part of a room or just reading in a chair and need more light, put a lamp on top of a short stepladder and you'll find light right at your elbow.

Build a tool caddy

Could you use an assistant to hand you tools? A short stepladder will do in a pinch. Set it up next to wherever you're working, and arrange your tools and supplies on the rungs. No more feeling around on the floor to see where you set down that hammer and no more clutching nails with your lips—just reach over to your materials ranged on the ladder.

Display knickknacks

Paint a wooden stepladder with bright, high-gloss enamel and use it to display teacups or figurines or any small knickknack that you fancy. It's an excellent talking point in a room. For a festive air, crowd small vases and jars of flowers all over the rungs and top step of the ladder. It's like having a flower festival in one spot.

lighter fluid

Even if you don't smoke and have no intention of refilling a cigarette lighter, a tiny container of lighter fluid is a powerful solvent that has additional uses beyond the obvious.

Take oil stains off clothes

Cooking stains can be nearly impossible to remove from clothes. They might be invisible to the naked eye when the item goes in the wash, then become an indelible ring after a trip through the washer and dryer. Squirt greasy areas with a little lighter fluid and then wash as usual.

Get a sticker off a paper book jacket

It's annoying when price stickers threaten to tear the glossy book jacket of that new hardcover. Use a few drops of lighter fluid and the sticker will lift off, leaving the jacket intact.

Remove lipstick stains

Forgot a lipstick in your pocket when you ran that load of clothes through the washer? Or worse, when you turned on the dryer! But you don't have to throw every item away. Apply lighter fluid directly to the stains, then wash again.

WAY BACK WHEN...

Steps to Safety

Fixing something you couldn't reach (though not changing a lightbulb) got easier after January 7, 1862. That's when the first U.S. patent for a safety stepladder was issued to John H. Balsley, a carpenter and a Dayton, Ohio, resident. Balsley ingeniously replaced round rungs with flat steps and placed hinges at the top of his ladder, allowing for easy folding and storage. Why was the stepladder not helpful in changing a bulb? The first public demonstration of Edison's lightbulb was still 17 years in the future!

Dissolve sticker residue

Lighter fluid is the easiest way to take stickers and labels off nearly any surface, from the bumper of your car to a glass bottle to a sticky sale tag on the jacket of a book. Drizzle a few drops directly from the bottle, then wait a few moments. Pull off any remaining sticker paper and use a paper towel to wipe off the glue residue.

magnets

Even a small magnet can be quite powerful, and they're enormously useful for cleanup around the house—they do a lot more than hold reminders and notices on the front of your fridge!

Hold paper clips

If you find that paper clips are scattered all over the surface of your desk or inside the drawers, don't use a magnet merely to pick them up but also to store them. Swing the magnet over the paper clips to gather them together, then put the magnet on the top of your desk as a sort of sculptural storage.

Gain More Counter Space

A magnetic strip hung horizontally above the countertop or stove keeps knives in reach but out of the way. (Knife blocks can have a sneakily large footprint that you'd probably rather use for your coffee maker.) Make sure the magnet is strong enough to hold your heaviest knife, and take care to dust frequently to keep knives clean.

Organize Your Ladder

Attach a round base magnet to the top of your ladder for an extra hand that can hold nuts, bolts, and screws, for you while you work. Round base magnets have a premade hole in the center, so all you need to do is drill a hole in the top of your ladder and secure the magnet with a bolt and nut.

Swing the magnet over paper clips to gather, then put the magnet on the top of your desk as a sort of sculptural storage.

Scotch Masking Tape

The monumental 3M company (formerly the Minnesota Mining and Manufacturing Co.) initially produced sandpaper. In 1925, employee Richard G. Drew noticed auto-body painters were aggravated with the tape they used for customizing. Drew decided to make a new product that didn't remove paint. A prototype combining cabinetmaker's glue and crepe paper didn't stick and earned the complaint: "Take this to those scotch (meaning cheap) bosses of yours and tell them to put on more adhesive!" Drew did, and Scotch masking tape, along with Drew's creativity, transformed 3M into an R&D-driven company.

masking tape

Designed to help autoworkers mask off and paint a clean edge on a car body, masking tape quickly proved to be ideal for a much wider variety of domestic tasks.

Tape kitchen chair bottoms

In most homes, kitchen chairs end up getting more use than nearly any other chairs in the house. They're scooted in and out, in and out all day long for meals, homework, and other projects. It's not surprising that the bases eventually wear and start to leave dark scuffs on the floor. Tape them up thickly with masking tape, and you'll find that the chairs slide smoothly, scuff-free.

Wrap crayons

Children love a fresh box of brand-new crayons, but the next thing you know, they're all broken. Little fingers find the breaking point of a crayon with astonishing ease. Make a new box go a little longer by wrapping each crayon's middle with masking tape.

Make labels

It's ridiculous to spend money on a label maker or on fancy labels if you have a roll of masking tape and a pen. Masking tape is durable but easy to remove. Use a strip for labeling lunch boxes, food storage containers, snow boots, schoolbooks, and more.

Pick up broken glass

You've swept up the big pieces of glass, but it's hard to be sure that every one of the tiny shards is gone. Find them by pressing down the sticky side of a few strips of masking tape, before you find them with your bare feet.

microfiber car polishing cloths

The space-age synthetic microfiber material, sold in multipacks to wash and polish cars, is extremely absorbent and durable, making it ideal for lots of other things besides making your wheels shine.

Polish windows and mirrors

Instead of a paper towel, use a microfiber cloth when you're washing windows and mirrors around the house. It will absorb the window cleaner and impart a radiant shine, and one cloth will do dozens of windows.

Dust furniture

When used dry, the microfiber cloth attracts and clings to dust. Get a chemical-free shine and sparkle on your furniture when you dust with microfiber.

Wipe your specs

The synthetic fibers of a microfiber cloth are extremely delicate and won't scratch the lenses of your glasses. From a large cloth, cut out a small square to fold and fit into your glasses case and keep the cloth reserved for just this purpose.

Dry a child's hair

Most little ones hate having their hair blow-dried almost as much as they hate having you rub their heads with a towel! Wrap a clean large microfiber cloth around your child's hair, and you'll find that it sucks out the moisture like magic. Hair dries fast and nobody has to cry!

paintbrushes

You won't find real sable paintbrushes for high-end craft work at your dollar store, but you will find an astonishing range of shapes and sizes of inexpensive paintbrushes—just right for all sorts of tasks other than applying paint.

Clean a keyboard

A small brush will help you clean crumbs and dust out of the cracks and crevices of your keyboard. Hold the keyboard upside down over a workspace using one hand and brush it vigorously with the other.

> A small brush will help you clean crumbs and dust out of the cracks and crevices of your keyboard.

Count your pennies!

Brush on kitchen glazes and sauces

Why spend money on a specialty food brush at a pricey culinary store? Buy a mid-size paintbrush and keep it exclusively with your kitchen utensils to brush on sauces or oils. Hand wash after each use.

Dust delicate items

A soft paintbrush is ideal for cleaning china figurines, chandeliers, lampshades—anything that you don't want to rub with a cloth. It's perfect for getting into the cracks and crevices of sculpted items, and it won't damage delicate parts.

Pretreat stains

A short stiff brush is perfect for working stain treatments into shirt collars or other dirty spots. Keep a brush near your laundry for just that purpose—there's no need to even rinse it out between uses.

paint scrapers

The thin, flexible blade of a paint scraper has a very straight, flat edge that makes it useful for a few things besides removing paint from glass, wood, and other surfaces.

Scrape off baked-on food

Keep a paint scraper in the kitchen solely dedicated to doing dishes. When you clean a glass or stoneware dish covered with baked-on food, it's much faster, easier, and neater to lightly scrape the surface with a paint scraper than to clog the fibers of a scrubbie.

Remove old drawer and cabinet liners

A paint scraper might have been made for this job. When you're replacing drawer and cabinet lining, whether paper or plastic, a paint scraper gets into the edges and lets you lift the liner along with any glue, as well as levering out tacks or small nails.

Use as a putty knife

A paint scraper is more flexible than most putty knives, allowing you to smooth spackle or even caulk into awkward spaces such as corners or curves.

Replace a spatula

A clean paint scraper kept solely for the purpose makes an ideal spatula for kitchen use. The thin metal makes it easy to prod and turn food while it's cooking, and the flexible blade makes it perfect for lifting out the first brownie or piece of pie from the pan.

pliers

Used for grasping and turning nuts and bolts, among other things, pliers seem industrial, but once you take a pair of pliers out of the workshop, you'll find they're indispensable around the house.

Remove pin bones from fish

That filet of salmon is about to go under the broiler when you spot a tiny bone protruding from the surface. Pin bones in fish can be nearly impossible to see but you'll feel them quickly enough if you accidentally bite down on one. Remove them by running your fingertips against the grain of the fish and using a pair of needle-nose pliers to jerk the bone out in the opposite direction from which it's pointing.

Hold a tack or tiny nail

Don't risk your thumbs when you're hammering in tiny tacks or delicate nails for a craft project. Grasp the stem with a pair of needle-nosed pliers and then apply the hammer. You'll save your fingers and get a better view of the task at hand.

Crack nuts

Use a large tongue-and-groove pliers for cracking nuts. The adjustable head lets you open everything from walnuts in the shell to little filberts.

Skin a chicken

The recipe calls for skinless chicken thighs, but the darn things keep slipping out of your hands as you try to pull. Hold the bone or firmly grasp the meat with a pair of clean new pliers kept exclusively for kitchen use, and pull the skin back with the other hand (grasping it with a paper towel if you still can't get a grip). It's the fastest, most efficient way to get the job done.

plungers

That rubber cup on the end of a stick seems to have only one use: unblocking a clog in a drain or toilet. But even a dollar-store plunger has uses that are hidden to the naked eye.

Deter mosquitoes

At the end of the season, you can get a bargain on citronella candles, whose pungent scent discourages insects. Push the wooden handle of a new plunger into the ground, and put the candle in the upturned cup.

Fix a dent in your car

It's such a simple ding but the cost may be a shocker if you take it to a body shop. Save your money and try a plunger instead. Dip it in water to help create suction, then push it over the dent and pull out briskly. It might just work the first time.

WHO KNEW? **DAWN DISHWASHING LIQUID CAN REPLACE A PLUNGER!**

If you don't have a plunger handy, here's a trick: Use Dawn dishwashing liquid to unclog your toilet. Squirt a generous amount of soap into the clogged bowl. Wait until the water level goes down, fill a bucket with cool water (hot water could crack the bowl), and then pour it into your soaped toilet from waist high. Your clog should clear—though you may need to repeat the procedure a few times. This only works if the clog is paper or organic.

---

rubber doorstops

These sturdy little triangles of rubber would seem to have a highly specific function—holding a door open but you can do more.

Prop a computer keyboard

Whether you want your keyboard to prop toward you or away from you—whichever position you find best for typing—two rubber doorstops will hold it securely and comfortably in place.

Put the brakes on rolling furniture

Having wheels on your bed or sofa is extremely handy for positioning it around the room wherever you want it. But once you've found the exact position, it can be extremely frustrating to make it stay there. Wedge rubber doorstops against each wheel on the bed or piece of furniture, turned inward to hide them, and your furniture won't move again until you're redecorating!

Shim a bookshelf

Bookshelves used to be a specialty item built by a carpenter, but fortunately, they're now easily available in all sizes to be constructed at home. Problem is, this type of flat-pack shelving can

teeter, especially if your walls aren't flat. Use rubber doorstops for a secure shim to tilt the shelf very slightly back to the wall for a safe and secure fit. If the stops are pressed up under the kick at the floor, they'll be unobtrusive.

sandpaper

Available in a range of grits, from so fine you could smooth your skin to extremely coarse for industrial use, sandpaper is useful for more than rubbing wood surfaces.

Polish away mineral and lime stains

Instead of using harsh chemicals to remove stains from an old toilet, very gently polish them away with sandpaper. Clean the toilet first as usual with cleanser and a brush. Then turn off the water supply to the toilet, flush, and use the finest grit sandpaper you can find to rub gently in a circular motion at the stains at the water line.

Smooth rough skin on your soles

No matter what you do, rough skin can build up on the soles of your feet, especially in summer when you might be wearing sandals or other open shoes. Experts warn against tools that shave off skin, and chemical smoothers can be harsh and abrasive. Instead, try a fine-grit sandpaper to buff off the rough edges and make your skin feel smooth and soft again. Be sure to slather on a rich foot lotion when you're done.

Sharpen tools

Quit using whetstones to sharpen chisels, axes and other tools. You can get an even sharper edge with sandpaper. Wet medium-grit sandpaper and lay it on a very flat and stable surface. The water will hold the sandpaper steady while you rub the edges of the tool in a regular circular motion, alternating sides. Hone the edge on a wet piece of super-fine grit paper.

Buy it for this, use it for that!

8 More Nontraditional Ways to Use

SANDPAPER

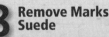
A DIFFERENT *Solution*

1 Sharpen Needles
Don't ditch dull needles. Instead, poke your old sewing needles through fine-grit sandpaper once or twice or twist them in a folded piece of sandpaper. They will be sharp and good-as-new in a jiffy. Point taken!

2 Save Shoes
Are your suede shoes feeling blue? Are they dirty and stained? Cheer them up! By very gently scuffing with sand paper, you can revive the nap and take off some stains.

3 Smooth Nails
It never fails: You're in a hurry and a nail breaks. If you can't find your emery board, don't dispair. A piece of fine-grit sandpaper will work just as well smoothing the snag.

4 Name Game
Cut the letters of your child's name out of sandpaper. Let your child feel the shapes and pick a favorite. Put a blank sheet of paper on top of the letter and let the little one rub over it with a crayon. The shape of the letter will appear like magic, promoting calls of "Let's do another!"

5 Outmart Slugs
Sanding disks (rounds pieces of sandpaper) are perfectly sized to fit under your potted plants. Why would you place them there? To keep slugs out! No slug enjoys oozing across an abrasive surface. Make certain that the circumference of the sandpaper is wider than that of your planter.

6 Create Keepsakes
Decorations made by hand become sentimental keepsakes. Seahorses, starfish, gingerbread houses—draw a pattern and trace it onto the smooth side of a sheet of sandpaper. Do this twice and then cut out your ornament. Spread glue on the smooth sides of the sandpaper, fold some yarn in half, and sandwich it between the two pieces with a loop sticking out. After your creation dries, you may decorate as desired.

7 Sharp Move
Have your little ones misplaced that plastic sharpener again? Sharpen dull crayons, pastels, and sidewalk chalk by rubbing them against a piece of sandpaper.

8 Remove Marks from Suede
A little fine-grit sandpaper and a gentle touch are great for removing (or at least minimizing) an ink stain or small scuff mark on suede clothing. Afterward, buff gently with a toothbrush or nailbrush. You might avoid an expensive trip to the dry cleaner.

Get out a little fine-grit sandpaper to help you remove stains from grout.

Restore a ping-pong paddle

That old wooden ping-pong set in the basement offered hours of fun, before the paddles' covering wore out. All you need is some glue, medium-grit sandpaper, and a pair of scissors. Strip off the old covering and cut two new sides to fit. Use a scrap of sandpaper to rub off the old glue, and then attach the new coverings. Once you get some new ping-pong balls, you're ready for tournament play!

Open stubborn jars

Keep a piece of medium-grit sandpaper in the kitchen for opening stubborn jar lids. The sandpaper, grit side down, will let you get a grip on the lid to turn it.

Get back your edge on scissors

Favorite kitchen shears lost their edge? Sewing scissors snagging on the fabric? You can pay to have them sharpened by a professional—or you can get excellent results by slicing up a sheet of medium- to fine-grit sandpaper with your dull scissors.

screening

A roll of metal or plastic mesh screening may look like it's calling you to (finally) re-stretch that saggy panel on your back door. But it might be suggesting something else.

Sieve lumps out of paint

A can of paint that sits for awhile can get lumpy, even if you still need it to touch up a wall in the living room. Sure, you could stretch a width of screen over a bucket and pour the paint through. Or, you could cut a circle of screen the width of the can and push it carefully to the bottom with a stirring stick pressed to the center, to keep the screen level. The lumps will sink down with the screen, allowing you to stir up the remainder and start painting.

Cover picnic food

Nothing ruins a bowl of potato salad at a picnic like finding flies hovering over it. Cut several squares of screen to keep on hand for outdoor entertaining. Lay them directly over bowls and pitchers. They're unobtrusive and highly effective.

Keep seeds safe

When your seeds are newly planted in the ground, the local birds and wildlife thank you for the buffet. Make sure more of your seeds get a chance to sprout by laying screening over a row of newly planted seeds until the first tiny shoots come up.

screwdrivers

A screwdriver is such a simple item—a flat (or Phillips) piece of metal to turn a screw. It's also the only tool for the job. When you need one, nothing else will do. But once you have one, it will also do a wealth of other things.

Prop open a window

You finally got that painted-shut window open by dragging the edge of a flat-head screwdriver along the painted sill, and now the doggone thing won't stay open! Turn the screwdriver upside down and push it against one side of the window, with the handle propped against the sill, and the flat head nestled against the bottom of the window. It will hold securely, without slipping.

Open a letter

Reach for a flat-head screwdriver when the mail arrives. The angled tip makes it easy to slip the head into the flap and slit the letter open.

Scrape off paint

Use the flat side of the tip to scrape any remains of paint off glass when you're painting windows. You can also use the sharp edge of the tip to scrape paint out of tracks and edges of wood when you're stripping paint off furniture.

Make a sturdy lever for prying

The beauty of a lever is that it exerts a great deal of power on the lifting end (assuming the fulcrum is close to that end) relative to the amount of exertion you apply at the opposite end. With that in mind, don't forget about your sturdy flat-end screwdriver when you need to lift something. With a small piece of wood as a fulcrum, you could even lift the leg of a sofa so you could shove in or remove the edge of a rug.

Plant seeds

A screwdriver is an ideal "sowing stick" for planting seeds. Push it straight down into the ground, wiggle around to open the hole, and then drop in the seeds.

Chip ice off the old block

If you've got a solid block of ice, as with store-bought ice that has thawed in the car and then refrozen into a hard mass in your home freezer, use your screwdriver like an ice pick, hitting the block with the flat head to break it up, and let the party start!

A screwdriver is an ideal "sowing stick" for planting seeds.

Remove staples

A flat-head screwdriver is as good as or better than a staple remover at prying out staples. Push it under the staple and lever it right out.

steel wool

When you're scrubbing crusted food off a cast-iron pan, steel wool is a lifesaver. It's tough and effective and can be used over and over. When it gets too rusty or dirty to use, just throw it out—it's very cheap. All of which makes it ideal for other uses in the home.

Give garden tools a rubdown

Give metal blades, tines, and shovels a blast of WD-40 and scrub off any dirt or rust stains with steel wool. Wipe the metal off with a dry cloth and put your tools away with a shine and a clean conscience!

Tell scuffs to get lost

Black heel marks on vinyl and linoleum floors are frustrating because they won't mop or wipe off, no matter how hard you scrub. A piece of steel wool will rub them away in a second. Scrub lightly, in small circles, and then wipe the area with a paper towel. Good as new!

Discourage rodents and other "boring" creatures

When it's cold outside, lots of little critters will expend lots of energy chewing through skirting boards. And carpenter bees don't care about the temperature while they're boring through the siding of your house. Outsmart the critters by stuffing holes and crevices with steel wool. It will give rodents something to chew on and quickly force carpenter bees to go looking for a new home.

Sharpen shears

Kitchen scissors, especially those you use for foodstuffs, can get dull quickly. Before you discard a well-used piece of steel wool, slice it to bits, directly into the garbage can, with your kitchen shears. Cutting through the fine metal threads will help bring the edge back to your scissors. Wipe the scissors with a damp sponge and then dry with a cloth before storing.

Rub crayon marks off walls

Little ones look at wallpaper and see a huge blank canvas. Parents look at the results of their handiwork ("But I only turned my back for a minute!") and see marks that seem like they can't possibly come clean. But before you repaper the hall, get a clean, new piece of unsoaped steel wool and scrub the crayon lightly, in one direction. You've got a good chance of returning the wall to its pristine state.

WD-40

Few homes are without the distinctive blue and yellow can of WD-40. It's the fastest and best way to stop hinges from squeaking, of course, but it's also a product that has inspired innovation among its users. You can find tales of WD-40 used for, among other things, uncoiling a python from a bus axle. Here are a few ways to start you thinking "outside the can."

Clean tough stains on clothes

WD-40 famously doesn't share its recipe, but it's easy enough to smell a petroleum product. Normally, that would suggest a potential grease stain if spilled on clothing, but, in fact, WD-40 is great at getting out a wide range of stains. As always, stains come cleaner when treated fresh, but if you can spray spots of tomato, tea, coffee, or blood with WD-40, then wash as usual, you may just get it out—with no grease spot remaining!

Remove spots from carpets and floors

Black scuffs and heel marks on linoleum, ink or wine on carpets and rugs, all can be difficult to remove to varying degrees. Spray with WD-40 and rub the floor or scrub the carpet, rinsing well with soap and warm water once the spot is gone.

Take dark stains off countertops

Spilled some blueberry jam? Let coffee or tea dry in? Dark colors can set into your countertops to stay, and no matter how you rub with a sponge or scrubbie, they won't budge. Try a spritz of WD-40 and they'll wipe right up. Be sure to wash it off and rinse well.

Make a blackboard look new

Wiping down a chalkboard with a wet sponge will certainly remove all the chalk, but it will leave a dusty residue over the board. Instead, clean a chalkboard with WD-40, and the whole thing will gleam like new.

Make a "dead" pen write again

Is your ballpoint truly out of ink, or is the tiny ball in the tip gunked up with dried ink? Before you toss it in the trash, find out by wiping the tip with a little WD-40 and a paper towel. There's a good chance your pen will live to write again.

Lubricate pins and needles

When you're sewing with a dense, heavy material, such as denim or tweed, it can be difficult to force the pins through the thick fabric. They'll slip through much more easily if you lubricate them first with WD-40. Dampen a cotton ball or crumpled paper towel with WD-40 and then wipe your pins on it.

Brighten lawn furniture

Faded plastic lawn chairs and tables may seem like a lost cause, but if you spray and buff them with WD-40, they'll not only look smoother and shiny, but the color actually appears to regain its luster.

Tell rabbits and rodents to bug off

If rabbits and other critters are digging and wriggling under your chain link fence to reach the tasty stuff in your garden, let them know their presence is highly unwelcome by spraying a generous amount of WD-40 along the base of the fence, directly on the metal.

Unstick gluey fingers

Accidentally sticking your fingers together with superglue can make anyone panic. Don't hop around in frustration, and don't slap your forehead with your gluey hand. Spray your sticky fingers with WD-40 and let them sit for a few minutes. They'll soon come unstuck. Use a bit more to remove any remaining residue—and be careful next time!

Spray and buff on faded plastic lawn chairs and tables to bring back the shine..

Loosen up a vertical blind

Vertical blinds should swing easily open at the lightest touch of your fingertips on the plastic or wooden stick that attaches to the mechanism. If you find you're having to twist hard, spray WD-40 directly on the mechanism at the top of the stick (or on the roller that holds the chain).

Help doors run in their tracks

Sliding glass doors look beautiful leading out onto a patio or deck, but any homeowner who's ever dealt with sticking doors knows that it ruins the illusion of a glass wall if you always have to put your back into it and force the door back and forth. Use WD-40 to keep your doors freely moving. Spray it generously all along the tracks, being careful to stay within the metal grooves, and then push the doors vigorously back and forth several times to distribute the lubricant.

Lubricate locks and deadbolts

You may not realize how much effort it takes when you struggle with a sticky lock. Spritz your key and the inside of the lock with WD-40, then insert the key and jiggle it. Also spray WD-40 on bolts and hinges so that every time, your doors will open and swing smoothly.

Silence a bed

Does your bed frame squeak, jingle or rattle every time you roll over at night? Get a peaceful night's sleep with WD-40. Reach under the bed frame and spray all metal joints, screws or hinges, then lie on the bed and roll and bounce until the lubricant works its way through each joint.

Take marks off car paint

With a spray of WD-40, you can remove the paint smear where another car bumped against yours in a parking lot, and you can get rid of dead bugs and road tar, both of which can damage paint if left unattended.

Repel wasps and hornets

In the spring, mist the undersides of eaves and the corners of your porch roof with WD-40 so that wasps and hornets don't build nests there.

Polish a Formica backsplash

A spritz of WD-40 and a wipe with a soft cloth will remove stains or streaks from the Formica backsplash in your kitchen and help repel grime. (Don't spray directly on the countertop.)

Prevent silver from tarnishing

Once you have cleaned decorative silver, you can keep it gleaming much longer if you mist the surface with a fine spray of WD-40, then buff with a soft lint-free cloth. Do not use this on silver that you will use for eating; however, it's ideal for, say, a decorative silver tea set that you keep on display, rather than using for tea.

Untangle jewelry chains

When necklaces are stored together in a jewelry box, it can be hard to avoid a tangle and even harder to unpick the knot without breaking a chain. Spray the snarl with WD-40, and use your fingers to gently loosen and untangle it.

weather stripping

A roll of weather stripping is an inexpensive fix that can save you big money when you seal off drafty windows and doorjambs. Once you've done that, see what else you can do with this handy material.

Make a secure tool grip

Wrap an overlapping spiral of weather stripping around the handles of your favorite tools, from hammers and axes to wrenches and screwdrivers. You'll get a padded, more comfortable handle and a much better grip for tough jobs.

Add a nonstick base to appliances

Many countertop appliances such as coffeemakers and electric can openers can skid or slip easily. Help them stay put by affixing a few pieces of weather stripping to the base of each appliance.

Give footwear a grip

Waterproof footwear, such as smooth, one-piece Wellington boots, are great at keeping out snow and ice, but not so terrific for keeping your footing. Get a grip by using rubber cement or superglue to attach strips of flat weather stripping under the heels and toes. You can use this trick with hip waders, to help you get a better grip on slick rocks in rivers and streams.

wire

The tool aisle has many types of wire, from insulated varieties meant for electrical work to rolls of shiny naked metal. Whichever you choose, there's a lot you can do with a roll.

Design homemade jewelry

A length of bright copper or nickel wire is a necklace waiting to happen. String on beads or pendants, sequins or buttons, and create a piece of jewelry that expresses you.

Make a handle

Got a bucket with a broken handle? Want to decorate a jar of jam with a handle? Loop covered wire around the neck of the container, then weave wire back and forth, making a U-shape across the top and twisting wire all around the U to make a comfortable carrying handle.

Create a candleholder

Wrap glass jars of different shapes and sizes with metal wire of various colors and thicknesses to make exciting and unique candleholders. You can make several patterns and add glass beads for color and flair. Be sure not to wrap so thickly that the light can't shine through.

Hang photos and cards

A doubled length of wire swooping between two nails is an ideal way to display photos or holiday and birthday cards. Use paper clips or wooden clothes pegs to hang the pictures off the wire, and change your own personal art gallery as the mood strikes you.

Wrap an overlapping spiral of weather stripping around the handles of your favorite tools for a secure grip.

wire brush

Like an industrial scrubbing brush but made with stiff wire bristles, a wire brush is primarily used for removing paint and cleaning off rust. If you pick up a couple from the dollar store, you can use them for more.

Clean concrete and brick flooring

Use a wire brush and a mild soap solution to scrub dirt and grime off garage floors and brick patios. Work in a circular pattern and use a gentle touch.

Remove moss from flagstones

Pour white vinegar straight over mossy flags and scrub off the moss with a wire brush. The brush will remove the existing moss, and the vinegar will help kill off the spores. If the flags are set in a very damp, shady area, the moss will inevitably creep back, but if it has merely crept into an area where you don't want it, a wire brush and vinegar should do the trick.

Texturize paint for a custom look

Use a wire brush to create patterns and designs on wood or plaster. Depending on your artistic ability, you can make circles or long curving lines, feathered edges or waves. Apply a thick coat of paint to a portion of the wall or item you're decorating, and experiment with your wire brush. If you don't like your initial efforts, paint over them and start again.

wood glue

Based on resin, wood glue is specially designed to attach the porous, uneven surfaces of wood. A thick layer dries to form a weak bond, but a thin layer makes an extremely powerful, water-resistant bond.

Remove splinters

Got a splinter in your finger that won't come out? It's amazing how something so tiny can torture you. Instead of prodding your sore digit with needles and tweezers, put a thin layer of wood glue over it. When it dries, peel the glue off. The splinter will lift out with it.

Fill nail holes in wood

Holes in wooden paneling are a real problem to fill. You can't just put anything in there or it will show. But if you have wood glue, you can mix it with sawdust and use this mixture to fill the holes. If the wood has a very dark finish, you may want to tint the wood glue and sawdust with a few drops of stain to match.

Create a clear varnish

Wood glue dries clear, making it ideal for varnishing craft projects. Mix it half and half with water, and use this mixture to paint over decoupage or papier-mâché. If you tint it with a few drops of fabric dye, the resulting varnish will have a translucent color.

WAY BACK WHEN...

Horse Hockey!

When you were young, did you ever ask for a pony and get handed a bottle of glue?

Even if you didn't have a relative with a questionable sense of humor, you may have heard that "horses are sent to the glue factory." Glue made of rendered animal parts was once the most popular type of adhesive used in woodworking, but this is no longer the case. Today, synthetic glues dominate the market. Elmer's Glue does not use animals or animal parts to make its best-selling product.

> If you have a splinter in your finger, put a thin layer of wood glue over it. When it dries, peel the glue off. The splinter will lift it.

work gloves

The work gloves you're looking for in the tool aisle of the dollar store are the thick rubber kind, rather than the thin rubber dishwashing gloves you see in the cleaning aisle. While they're intended for industrial uses, they have other domestic purposes you may have never imagined.

Open jar lids

A durable rubber work glove is the best way to "get a grip" on a stubborn jar lid. Keep one in your utensil drawer and you'll never beat a jar of pickles in frustration on the countertop again.

Put a frozen "hand" in your punchbowl

Having a Halloween party? Here's what to drink: Fill a rubber glove with water, tie off the wrist, and freeze it solid. In a punchbowl or large mixing bowl, combine half cranberry juice, half ginger ale. Remove the hand from the freezer and snip the glove off with scissors. (Trying to tear it off will break the fingers.) Float the icy hand in the punch. Accept compliments.

Serve Thanksgiving dinner

Large birds are often too big and bulky to remove from roasting pans with tongs or a spatula. If you need to move a warm bird from pan to platter, slip on a pair of clean gloves and lift the bird from underneath. Your hands make the best tools.

Remove pet hair

A rubber glove is a pet-hair magnet. If you've gone through more vacuum bags (and vacuums!) than you care to count in cleaning pet hair off your sofas and chairs, all you need is a supply of dollar store rubber work gloves. Put them on and don't forget to fondle the throw pillows while you're at it. Pet hair will practically leap off your sofa and onto your gloves.

Sort recyclables

If you're like many of us, during the week you toss all your glass and cans and containers higgledy-piggledy into your recycling bin. Then you may have to hurriedly sort it out before pickup day. Make the job easier by keeping a sturdy pair of durable rubber work gloves right next to the recycling bin. Put them on each time you have to sort, to avoid nicks from open can lids and yucky drips from rinsed containers.

INDEX

A

acne, 49
Adams, Thomas, 21
address book replacement, 202
adhesive bandages, 48
    alternative, 67
    removing, 50
adhesive fabric spray, 160
adhesive tape, 10–11, 186–87, 207–8
Adolph's Meat Tenderizer, 29
air conditioners
    cleaning, 16, 109, 132
    sealing room vent for, 203
air freshener, alternative, 42, 84
air travel, aromatherapy for, 56
algae, removing, 107
allergy attack, preventing, 70
allergy self-test, 48
alligator clips, 216
all-purpose cleaners, 26, 45
aluminum cookware, discolored, 24
aluminum foil, 104, 130–31
aluminum pie pan, 131
ammonia, 105
antacid tablets, 48–49
ant bites, 75
ant control, 25, 38, 86, 109, 149, 186, 193, 219
antistatic fabric spray, 105–6
applesauce, 14
appliances. *See* kitchen appliances; specific appliances
appliqués
    bathtub, 132–33
    fabric, 174
Armor All Protectant, 82
aromatherapy, for air travel, 56
arthritis, 33, 88, 182
ashtray, outdoor, 87
aspirin, 11, 49
athlete's foot, 16, 49

B

babies. *See* children
baby blankets, making, 164
baby clothes, washing, 17
baby food, freezing, 140, 142
baby oil, 50, 65
baby powder, 11, 50–51
baby shampoo, 51–52
baby wipes, 52
back massage, 97
backpacks, 138, 164, 165, 174
back pain, 29, 31
back scratchers, 55, 60
backsplash, cleaning, 238
back support, for driving, 127
bacon grease, 131, 145
bad breath, 63
Baggies, 154
baked goods, testing doneness of, 176
baking soda, 14–17
balloons, 11, 187–88
Balsley, John H., 226
Baltzley, Louis E., 189
bandages
    adhesive, 48, 50, 67
    keeping dry, 151, 188
bandannas, 78
Ban Roll-On deodorant, 58
barrette, alternative, 167
baseball mitt, reconditioning, 32
basil, planting, 86
baskets, 160–62
baster, 132
bath oil, 52–53
bathroom
    deodorizing, 84
    magnetic holder in, 202
    mildew in, 56, 218
bathroom floor, removing hair from, 116
baths
    additives for, 30, 31
    for children, 92
bathtub appliqués, 132–33
bathtub ring, removing, 24
bathtubs
    removing paint splatters from, 91
    repairing scratched, 195
    replacing plug in, 89
bat repellent, 117

batting, 162
beading, 163
beads
    history of, 163
    picking up spilled, 205
beanbags, making, 18
beans, dried, 14, 18
bed frame, squeaky, 238
belts, alternative, 99, 165–66, 217
Bentz, Amalie Auguste Melitta, 137
berries
    freezing, 141
    hulling strawberries, 134
bias tape and binding, 164
bibs, baby, 78, 166
bicycle
    leveling, 98
    shining, 113
bicycle seat, rain-proofing, 72
binder clips, 189
binders, 188–89, 198
birdbaths
    alternative, 87, 153
    mosquito repellent for, 42–43
bird droppings, removing, 45
bird feeder, protecting from squirrels, 34, 37
blackboard
    cleaning, 237
    making, 195
blackout window covers, 143, 223
blankets
    baby, 164
    fleece, 172
bleach, 106–7
bleach spots, covering, 177
bleeding
    from cuts, 67
    nosebleeds, 64, 108
    from shaving, 49, 66
blender, cleaning, 111
blinds
    cleaning, 43, 72, 73, 82, 88, 105
    unsticking opener on, 238
blisters, 54, 58, 222
bloodstains, 24, 30, 237
book covers, 178, 212, 213
bookmarks, 163, 167, 201, 203, 207
books
    mildewed or musty, 15, 83, 85

removing price sticker from, 227
sealing, 166
storing, 104
tracking already-read, 202
bookshelf shims, 152, 232
boots
alternative, 114
attaching grips on, 239
repairing ripped, 224
shaper for storing, 119, 191
bottle caps
removing, 98
substitute for missing, 143
bottle openers, 134
bottles, 133
deodorizing, 15, 31
spray bottles, 122–23
squeeze bottles, 95–96
water bottles, 45
bows, stiffening, 173
box cutters, 216–17
boxes, 189–90
bracelets
for calorie counting, 163
materials for making, 58, 80, 99, 169, 179, 183, 216
brass, cleaning, 25
bread, 18–19
baking, 123
freezing, 146
keeping fresh, 200
bread crumb alternative, 34
bricks, cleaning, 117
broiler flare-ups, preventing, 19
broken glass, 222, 224, 229
brooch, attaching with magnet, 204
broom, storing, 120, 203
brownies, precutting, 141
brown sugar, freshener for, 28
bruises, 68–69
brushes, cleaning, 16
bubble bath, 53, 65
bubble wrap, 190–91
buckets, 10, 78–79, 134–35, 239
bulbs (flower)
marking location for, 89, 166, 208
protecting, 50, 51, 116
bumper sticker, removing, 55, 227
bungee cords, 79–80, 182, 217
bungee jumping, origin of, 80
burgers
freezing, 86

marking doneness of, 156
burlap, 80
burned pots
cleaning, 15, 35, 113, 117
preventing, 18, 164, 165
burn marks
on carpet, 210–11
on clothing, 111
burns
minor skin, 74
mouth, 39
butter, 19–20
shaping, 140
softening, 157
buttons, 164–65
cutting from clothing, 56
protecting decorative, 104
securing, 101, 173, 206
sewing on, 58, 73
Velcro replacing, 182

C

cabbage, odor when cooking, 18
cabbage worms, 35
cabinets. See kitchen cabinets
cactus, replanting, 208
cake pan, greasing, 154
cakes
decorating, 96, 123, 125, 157
made with soda, 37
preserving freshness of, 39
preventing stale, 126
protecting from ants, 186
calamine lotion, 53–54
calorie-counting bracelet, 163
camera, rain-proofing, 72
camping, 134, 191, 225
candleholders, making, 239
candles, 80–81, 135
lighting, 156
mirror reflecting, 68
candle wax drips, removing, 117, 144
candy garden, in flowerpot, 87
candy tins, 192
canker sores, 16, 48
can opener, cleaning, 146, 157
cans, 135
cap erasers, 192
car battery corrosion, 37
car care
cleaners for, 44, 52, 53, 61, 123, 238

cleaning chrome, 37, 69, 114, 123
cleaning headlight and taillight covers, 75
cleaning hubcaps, 114, 117
cleaning whitewall tires, 117
cleaning windshield wiper blades, 105
de-icing, 94, 108, 204, 206, 207
deodorizing, 56
detailing interior, 137
detecting oil leaks, 60
hiding spare key, 222
oil changes, 153
organizing, 78–79, 210
protecting interior, 109, 167
removing dents, 231
removing paint smears, 238
removing tree sap, 28, 121
scratch repair, 69, 195
securing floor mat, 181
shading steering wheel, 92
taping permit sticker, 186
when parking, 98
on winter ice, 133
carpal tunnel syndrome, 209
carpenter bees, 236
carpet
deodorizing, 51
removing stains from, 22, 52, 62, 71, 118, 237
repairing burns on, 210–11
reviving fibers of, 43
carrot seeds, sowing, 23
carryalls, alternative, 78, 79
car seat, cushioning, 191
carsick odor, 44
car wax, 10, 81–83, 218–19
casserole topping, 34
cast, keeping dry, 151
cat litter, 83–84, 133, 139, 148
cats
belly-scratcher for, 55
brushing, 60
discouraging clawing by, 224
keeping off countertop, 123
keeping off furniture, 188
keeping out of sandbox, 43
pooper scooper for, 95
protecting tree ornaments from, 156
skin problems in, 69
toys for, 173, 225
caulk, 219
caulk tube or gun
extending, 207

stopper for, 136
cayenne pepper, 33–34
C-clamps, 220
CDs
    removing stuck, 206
    skipping, 82
cedar chips, 107
cell phone
    drying out, 83
    removing scratches on, 75
chairs
    preventing scuffs from, 228
    upholstering, 150–51
chalk, 193, 233
chalk lines, preserving, 62
chamomile tea, 20–21
chandelier, cleaning, 88
changing pad, 147, 178
chapped hands, 66
charcoal briquettes, 84–85, 220
cheese, preserving freshness of, 19–20, 39
cheesecloth, 136
cheese grater, cleaning, 73
Chesebrough, Robert A., 70
chest rub, 54–55, 65
chewing gum, 21–22, 200–201, 217
chicken
    skinning, 231
    trussing, 97
child-proofing, 138, 162, 210
children
    baby bibs for, 78, 166
    baby blankets for, 164
    baby mobile for, 136
    bathing, 92
    changing pad for, 147, 178
    clothing for, 17, 108, 147, 154, 160, 167
    crafts for, 145, 152, 164, 169, 177, 183
    decorating room for, 26
    entertaining, 22, 96, 179, 190–91, 223, 233
    foods for, 27–28, 140, 141, 142, 152, 161
    hair-drying for, 229
    Halloween and, 54, 104, 145
    high chair protection for, 132, 178
    ice packs for, 122
    kiddie tables for, 135
    mini snow shovel for, 85
    protecting in shopping cart, 178
    securing sippy cups of, 132
    skin rashes on, 30
    string phone for, 140
    tick repellent for, 42
    toys for, 85, 87, 138, 170–71, 173
    utensils for, 152
    wading pool safety for, 133
    waterproofing shoes of, 154
chile burns, 39
china, repairing nicked, 195
chlorine green hair, 25
chocolate curls, making, 157
chocolate stains, 30
Christmas cards, displaying, 216, 239
Christmas gifts, tracking already-given, 202
Christmas tree. See also holiday decorations
    decorating, 180
    disposing of, 149
    hangers for, 216
    pruning, 225
    two-dimensional, 91
Christmas tree stand, 79
chrome, cleaning, 37, 69, 123
church-key bottle opener, 134
cinnamon-sugar shaker, 153
cleaning and home supplies, 102–27
Cline, Elmer, 19
clipboard, 194–95
Clorox bleach, 106
clothesline, for travel, 217
clothespins, 108, 166–68
clothing. See also specific items of clothing
    burn marks on, 111
    children's, 17, 108, 147, 154, 160, 167
    dust covers for, 109, 147
    hanging, 108, 119, 190
    laundering (see laundry)
    preventing creases in, 119, 190, 194, 212
    quick drying of, 127
    rejuvenating, 165
    removing lint and "pills" from, 222
    removing stains from, 22, 24, 52, 55, 93, 111, 195, 226, 227
    removing tar from, 36
    static cling on, 61, 130
    storing, 104, 147, 160–61, 220, 221
    wrinkle remover for, 126
club soda, 22
coasters, alternative, 86, 143
coat hangers. See hangers
coffee, 23
coffee filters, 137–38
coffee reservoir, overfilled, 132
coffee stains, 30, 226, 237
cola, 37
colanders, 138
cold cream, 54, 55
cold pack, 154, 187–88
cold sores, 44
collars, softening, 212
combs, 55–56
    cleaning, 16, 186
compass, made from cork, 203
compost, 41, 109
computer keyboard
    cleaning, 198, 229, 230
    missing feet on, 133
    propping up, 232
    protecting, 151
concrete, cleaning, 26, 37, 83, 240
condiments
    catching drips from, 143
    holders for, 96
congestion, chest and sinus, 31, 34, 54
conjunctivitis, 51
contact information, organizing, 188, 202
container gardening, 78, 85
containers
    food storage, 79–80
    marking liquid content of, 209, 210
    plastic, 107, 149–50
contractor bags, 108–9, 221
cookbooks
    page opener for, 167, 189, 220
    protecting from splatters, 114, 189
cookie cutter, alternative, 142
cookies
    keeping fresh, 19, 211–12
    potato chips in, 35
    protecting from ants, 186
    scooping dough for, 140
    sprinkling sugar on, 153
cookie sheets, storing, 127
cooking odors, 18, 44, 45
cookware
    discolored aluminum, 24
    removing rust from, 15

scorched, 15, 18, 35
coolers
    deodorizing, 41
    storing, 220
copper, cleaning, 25, 26
corkboard cover, 213
corn
    bread for buttering, 19
    removing silk from, 120
    sweetening, 30, 31
corn removal, on foot, 49
cornstarch, 23–24
correction fluid, 194, 195
cosmetics
    case for, 209
    packing, 154
cotton balls, 56, 65
cotton swab, 56–57, 65
coughs, 54
countertops
    cleaning marble, 17, 27
    keeping cat off, 123
    removing dough from, 91
    removing rust rings from, 83
    removing stains from, 237
    scorch marks on, 83
    scratched, 82
    securing appliances on, 239
    spoon rest for, 143
coupon holders, 167, 197
crab bait, 22
cracks
    in clay flowerpot, 201
    cleaning, 156, 230
    in dog dish, 21
    in plaster, 219
    in trash can, 224
craft apron, 222
craft supplies
    cleaning up, 85, 115
    for kids' projects, 145, 152,
        164, 169, 177, 183
    varnish, 240
crayons, 196
    coloring, 196
    preventing breakage of, 228
    removing marks from, 28, 71,
        210, 236
    sharpening, 233
cream of tartar, 24–25
creased clothing, preventing,
    119, 190, 194, 212
crumbs, making, 149
cupcakes
    distributing batter for, 132
    toppings for, 27, 153

cup hooks, 221
curlers, alternative, 130
curtain rings, 138
curtains
    drop cloths as, 223
    hemming, 175
    made of buttons, 165
    making café, 175
    tiebacks for, 165
cushions
    securing to chair, 197
    weatherizing, 177–78, 223
cuts, 67, 70
cutting board
    cover for, 157
    securing on counter, 210
cutworms, 119

D

dance party, on bubble wrap,
    190–91
dashboard, cleaning, 52
Dawn dishwashing liquid, for
    unclogging toilet, 231
decks, removing bird droppings
    from, 45
decorating
    with boxes, 190
    with flowerpots, 87
    with mirrors, 67–68
decorations. See also holiday
    decorations
    sandpaper, 233
decorative balls, made from
    twine, 100
decorative storage boxes, 160
deer deterrent, 34
dental floss, 57–58
dents, car, 231
dentures, cleaning, 22
deodorant, 58, 63, 65
deodorizers
    baby powder, 51
    baking soda, 14, 15, 16
    bread, 18
    charcoal briquettes, 84, 85,
        220
    coffee, 23
    dryer sheets, 112
    Epsom salt, 59
    essential oils, 56
    hydrogen peroxide, 63
    kitty litter, 83, 84
    mustard, 31

peanut butter, 33
    spices, 38, 39
    tea, 40
    tomato juice, 41
    vanilla, 42
    vinegar, 44, 45
desserts, decorating, 96
diamonds, cleaning, 22
diapers
    fleece-lined, 172
    securing, 205
    storing soiled, 148
dining chair, upholstering,
    150–51
Diserens, Helen Barnett, 58
dishes, removing baked-on food
    from, 230
dishwasher
    cleaning, 26
    deodorizing, 14
dishwasher detergent, 111
dishwashing liquid, 17, 109–11
documents, storing, 119
dog bed, making, 162
dog dishes
    alternative, 86, 141, 149
    cracked, 21
dog food, 153, 167
doghouse, insulating, 191
dogs
    beans for training, 18
    belly-scratcher for, 55
    as fast eaters, 141
    fleecy toy for, 173
    giving medicine to, 33
    pooper scooper for, 95
    protecting car seat from, 167
    skin problems in, 69
    washing, 124
dollar stores. See also 99 cent
    stores
    food items from, 12
    gardening and outdoor supplies
        from, 76
    housewares from, 128
    school and party supplies
        from, 184
    tools from, 214
door hanging, making, 169
doorknob, protecting from
    paint, 131
doors
    preventing slamming of, 99
    squeaky hinges on, 81, 113–14,
        124
    stopping drafts from, 171
    unsticking, 73, 193, 238

doorstops, rubber, 232
double-stick tape, 197
down-filled items, fluffing in dryer, 98
drafts
    plugging, 120, 151, 162, 171
    testing for, 81
drains
    preventing clogs in, 124
    retrieving dropped items from, 99, 136
    unclogging, 17, 37
draperies, clipping shut, 108
drawers
    liners for, 144, 178
    removing liners from, 230
    unsticking, 81, 135, 219
drawstring bag, repairing, 164
dresses
    flapper-style, 180
    made from pillowcase, 147
    securing on hangers, 210
Drew, Richard G., 228
D-rings, 165–66
drinking glass, lid for, 143
drop cloths, 150, 222, 223
dropper, drinking straw as, 155
dryer door seal, leaking, 212
dryer sheets, 111–12, 167
Duane Reade drugstore, 24
duct tape, 222, 224
dusting aids
    cotton swabs, 57
    gardening gloves, 88
    microfiber cloth, 229
    paintbrush, 229, 230
    pipe cleaners, 178–79
dustpan, 85, 131, 139
dust repellents, 105, 109
dusty room, concealing, 81
duvet covers, 181
DVDs, removing stuck, 206
dyes, 168

E

earache, 50, 64
earrings
    for decorating magnet, 203
    making, 216
    replacing back of, 192
    storing, 141, 143
Easter egg decorating, 81, 196

eczema, 88
eggs
    fluffing, 35
    poaching, 135
    separating, 139
egg whites, freezing, 141
elastic cord and tape, 168–69
electrical cords, corralling, 156, 211
electronic equipment, protecting from static electricity, 106
Elmer's Glue, 174, 240
embroidery hoops, 169
emery board, 58–59
envelopes, 197–98
    handmade, 174
    sealing, 196
Epsom salt, 59–60
eraser, 198–99
    cleaning, 59
extension cords, storing, 79, 119, 135
eyebrows
    plucking, 64
    taming, 66, 74
eyeglasses
    cleaning, 229
    preventing foggy, 71
    removing hairspray from, 71
    screws in, 101, 126, 206, 208
    securing popped lens in, 21
eye makeup, removing, 52
eye mask, bandanna as, 78
eye pencil, sharpening, 156–57
eye puffiness, 63
eye shadow applicator, 57

F

fabric, 169–70
fabric softener, 112–13
face masks, 225
facial exfoliator, 49
facial lines, 63
facial toner, 21
fat replacement, for baking, 14
faucet, dripping, 125
felt, 170–72
fevers, 122
fiberfill, 162
fingernails
    smoothing broken, 94

strengthening, 88
finger paints, 152
finger splint, 152
fireplace, cleaning, 15–16, 23, 117
fire starters, 56, 97, 127, 196
first-aid kit
    making, 209
    securing in car, 181
fish
    cleaning fresh-caught, 35
    freshening thawed, 30–31
    removing odor from, 14, 33
    removing pin bones from, 231
fish food shaker, 206
fishing bait, 23, 38
five-and-dime stores, 9–10
fleas, 60, 75, 107, 110
fleece, 172–73
floors. See also wood floors
    cleaning, 83, 240
    hiding scratches on, 72
    removing hair from, 116
    removing hair spray from, 71
    scuffs marks on, 93, 171, 228, 236, 237
    squeaky, 51
flour, 25
    dusting food with, 153
    storing, 142
flowerpots, 85–86, 87, 139. See also planters
    alternative, 78
    drainage for, 89, 139
    filling crack in, 201
    keeping soil in, 80, 111–12, 137
    preventing scratches from, 92
flowerpot saucers, 86
flowers
    arranging in vase, 155, 168, 186
    balloon holder for, 187
    drying, 84
    made from felt, 172
    preserving fresh-cut, 37, 45, 61, 106
    splints for bent, 57, 126, 207
    stakes for, 199
    vases for (see vases)
food brush, alternative, 230
food covers, 234
food scraps, disposing of, 144, 200

food skewers, 152, 176
food storage
    at campsite, 134
    insulation for, 191
food storage containers, protecting, 79–80
foot care
    exercise, 208
    massage, 89, 97
    odor control, 40, 58, 59
    for rough soles, 232
    soaks, 16, 40, 68
    for sore feet, 55
foot cream alternative, 36
foot powder, 60
fray preventer, liquid, 173–74
freezer
    deodorizing, 23
    increasing efficiency of, 133
    removing ice buildup from, 92–93
freezer bags, 153–54
Frisbee, 86
frost protection, for plants, 91
frozen foods, insulating, 190
fruit
    kebabs, 176
    ripening, 144
    washing, 17
fruit pies, boil-overs from, 35, 130
fruit snacks, frozen, 141
Fuller, Henry V., 24
funnels, 139–40
    alternative, 137, 197
furniture. See also wood furniture; specific furnishings
    baby-proofing, 162
    cat-proofing, 188, 224
    covering, 222
    dusting, 229
    filling scratches on, 74, 83, 135, 196
    patio, 82, 107, 237
    preventing scratches on, 92
    protecting floor from, 171
    protecting outdoor cushions on, 177–78
    refinishing, 95, 98, 168
    removing crayon marks from, 28
    removing scuff marks from, 192
    removing water rings from, 43, 74
    reupholstering, 150–51, 175 76
    securing wheels on, 232

wobbly, 152, 201
furniture polish, 113–14
    alternative, 32, 38
    removing excess, 23
furrowed brow, removing, 186

G

gallon bags, 114
galoshes. See also boots
    shining, 36
game piece replacements, 164
garage, parking in, 98
garage floor, cleaning, 83, 240
garbage can, deodorizing, 15, 16, 84
garden
    bulb protection, 50, 51
    charcoal groundcover, 220
    container plants, 78, 91
    fertilizers, 23, 40, 41, 60
    on fire escape, 134
    flowerpots, 85–86, 87
    flower splints, 57, 126
    frost protection, 91
    mildew prevention, 43
    mirror in, 68
    pest control, 35, 39, 105, 107, 110, 116, 119, 150, 187, 237
    plant labels, 95, 152
    rosebushes, 40, 41, 60
    saving information on, 95, 188, 201
    seed care, 59, 140, 141
    seedlings, 118, 138
    stakes, 199
    tomato plants, 15, 119
    watering, 105, 126
    weeds, 16, 109, 155
    window-box greenhouse, 136
gardening and outdoor supplies, 76–101
gardening gloves, 88
garden tools, cleaning, 157, 236
garlic chips, 108
gift card holders, 197
gift ribbon, 199
gifts
    for gardener, 87
    tracking already-given, 202
giftwrap alternatives, 78, 92–93, 130, 144, 148
gift-wrapping, 174, 180, 189–90, 199, 200
glass cleaner, 114–15

glass table, removing scratches in, 74
glassware
    cleaning, 35, 45, 107
    cover for, 143
    unsticking, 43
glitter glue, alternative, 62
gloves
    gardening, 88, 90
    repairing, 204
    rubber, 90
    work, 241
glue
    alternative, 62, 63
    made from animal parts, 240
    wood, 240
glue cap, preventing sticking of, 70
glue sticks, 174–75
golf balls, 88, 89
golf scores, tracking, 163
golf tees, 89
Graham, Bette Nesmith, 194
grains, storing, 142
grapes
    freezing, 141
    storing, 138
grass growth, between pavers, 16
grass seed, scattering, 153
grease
    bacon, 131, 145
    preventing odor from, 44
    removing from food, 146
    removing from hands, 53
    stopping spitting of, 131
    grease stains, 111
greeting cards
    displaying, 239
    homemade, 95
griddle, polishing, 35
grilling food, 104, 114, 152–53
grill scraper, 134
groceries, 12–45
grocery bags, 199–200
groundhog deterrents, 34, 84
grout
    cleaning, 74, 192, 234
    repairing, 219
gum. See chewing gum
gum pain, 64
gutters, repairing leaky, 222

H

hacksaws, 225
hair
    chlorine in, 25
    coloring, 62
    conditioning, 20, 28, 43, 61
    damaged, 32–33
    degreasing, 111
    dry, 51, 61, 66
    drying, 229
    fasteners for, 167, 176, 209, 216
    lightening, 20–21, 40
    shining, 39
    taming wild, 105
hair bands, storing, 119
hairbrush, 60
    cleaning, 16
hair conditioner, 61
hair spray, 61–63, 65
Halloween costumes, 104, 180, 221
Halloween makeup, 54
Halloween masks, 145
Halloween punchbowl novelty, 241
hammering nails, 56, 98, 166
hammers, 98, 225–26
hamper, deodorizing, 112
hamster tunnels, 119
handbags
    cleaning, 198
    repairing, 166, 176
    storing, 112, 212
handle, making, 239
hands
    cleaning, 20, 32, 39, 53, 71
    exercise for, 209
    gloves for, 88, 120–21, 241
    massage for, 89
    moisturizing, 66, 148
    removing superglue from, 69–70, 237
    rubber glove substitute for, 154
    sweaty, 58
hand soap, alternative, 53
hangers, 136
    alternative, 194
    padding for, 119, 190
    securing clothes on, 210
    for umbrella repair, 206
    for wreath making, 213
hangnails, 67

hats, storing, 212
headaches, 34, 78
headlight covers, cleaning, 75
health and beauty items, 46–75
heartburn, 21, 201
heating pad, making, 175
heat rash, 53
heavy objects, moving, 80
hedge trimming, 97
hemming
    curtains, 175
    skirts, 108
hemorrhoid cream, 63
hem repairs, 197, 211, 222
herbs
    cheesecloth wrap for, 136
    drying, 136, 144–45
    freezing, 141
hiccups, 118
high chairs
    floor cover under, 223
    protecting baby in, 132, 178
Hirsch, Benjamin, 218
hives, 54
holes, plugging, 89, 94, 101, 104, 193, 200, 219, 240
holiday decorations
    cat playing with, 156
    Christmas stockings, 182, 183
    Christmas-themed boxes, 190
    Easter eggs, 81, 196
    fragrant ornaments, 14
    garlands, 165
    hangers for, 164
    making, 169
    napkin rings, 179
    popcorn garlands, 34
    storing, 212
    tinsel, 106
    twine balls, 100
    wrapped picture mats, 213
    wreaths, 174
holiday lights, 91, 168, 220
home repairs
    adhesive fabric spray for, 160
    caulk for, 219
    mirrors aiding, 68
hornets, 29, 238
hotel rooms
    musty-smelling, 112
    shutting draperies in, 108
hot packs, 18, 187–88
hot-water bottle, 121

hot water heater, insulating, 161, 162
houseplants. See also plants
    cleaning leaves on, 28, 53, 88, 122
    removing bugs from, 116, 121
    repotting, 80
    watering, 125, 126, 132, 208
housewares, 128–57
hubcaps, cleaning, 114, 117
hydrogen peroxide, 63–64

I

ice, crushing, 226, 235
ice cream cone drips, preventing, 27–28
ice cream scoops, 140
ice cubes, 142
ice cube trays, 140–42
ice hand, for Halloween punch-bowl, 241
ice packs, 64, 122
ice scraper, 91–92
index card box, 201–2
index cards, 201
inhaler rubs, 225
ink stains, 63
insect bites and stings, 16, 29, 58, 59, 62, 75, 105, 115, 122–23
insect control. See also pest control
    ants, 25, 38, 86, 109, 149, 186, 193, 219
    fleas, 60, 75, 107, 110
    for houseplants, 116, 121
    mosquitoes, 20, 42–43, 53, 55, 231
    moths, 107, 116–17
    natural insecticide for, 62
    nematode worms, 39
    removal methods for, 116, 121
    repellents for, 53, 55, 56, 104
    roaches, 39
    ticks, 42, 55, 116
    toads for, 86
    wasps, 149, 200, 238
interfacing, 175–76
iron, cleaning, 127, 207
ironing board cover, 92, 130
itchy skin, 30, 32, 55, 59, 72, 75, 105

J

jacket buttons, replacing, 165
jar lids, 143
    opening, 120, 234, 241
jars, 142, 202
    as candleholders, 239
    deodorizing, 38
    wire handle for, 239
jeans, hemming, 222
Jell-O cubes, 141
jewelry. See also bracelets; earrings; necklaces
    brooch, 204
    cleaning, 22, 26, 74, 112–13, 115
    materials for making, 58, 80, 99, 179–80, 183, 216, 239
    skin discoloration from, 69
    storing, 141, 143, 183, 187, 192
jewelry box, decorating, 163
Johnson's Baby Powder, 51
jugs, in freezer, 133

K

ketchup, 25–26
key chain, alternative, 207
keys
    finding, 58, 69, 101, 138, 156, 163, 167
    hanger for, 221
    hiding spare, 222
    paper clip as, 206
kiddie tables, 135
kindling, fire, 97, 127, 139
kitchen appliances
    covering, 73, 190
    securing on countertop, 239
    shining, 218
kitchen cabinets
child-proofing, 210
liners for, 155
removing liners from, 230
kitchen chairs, preventing scuffs from, 228
kitchen rags, 170
kitchen tool hanger, 164
kitchen towel hanger, 169
kitty litter, 83–84, 133, 139, 148
K-Mart, 10

kneeling pad, 92
knickknacks, 88, 163, 226
knife
    camping, 225
    dental floss as, 57
    holder for, 227
    sharpening, 94
knitting, 100, 101
knitting needles, 176
Kool-Aid, 26
Kresge, Sebastian, 10
Kress, Samuel, 10

L

labels
    garden, 95, 152
    handmade, 160, 228
    mailing, protecting, 81
    paint can, 205
    removing, 93
ladders, 79, 210, 226, 228
lamps, made from twine, 100
lamp shade, trimming, 180
lamp stand, 226
laundry
    bleach spots on, 177
    bucket for soaking, 78
    delicate items, 71, 110
    fluffing down-filled, 98
    instruction card for, 201
    pretreating, 95, 110, 230
    stain removal for (see specific stains)
    storing stain removers for, 123
    travel clothesline for, 217
    vinegar rinse for, 44
    whitening, 16
laundry bags, for travel, 146, 147, 148
lawn, watering, 109
leaf bags, 92–93
leaf collector, when raking, 150
leather furniture, 192
leather gloves, 90
lemon juice, 26–27
    extracting, 126
letter opener, alternative, 235
lettuce
    crisping, 27
    drying, 146–47
lever, screwdriver as, 235

library card, protecting, 186
lightbulbs, outdoor rusting and, 66
lighter fluid, 93, 226–27
linen closet liners, 213
lint remover, duct tape as, 222
lint roller, 115–16
lip balm, 65, 66
lip pencil, sharpening, 156–57
lipstick
    fixing broken, 94
    ingredients in, 66
lipstick stains, 55, 227
liquid fray preventer, 173–74
Liquid Paper, 194
locks
    baby-proof, 138
    lubricating, 208, 238
    paper clip opening, 206
    winter protection for, 94, 125, 204, 206, 207
lotion, 66–67
luggage
    deodorizing, 112
    identifying, 199
    laundry bags for, 146, 147, 148
    packing, 114, 154
    sealing overstuffed, 217
    strapping on car roof, 182

M

magazines, storing, 79
magic tricks, 203
magnets, 202–4, 227–28
mailing labels, protecting, 81
mailing reminder, 167
makeup, storing, 161
maple syrup, rationing, 95–96
marbles, 133, 204
marble surfaces, cleaning, 17, 27
marinades, 114
marking pens, 177
marshmallows, 27–28
masking tape, 205–6, 228–29
massages, 89, 97
matches, 94, 213
mats
    car floor, 181
    under planters, 155
    weaving, 182–83
mattress cover, alternative, 147

matzo balls, club soda in, 22
maxi pads, 67
mayonnaise, 28
McCrory's, 9
mealybugs, on houseplants, 121
meatballs, preparing, 140
meat fork, 90
meat mallet, alternative, 225
meat tenderizer, 29–30
medicine cabinet
    essentials in, 65
    organizing, 203
Melitta Coffee Filters, 137
metal files, unclogging, 193
metal grooming tools, organizing, 202, 203
mice
    bait for, 33
    blocking entry of, 124, 135
    disposing of dead, 118
microfiber car polishing cloths, 229
microwave oven
    cleaning, 17, 27
    deodorizing, 42
migraines, 34
mildew
    in bathroom, 56, 218
    on books, 15, 83, 85
    on garden plants, 43
    preventing, 145, 220, 223
milk, 30–31
mirrors, 67–68
    car, 108
    cleaning, 229
    defogging, 38, 83
    writing message on, 75
mittens, 108, 160, 167
mobile, for baby, 136
modeling clay, homemade, 14
mold, preventing, 20, 39, 85, 138, 144
moldings, paint touch-ups on, 195
moles (animal), 84
money clip, alternative, 189
mop, storing, 120
mopping cloths, fabric, 170
mosquito bites, 16, 29, 62, 75, 105, 122–23
mosquito repellents, 20, 42–43, 53, 55, 231
moss, removing, 107, 240
mothballs, 116–17, 220

moth repellents, natural, 107, 116–17
mouthwash, 65, 68–69
muscle aches and soreness, 18, 31
mushrooms, storing, 144
mustache, grooming, 66
mustard, 31

N

nail care, 28, 88, 94, 233
nail holes, plugging, 89, 94, 219, 240
nail polish, 69
    fixing chipped, 66
    on pedicures, 122
    removing, 57
    spilled on carpet, 62
nail polish remover, 69–70
nails (hardware)
    corralling spilled, 202, 204
    hammering, 56, 98, 166, 231
    protecting wall from, 187
    removing, 95
    storing, 97, 98, 202, 228
napkin rings, alternative, 179
napkins, alternative, 78, 170, 175, 223
necklaces
    broken, 192, 205
    materials for making, 58, 80, 99, 179–80, 216, 239
    preventing knots in, 187, 207, 221
    untangling, 51, 238
needles. See also pins and needles
    sharpening, 59, 233
    storing, 81
    threading, 63
needlework, 123, 177
nematode worms, 39
newspaper clipping, preserving, 22
99 cent stores, 9–10. See also dollar stores
    cleaning and home supplies from, 102
    gardening tools from, 90
    health and beauty items from, 46
    notions from, 158
nosebleeds, 64, 108
no-sew/iron-on hem tape, 175

notepaper, decorating, 180
notions, 158–83
nutcrackers, alternative, 220, 226, 231

O

oatmeal, 14, 32
oil (cooking)
    absorbing excess, 200
    filtering, 137–38
    olive, 32–33
    vegetable, 42–43
oil change (auto), 153
oilcloth, 177–78
oil leaks, engine, 60, 83
oil stains, 83, 93
olive oil, 32–33
onions
    keeping fresh, 19, 20
    preventing tears when cutting, 81, 225
Oriental rugs, cleaning, 40
ornaments, holiday. See holiday decorations
oven cleaner, 117
    odor from, 44
oven liner, 130
oven mitt, making, 162
oven rack, cleaning, 108–9

P

packing materials, 34, 112, 125, 126, 148, 212
paint
    correction fluid touching up, 195
    disposing of, 84
    dripping down can, 131, 145
    for finger painting, 152
    for flowerpots, 87
    Kool-Aid for coloring, 26
    magnetized, 203
    marks on car, 238
    neutralizing odor of, 42
    no-mess pouring of, 132
    palette for, 86
    protecting door parts from, 70, 131
    recording name of, 152
    removing from bathtub, 91
    removing from skin, 50
    removing from window glass, 217, 235

removing lumps in, 234
spray, containing, 93
storing leftover, 114, 133
testing quality of, 48
texturizing, 240
unsticking windows from, 217

paintbrushes, 229–30
cleaning, 113
covers for, 148, 205
reviving, 44

paint cans
keeping clean, 210
labeling, 205

painted surfaces, cleaning, 19, 123

Painter, William, 134
paint scrapers, 230
pajama pillow, 183
Palcher, Joe, 82
pancake batter, 22, 96
pants
preventing creases in, 119, 190, 194
reinforcing pockets in, 175
removing cat hair from, 106
removing scorch marks from, 111
repairing split, 211
repairing zipper on, 101

panty hose runs, 62, 73, 113, 209
paper bags, 117–18, 143–45
paper clips, 206–7
corralling, 202
magic trick with, 203
storing, 227

paper plate holder, 86
paper plates, 145
paper towels, 118, 120, 146
rags replacing, 170

paper towel tubes, 119
parchment paper, 127
party favors, 134
party game, 204
party straws, 155, 207
party supplies, 184–213
pasta platter, warming, 138
pastry trimmer, 217
patio furniture, cleaning, 82, 107, 237
patios, cleaning, 45, 240
patterns, for sewing, 176, 216–17
pencil, 208–9

pencil case, 209
pens
cleaning ballpoint on, 237
holders for, 181, 206

pepper, 33–34
permit sticker, securing, 186
pest control. See also insect control
bats, 117
cabbage worms, 35
at campsites, 134
cats, 43
deer, 34
in garden, 105, 107, 110, 116, 119, 187, 237
groundhogs, 34, 84
mice, 33, 124, 135
moles, 84
rabbits, 187, 237
raccoons, 60, 80, 188
skunks, 188
slugs, 85, 150, 193, 233
squirrels, 34, 37
steel wool for, 236

pesticide residue, on produce, 17
pesticides, natural, 25, 50, 51
pet bedding, 212
pet food bag, closing, 220
pet hair, removing, 62, 106, 115, 121, 122, 205, 222, 241
petroleum jelly, 70, 88
pets. See cats; dogs
photographs
displaying, 189, 194, 202, 203, 216, 239
filters for taking, 138
protecting, 124–25

piano keys, cleaning, 75
pickpockets, foiling, 56
picnic supplies, 151, 155
picture frames
alternative, 169, 194
antiquing, 72
decorating, 165, 180
gift-wrap art in, 213
hanging, 179
holiday-themed, 213
school, 208

pies
fruit boil-overs from, 35, 130
stacking, 131

piggy bank, homemade, 142
pillowcases, 146–47, 183
pillows
for camping, 191
garden furniture, 223

pill swallowing, easing, 20
pimples, 63, 75, 115
ping-pong paddle, restoring, 234
pinkeye, 40
Pink Pearl eraser, 198
pins and needles. See also needles
lubricating, 237
picking up spilled, 204
storing, 81, 199

pipe cleaners, 178–79
place mats, alternative, 178
planters. See also flowerpots
decorating, 100, 165
hanging, 99
paper bags as, 118
protective mats under, 155
using less soil in, 85, 139, 148

plants. See also garden; house-plants
fertilizing, 23, 94
frost protection for, 91
makeshift saucer for, 73
mildew on, 43
pedestals for, 139, 190
replanting cactus, 208
slug repellent for, 233
watering, 105

plaster
preventing drying of, 44
repairing, 95

plastic bags, 147–49. See also sandwich bags
plastic containers, 149–50
removing stains from, 107

plastic grocery bags, storing, 119
plastic tablecloths, 150–51
plastic wrap, 150, 151, 187
plates, disposable, 131
playing cards, cleaning, 25
Playtex gloves, 121
play zone, 223
pliers, 231
plungers, 70, 231
pockets, preventing wear of, 175
poison ivy, killing, 36
poison ivy rash, 59, 72, 110, 121
Polarfleece, 172
poncho, making, 173, 221, 222
Pond, Theron T., 54
Pond's Cold Cream, 54
popcorn, 34, 144

Popsicle sticks, 152
potato chips, 34–35
pots and pans, 152–53
  burned
    cleaning, 15, 35, 113, 117
    preventing, 18, 164, 165
  copper, 26
  greasing, 123
potting soil
  reducing use of, 85, 139, 148
  scooping, 140
price tags, removing, 33, 45, 198, 227
pruning shears, 90
  disinfecting, 107–8
  removing sap from, 69
pumpkin seeds, baking, 200
putty knife, alternative, 230

Q

quarters, stored in car, 192
quilts
  fastening cover on, 181
  restoring, 164
  stuffing for, 162

R

rabbit deterrents, 187, 237
raccoon deterrents, 60, 80, 188
rags, kitchen, 170
raisin "submarines," 22
receipts, shredding, 197
recipe cards, 201
recyclables, sorting, 241
refrigerator
  attaching pen to, 181
  deodorizing, 23, 40, 41, 84
  drawer liners for, 120, 127
  polishing, 82
  posting photos on, 202, 203
  shelf protectors for, 86
  storing vegetables in, 120, 122
remote controls, corralling, 161, 190
repair clamps, bungee cords as, 79, 80
ribbons, 179–80, 199
  alternative, 100
  reinforcing, 186
rice, making fluffy, 27

ring around the collar, 71
rings, removing stuck, 63, 115
roach control, 39
rocking chair, protecting floor from, 187
room decluttering, 78
root vegetables, storing, 80
rope, made from plastic wrap, 151
rosebush fertilizers, 40, 41, 60
rubber bands, 209–10
rubber cement, 210–11
rubber doorstops, 232
rubber gloves, 90, 120–21
rubbing alcohol, 121–22
rugs
  cleaning, 22, 40
  reviving fibers in, 43
  securing, 197
rust prevention
  on outdoor lightbulbs, 66
  on shower curtain rod, 157
  on tools, 61, 83, 84, 193
rust stains, 17, 26, 37, 83, 93
RVs, deodorizing, 220
Rypinski, Alan, 82

S

sachets, 107
salad, tossing large, 108
salt, 35–36
  lemon juice replacing, 27
salt rings, removing from footwear, 45
saltshakers, 153
  refilling, 197
sandals
  nonslip bottom for, 132
  polishing, 125
sandbox, keeping cats out of, 43
sandpaper, 194–95, 232–34
sand shovel, 139
sand toys, 87
sandwich, potato chip, 35
sandwich bags, 124–25, 153–54.
  See also plastic bags
Saran Wrap, 150
saw blade, lubricating, 135
scarf, fleece, 172–73
school papers, corralling, 194
school supplies, 184–213

Schrafft's candy tins, 192
scissors
  cleaning, 45
  for garden chores, 90
  sharpening, 234, 236
scoops
  dustpan as, 139
  ice cream, 140
  saucepan as, 153
scorch marks
  on clothing, 24
  on cookware, 15, 18
  on countertop, 83
Scotch masking tape, 228
scouring pad, for grill, 104
scrapbook, decorating, 213
scrapes, 70
scratches
  bathtub, 195
  car, 69, 195
  countertop, 82
  from flowerpots, 92
  furniture, 74, 83, 135, 196
  skin, 88
  smartphone, 75
  wood floor, 72, 92, 171, 187
screening, 224, 234–35
screwdrivers, 193, 235–36
screw holes, tightening, 101, 104
screws
  in eyeglasses, 101, 126, 206, 208
  lining up for assembly, 197
  securing in tight spots, 210, 211
  storing, 202, 228
scuff marks
  on floors, 93, 171, 228, 236, 237
  on leather furniture, 192
  on pencil eraser, 59
  on shoes, 53, 75
seedlings
  planting, 118
  watering, 138
seed packets, 94–95, 201
seeds
  planting, 59, 140, 141, 235
  protecting from wildlife, 234–35
sewing
  hiding repairs from, 177
  patterns for, 176, 216–17
  pillowcase dress, 147
  preventing tangled thread when, 73, 112

protecting fingers when, 48
refashioned T-shirt, 168
seam-pinning alternative for, 174
sharpening needles for, 59, 233
skirt hems, 108
socks, 98
storing supplies for, 81, 192, 199
supplies for (see needles; pins and needles)
shampoo, 32, 71
shaving cream, 71
   alternative, 30, 61
shaving cuts, 49, 66
sheet sets, storing, 144
shingles pain, 69
Shinola shoe polish, 72
shoelaces
   alternative, 99, 101, 179, 199
   loosening knotted, 23
shoe polish, 72
shoes
   cleaning, 105, 115, 198, 233
   deodorizing, 39, 112
   hygienic foot covers for, 148
   making insoles for, 171
   packing, 72, 147
   polishing, 50, 52, 62, 66, 67, 125, 137
   removing salt rings from, 45
   removing scuffs from, 53, 75
   storing, 166, 191
   stretching, 121
   waterproofing, 154
shopping cart, protecting baby in, 178
shopping lists, 197, 201
shortening, 36–37
shovels
   sand, 139
   snow, 36, 83, 85, 218
shower, campsite, 134
shower cap, 72–73
shower curtain rod, lubricating, 157
shower curtains, 150, 154–55
shower doors, cleaning, 52–53, 71, 110, 113
showerhead, descaling, 124
showering, with vinegar, 96
shower tiles, cleaning, 111
signature, on handmade items, 177
silk, washing, 71
silver tarnish

preventing, 84, 238
removing, 24, 25, 112–13, 125
sink
   cleaning, 25, 60, 75, 118
   leaky faucet on, 125
   skirt for, 182
   unblocking drain in, 17, 37
sippy cup spills, preventing, 132
skin care
   face masks for, 28, 32
   for itchy skin, 30, 32, 55, 59, 72, 75, 105
   milk bath for, 30
   for minor burns, 74
   Pond's Cold Cream for, 54
   removing furrowed brow, 186
   removing rough patches, 59
   for rough feet, 232
   sugar scrub for, 39
   toner for, 21
skirts
   hanging, 167
   hemming, 108
   for sink, 182
skunk deterrents, 188
skunk spray, deodorizing, 31
sled, alternative, 221
sled runners, lubricating, 135
sleeping bag, cushioning, 191
slipcover, dyeing, 168
slippers, nonslip bottom for, 132
slugs, 85, 107, 150, 193, 233
smartphone
   drying out, 83
   removing scratches from, 75
smoke detector, hanging, 181
smoke odor, 45
smoker, flavoring wood chips in, 40
snack bags, sealing, 166, 188, 189
snack basket, 161
sneakers
   cleaning, 75, 105
   protecting, 123
snoring, preventing, 98–99
snow games, 96
snow shovel
   dustpan as, 85
   repelling snow from, 36, 83, 218
soaker hose, 90
soap, 73
   extending life of, 130
   hand, 53
soap holder, 86, 122

soap scum
   preventing, 113
   removing, 52–53, 71, 110
soap suds, minimizing, 36
sock puppets, 164
socks, sewing, 98
soda, 37
soft scrub, homemade, 24
sore throat, 27, 41
soups, decorating, 96
Spam, 38
Spanel, Abram Nathaniel, 121
spatulas, 91, 95, 107, 164, 230
spices, 38–39
splinter removal, 59, 186, 240, 241
splints
   for bent flowers, 57, 126
   finger, 152
sponge, 122
spoon, Popsicle stick as, 152
spoon rest, 143
sports cream, heating, 151
spray bottles, 122–23
spray starch, 123
squeaks
   bed frame, 238
   door hinges, 81, 113–14, 124
   floor, 51
   steps, 208
squeeze bottles, 95–96
squirrels, protecting bird feeder from, 34, 37
stainless steel sink
cleaning, 60
polishing, 25
removing rust from, 93
stain pretreaters, 110, 230
stain removers. See also specific stains
   baby wipes, 52
   baking soda, 15, 16, 17
   bleach, 107
   bread, 19
   club soda, 22
   cold cream, 55
   cornstarch, 24
   correction fluid, 195
   cream of tartar, 24
   dishwasher detergent, 111
   dishwashing liquid, 110
   emery board, 59
   eraser, 198–99
   hair spray, 63
   Kool-Aid, 26

lemon juice, 27
lighter fluid, 93, 226, 227
meat tenderizer, 30
paper bags, 117–18, 144
salt, 35
sandpaper, 232, 233, 234
shaving cream, 71
soda, 37
storing, 123
WD-40, 236–37
stairway
   lighting, 91
   squeaky steps on, 208
staples, 211, 236
static cling, 61, 130
static electricity, 66–67, 105, 106
steaks, marking doneness of, 156
steam iron, adding water to, 96
steel wool, 123–24, 236
   storing, 147
steering wheel, providing shade for, 92
stepladder, 210, 226
sticker residue, removing, 227
sties, preventing, 51
stock (soup)
   cutting bones for, 225
   straining, 146
stocking runs, 62, 73, 113, 209
stomach problems, 17, 21
Stone Straw Corporation, 207
storage bags, 124–25, 153–54
storage boxes
   decorative, 160
   lining, 104
stove gaskets, cleaning, 156
stovetop
   cleaning, 15, 35, 91, 110, 179
   protecting drip pans on, 130
strainer, cheesecloth as, 136
strawberries, hulling, 134
straws, 155, 207
string, 97, 125
   dispenser for, 133, 140
   reinforcing, 186
string lamps, 100
string phone, 140
stud (wall), finding, 203
stuffed animal
   repairing, 173, 176
   secret safe inside, 183
suede, cleaning, 19, 59, 198, 233

sugar, 39, 153
suitcases. See luggage
sunburn, 15
superglue, removing from hands, 69–70, 237
swatch portraits, 169
sweaters
   moth repellent for, 116–17
   washing, 44, 93
sweaty palms, 58
swim goggles, de-fogging, 75

T

tablecloths
   alternative, 155, 222
   dyeing, 168
   felt liner under, 171
   plastic, 150–51
   removing candle wax from, 144
table-setting caddy, 161–62
taco salad shell, making, 130
Taggart Baking Company, 19
taillight covers, cleaning, 75
tape measure, alternative, 125
tarps, securing, 167
tar removal, from clothing, 36
tattoos, removing temporary, 55
tea, 40–41
   chamomile, 20–21
teacher notes, securing, 198
tennis balls, 97–99
terrarium, making, 142
thank-you notes, 161
thermos
   cleaning, 49
   deodorizing, 15, 38
ticks, 42, 55, 116
tie rack, making, 89
tile, cleaning, 24, 192
tinsel, 106
tissue paper, 211–12
toads, for insect control, 86
toilet
   cleaning, 37, 49
   overflowing, 67
   removing stains from, 232
   unclogging, 231
   water saver for, 133
toiletries, storing, 161
tomato juice, 41
tomato paste, freezing, 141

tomato plants
   pest control for, 119
   sweetening, 15
tomato stains, 107, 237
tongue biting, 68
tool belt, making, 183
tool grip, 238, 239
tools, 214–41
   attaching to stepladder, 210, 226
   carryall for, 79
   cleaning garden, 157, 236
   preventing rust on, 61, 83, 84, 193
   sharpening, 232
   storing, 160, 191, 202
toothache, 64, 118
toothbrush, 65, 73–74
   cleaning, 16, 68
   ID marking on, 69
   storing, 63, 64, 221
toothpaste, 74–75
toothpicks, 125–26, 156
tote bag, closure for, 166
towel rack, making, 221
towels, 126–27, 160, 169
toys
   bath, 138
   cleaning up tiny, 85, 213
   felt scraps for, 170–71
   pet, 173, 225
   rag doll, 183
   repairing inflatable, 219
   sand, 87
transplanting spade, 90
trash can
   protecting from animals, 80
   repairing cracked, 224
travel documents, organizing, 189
trees
   protecting from lawn mower, 191
   pruning, 107–8, 225
   training branches on, 217
tree sap, removing, 20, 28, 69, 71, 121
trimming (for fabric), 180
trowel, 90
trug, 90
T-shirts
   decorating, 177
   refashioning, 168
tuna can rings, for food presentation, 135
turkey, moving to platter, 241

Turtle Wax, 218
twine, 99–100, 133
twist ties, 101, 156

U

umbrella
    covering wet, 149
    repairing, 206
    storing, 122
upholstering dining chair,
    150–51
upholstering furniture, 175–76

V

vacuum nozzle, filter for, 136
vanilla, 42
varnish, for craft projects, 240
Vaseline, 70
vases
    cleaning, 48, 49
    freshening water in, 220
    marbles enhancing, 204
    preventing leaks from, 147
    securing, 174–75
vegetable garden, pest control
    for, 105, 116
vegetable oil, 42–43
vegetable peelers, 156–57
vegetables
    cleaning, 74
    garden stakes for, 199
    storing, 80, 120, 122
    washing, 17
Velcro, 181–82
vents, sealing, 203
vinegar, 43–45, 96, 124
vomit odor, 44

W

wading pools, nonslip bottom
    for, 133
waffle batter, club soda in, 22
walkways
    cleaning, 107
    lighting, 91
wallet protector, 56
wall hangings, making, 169
wallpaper

cleaning, 17, 19, 199, 236
    removing, 113
    securing curls in, 160
walls
    cleaning, 48, 123, 198–99, 210
    paint touch-up on, 195
Walmart, 10
Walton, Sam, 10
wart removal, 48
washcloth, 154
wasp nests, 200, 238
wasp sting, 29
wasp trap, 149
wastebasket
    deodorizing, 112
    liner for wicker, 147
water bottles, freshening, 45
watering can, 90
watermelon balls, 140
water rings, removing from wood,
    43, 74, 124, 218
wax paper, 127, 157
WD-40, 91, 236–38
weather stripping, 238–39
webbing, 182–83
weeds
    killing, 109
    preventing, 16, 155
wheelbarrow, 90
whipping cream, fluffing, 35
whitewall tires, cleaning, 117
Wiley, Ralph, 150
wind chimes, 87
Windex, 115
window-box greenhouse, 136
window frames, cleaning, 81–82
windows
    blackout covers for, 143, 223
    broken glass in, 222, 224
    cleaning, 117, 123, 229
    curtain of buttons for, 165
    painting snowflakes on, 195
    propping open, 235
    removing paint from, 217, 235
    stopping drafts from, 120, 151,
        162, 171
    unsticking, 80, 217, 219
window screens, cleaning, 111
windshield
    cleaning, 52, 67
    de-fogging, 71
    ice repellent for, 145
    rain repellent for, 14–15
    removing bird droppings from,
        45

winter cover for, 93
windshield wiper blades
    cleaning, 105
    de-icing, 122
wine, freezing leftover, 142
wine corks, 126, 127
winter attire, storing, 160–61
wire, 239
wire brush, 240
Wonder Bread, 19
wooden doors, unsticking, 73
wood floors. See also floors
    cleaning, 114–15, 117–18
    hiding scratches on, 72
    leveling, 91
    preventing scratches on, 92, 171,
        187
wood furniture
    coasters for, 86
    crayon marks on, 28
    felt liner for, 171
    polishing, 32, 38, 83
    protecting from spills, 155
    water rings on, 43, 74, 124, 218
    wood glue, 240
wood paneling
    cleaning, 43
    plugging holes in, 240
woolens, moth repellent for,
    116–17
Woolworth's, 9–10, 198
workbench, organizing, 142, 192,
    202
work gloves, 241
wrapping paper, 212–13
wreaths, making, 174, 213
wrinkles, clothing, 126

Y

yarn
    dispenser for, 139
    storing, 119
yoga band, making, 168, 217

Z

zippers, 183
    malfunctioning, 63, 73, 81, 101,
        208

PHOTO CREDITS